BREAKTHROUGH
BRANDING

BREAKTHROUGH BRANDING

Positioning your library to survive and thrive

SUZANNE WALTERS AND KENT JACKSON

Neal-Schuman

An imprint of the American Library Association

Chicago 2013

Printed in the United States of America
17 16 15 14 13   5 4 3 2 1

Extensive effort has gone into ensuring the reliability of the information in this book; however, the publisher makes no warranty, express or implied, with respect to the material contained herein.

ISBNs: 978-1-55570-766-8 (paper); 978-1-55570-867-2 (PDF).

Library of Congress Cataloging-in-Publication Data

Walters, Suzanne.
    Breakthrough branding : positioning your library to survive and thrive /
    Suzanne Walters and Kent Jackson.
      pages   cm
    Includes bibliographical references and index.
    ISBN 978-1-55570-766-8 (alk. paper)
    1. Libraries—Marketing. 2. Branding (Marketing) I. Jackson, Kent, 1945-
  II. Title.
  Z716.3.W235 2013
  021.7—dc23   2013005134

Book design in Chapparal Pro, Interstate, and Popular by Kimberly Thornton.

♾ This paper meets the requirements of ANSI/NISO Z39.48–1992 (Permanence of Paper).

contents

List of Illustrations / xiii

Preface / xv

Acknowledgments / xxi

SECTION I: BRANDING

Chapter 1 **What Is a Brand?** **3**

Knowing a Brand Means Experiencing a Brand 4

What Good Brands Have in Common / 5

The Concept of Brands and Branding Is Evolving / 5

Branding—An Idea Whose Time Has Come 6

Branding Inspires Action 6

It Begins with the Basics 7

The Readily Observable Elements of a Brand / 7

The Tangible Elements of a Brand / 8

Experiential Elements of a Brand / 8

The Origin of Intentional Elements of a Brand / 9

Advanced Branding and the World of Libraries 9

The Three Dimensions of Branding / 10

Application to Libraries / 10

Summary 15

References 15

Chapter 2 **Assessing Your Library Brand** **17**

Start with Your Own Intuition 18

Power of the Brand Story / 18

Revisit the Bubble Room / 19

*Ask Customers, Colleagues, and Community
Leaders / 20*

**The Nexus—Forging a Purpose and Focusing Your
Library** 20

Taking Stock of Your Library Brand 21

Start with Mission and Values—Why You Are Here / 22
Consider Your Vision—Where You Are Going / 23

Assessing Your Situation with SWOT 23

Internal Strengths and Weaknesses / 24
External Opportunities and Threats / 26

Team Involvement 26

Using Market Research 27

What Constitutes Market Research? / 28
Understanding the Competitive Market / 32
Assessing Market Share and Mind Share / 33
Assessing Brand Equity / 34

**Implications for Planning and the Formulation
of Strategy** 35

Summary 35

References 36

Chapter 3   **Developing Your Library Brand**   **39**

Your Brand Is a Living Thing 40

A Path to Follow 40

Who Should Be Involved in the Process? / 41
Use of Outside Experts / 41

Relating the Branding Process to Planning 42

People, Protocol, and Process 43

A Disciplined Approach 45

Step 1—Brand Assessment / 45
Step 2—Brand Discovery / 45
Step 3—Brand Creative / 46
Step 4—Brand Plan / 47
Step 5—Brand Implementation / 48

Internalizing Your Brand 49

Brand Management / 51

Building Brand Equity / 52

Summary 52

References 53

SECTION II: **POSITIONING**

Chapter 4 **Defining a Positioning Strategy**
Why Is It Important to Your Library? **57**

What Is Positioning? What Is a Positioning Strategy? 58

Secrets of Positioning: Identifying Target Markets and the Competition / 58

Using Positioning to Differentiate Your Library in the Marketplace 59

Positioning Differentiates Your Products and Services / 60

Examples of Positioning within the Commercial Marketplace / 61

Your Library Has a Position in the Marketplace 62

Conducting Market Research to Understand Your Position within the Community / 63

Market Research Methodology / 63

The Integration of Branding and Positioning 64

Brand Loyalty / 64

Brands Evoke Feelings and Emotional Attachment / 65

Positioning and Branding 65

Is the Branding Process Necessary to Position the Library? / 67

Strategic Planning and Strategic Positioning 67

Summary 69

References 69

Chapter 5 **Understanding Segmentation**
Selecting Your Target Markets   **71**

Using Market Research to Understand Target Markets 72

Getting the Market Research Assistance You Need / 73

Using Professional Market Research Teams / 74

Using Primary and Secondary Resources / 74

Understanding Qualitative and Quantitative Research / 75

*Understanding Segmentation Analysis and Targeting
Your Audience / 78*

Cluster Systems: PRIZM and VALS / 81

Selecting Your Target Markets 82

Criteria for Evaluating Your Target Market / 82

Selecting Your Target Markets (Market Segmentation) / 84

Choosing the Approach for Your Library / 86

*Successful Market Segmentation Research—Columbus
Metropolitan Library / 86*

Summary 90

References 91

Chapter 6 **Crafting a Desired Positioning Strategy**
Achieving a Distinctive Difference   **93**

Understanding Positioning as It Relates to the Brand 95

Behavior-Focused Positioning / 95

Barrier-Focused Positioning / 95

Benefit-Focused Positioning / 95

Competition-Focused Positioning / 96

Focus on Repositioning / 96

Determining How to Position Your Brand 97

The Positioning Statement 97

Positioning Drives the Creative Process / 97

Crafting a Positioning Statement / 98

Value Propositions 99

Value Propositions and Taglines / 99

Where to Begin / 100

*Relationship of the Positioning Statement and the Unique
    Value Proposition / 101*

Developing Goals and Objectives for Target Audiences 104

Summary 104

References 106

SECTION III: PROMOTION

Chapter 7 **Positioning and Marketing Strategies**
**Introduction to Positioning
and the Marketing Mix**   **109**

What Is the Marketing Mix? 110

Marketing Mix, Branding, and Positioning / 111

Selecting the Right Marketing Mix for Your Library / 111

Product/Service—The First "P" 111

The Core Product / 112

The Actual Product / 113

The Augmented Product / 113

The Potential Product / 113

The Product Life Cycle / 114

Place Strategies 115

Distribution Channels as Place Strategies / 117

Objectives for Place Strategies / 118

Price Strategies 119

Pricing Strategies and Value / 119

How Organizations Decide on Pricing Strategies / 120

*Libraries and the Common Positioning Premise—
    "Free" for All / 121*

Enhancing the Brand through Pricing / 122

Monetary and Nonmonetary Costs / 123

Competitive Behavior and Pricing / 123

Pricing Strategies Built on the Brand and Positioning Statement / 124

Pricing Strategy Based on Product or Service / 124

People Strategies—The Fifth "P" for Consideration 125

The Customer Life Cycle / 126

Summary 127

References 129

Chapter 8   **Promoting Your Brand**   **131**

Concept of Promotion 131

Brand Architecture and Promotion 132

Developing Your Brand Architecture / 133

Applications to New and Existing Brands / 134

Revisiting Brand Architecture to Bring Clarity and Focus to the Brand / 135

Investing in Brand Identity / 135

Brand Architecture in Summary / 143

Developing Your Promotional Plan 144

Developing a Creative Brief / 145

Messages and Messengers / 145

Creative Strategy / 146

Selecting Communication Channels 146

Varieties of Communication Channels and Media Vehicles / 146

The Website / 150

Facilities and Physical Environments as Communication Tools / 150

Public Relations 151

Public Relations Tools / 151

Public Relations and Libraries / 153

Nontraditional and New Media Channels 154

Social Media / 154

Evaluation—You Get What You Measure 155

Building Brand Champions 157

Using Internal and External Design Teams / 158
Developing Brand Standards and Guidebooks / 158
Managing Consistency and Integrity of the Brand / 158

Summary 159

References 161

Chapter 9   # Advocating for Libraries   **163**

OCLC Study *From Awareness to Funding* 165

Columbus Metropolitan Library / 166
Queens Library: Positioning through Advocacy / 168
Anythink Libraries and Advocacy / 169
*Wyoming State Library: Forging Strong Community
    Grassroots Advocacy Programs* / 169

Turning Adversity into Advantage 170

Using Adversity to Reposition Your Library / 171
The Rebirth of the Grand County Library District / 172

**Positioning the Library within the Brand
    of a University** 174

A Final Word about Leadership 175

Summary 179

References 180

About the Authors / 183

Index / 185

list of illustrations

Figure 1.1 Brand Dimensions 10

Figure 1.2 Library Brand Identity—Do Customers Know Who We Are and What We Offer? 11

Figure 1.3 Library Brand Personality—Do We Convey a Personality Customers Can Relate To? 13

Figure 1.4 Library Brand Image—Sets Expectations and Inspires Confidence 14

Figure 2.1 Brand Premise and Brand Promise 18

Figure 2.2 Brand Story 19

Figure 2.3 Nexus for Change 21

Figure 2.4 Brand Promise—The Sweet Spot 22

Figure 2.5 SWOT Analysis 24

Figure 2.6 Brand Essence 25

Figure 2.7 Strategic Purpose and Focus 26

Figure 2.8 Research Sequence and Application 28

Figure 2.9 Research by Source and Type 30

Figure 3.1 External and Internal Brand Perspectives 40

Figure 3.2 Brand Process 41

Figure 3.3 Strategic Brand Planning 42

Figure 3.4 People, Protocol, and Process 44

Figure 3.5 Customer Experience Map 47

Figure 4.1 OCLC Logo 61

Figure 4.2 Anythink Logo 63

Figure 4.3 Columbus Metropolitan Library Logo 66

Figure 4.4 Purpose of Columbus Metropolitan Library 66

Figure 4.5 Vision of Columbus Metropolitan Library 66

Figure 4.6 Values of Columbus Metropolitan Library 66

Figure 4.7 External Audiences of Columbus Metropolitan Library 66

Figure 4.8 Arapahoe Library District Logo 67

Figure 5.1   Target Your Market *74*

Figure 5.2   Seattle Public Library *76*

Figure 5.3   Demographic, Geographic, and Behavioral Segmentation for the Apple iPhone *79*

Figure 5.4   Three-Legged Stool—Positioning, Barriers, and Benefits *81*

Figure 5.5   Selecting Your Target Audience *82*

Figure 5.6   Wyoming Librarian *83*

Figure 5.7   Wyoming Mudflap Girl *83*

Figure 6.1   Seth Godin's Purple Cow *94*

Figure 6.2   Wyoming Libraries and the Mudflap Girl *96*

Figure 6.3   Revitalize Our Offering from the Anythink Brand Book *98*

Figure 6.4   Examples of Value Propositions *100*

Figure 7.1   Columbus Metropolitan Library Homework Help Centers *110*

Figure 7.2   The Marketing Mix *111*

Figure 7.3   Core Product, Actual Product, Augmented Product, Potential Product *112*

Figure 7.4   Product Life Cycle Curve *115*

Figure 7.5   Staff Manifesto of Anythink *126*

Figure 7.6   Staff Manifesto of Anythink, Part Two *127*

Figure 8.1   Columbus Metropolitan Library Brand Personality *136*

Figure 8.2   Columbus Metropolitan Library Logo *137*

Figure 8.3   Anythink Banners *138*

Figure 8.4   Brand Touch Points *141*

Figure 8.5   Anythink Bookmobile *143*

Figure 8.6   Transit Ad for Queens Library *148*

Figure 8.7   Love @ Queens Library *149*

Figure 8.8   Eat @ Queens Library *149*

Figure 8.9   Surf @ Queens Library *149*

Figure 8.10 Wyoming Trojan Horse *152*

Figure 8.11 Wyoming Windmill Eiffel Tower *152*

Figure 8.12 Columbus Metropolitan Library Levy Campaign *154*

Figure 9.1   Brand and Chaos *164*

Figure 9.2   Geek the Library Campaign *167*

Figure 9.3   New Granby Public Library *173*

Figure 9.4   Artist's Conception of Penrose Library, University of Denver *177*

preface

N 2006 AN ORGANIZATION CALLED PUBLIC AGENDA, with the support of the Americans for Libraries Council and the Bill and Melinda Gates Foundation, published a comprehensive report titled *Long Overdue* that insightfully examined how the public and our leaders view libraries. The report was intriguing, characterizing libraries as among the most appreciated of social enterprises while paradoxically revealing a widening disconnect between public adoration and the willingness to fund libraries at the local level (Public Agenda 2006).

Two years later, an organization called OCLC, a branded acronym for Online Computer Library Center, Inc., joined with the Bill and Melinda Gates Foundation and Leo Burnett USA, one of the world's largest brand marketing firms, to address this gap as documented in a publication titled *From Awareness to Funding: A Study of Library Support in America* (DeRosa and Johnson 2008). Following is a summary of their findings: "Findings suggest that there is sufficient, but latent, support for increased library funding among the voting population. There is evidence that a large-scale library support campaign could make a difference."

The report concludes by emphasizing three keys to campaign success:

- Making libraries relevant
- Instilling a sense of public urgency for support—along with schools, fire, and police services
- Engaging the community in conversations about the importance of libraries as a "transformative" force in shaping the future of our communities

With an eye on these important and seminal efforts, the authors of this book were moved to collaborate on a branding approach *just for libraries*. It was our primary interest to enable libraries to methodically close this gap—to survive and ultimately thrive as noble public investments through the clear understanding and application of the principles of branding, positioning, and promotion.

Why just for libraries? Suzanne Walters has become well connected with libraries over the years, having been among the first to serve in the role of a marketing director for a large urban library and as a consultant, trainer, educator, and author of several books on library marketing. Well respected by the library community, Walters firmly believes that the branding, positioning, and promotional needs of libraries are unique. Dr. Kent Jackson has long been involved with the practical side of enterprise branding and promotion, and he shares Walters' fascination with the unique characteristics and dynamics of libraries that play a special and integrative role in the communities they serve. While both authors believe that marketing concepts derived from and applied to other business and social enterprises offer useful perspectives, libraries present a truly unique balance of opportunity and challenge in today's multimedia environment.

On the opportunity side, the public's perception of libraries is a powerful marketing asset. Libraries are experiencing unprecedented demand for services while establishing enduring connections with their customers. Libraries are at once addressing basic needs from literacy to employment while fulfilling the special interests and aspirations of their customers. Libraries are as much partners as they are competitors with institutions and organizations that also serve the public interest, whether in education, health care, public services, or entertainment and cultural programming. And, the library culture includes people who are passionate about their work, share a strong public service mentality, and are accustomed to a collaborative approach to problem solving—all attributes that afford a profound strategic advantage when properly applied to the tasks of branding, positioning, and promotion.

On the challenge side, libraries are enterprises that require an inherently complex approach to marketing. While they represent internal cultures with attributes highly oriented to service, they also tend to be skeptical of marketing—seeing the two as somehow in conflict with each other. Libraries are traditionally viewed as quiet places to be, as quiet purveyors of a service, and therefore seldom inclined to promote what they do. Their markets—their customers—are wide ranging; their mission statements are sweeping. Whereas for most social and business enterprises a good strategy is one that is narrow in focus and message, libraries are inclined to the opposite. And while most enterprises wisely avoid the claim to be "all things to all people," libraries embrace this mission.

Also challenging is the manner in which libraries exchange value with their customers. Unlike most enterprises where customers expect to give and/or do something significant in exchange for a benefit received, libraries promote most of their offerings as free and easy to access and use. Thus, a free-and-easy exchange with minimal obligation is implied at the time of transaction. In reality, there is an exchange value—paid in taxes and related fees—that often is revealed as fines for overdue books or in reduced offerings when resources wane, budgets erode, elections fail, or doors close. This real and perceived ambiguity and delay in expression of the exchange value contributes substantially to the "gap" between public appreciation and financial support.

How and why is this book different? While marketing books and resources for libraries have become more common (including those authored by Walters), the focus of this book is unique in several ways. Here the authors encourage you to seek a "higher ground" and look at library marketing through the lens of three key and integrated elements—branding, positioning, and promotion. On one hand, we offer an approach that goes deep, focusing on the very essence of the library enterprise— your raison d'être. On the other hand, we show you how to develop and translate deep insights about the customers you serve and how to best approach and engage them in your offerings. Throughout this book we share case examples from the field that demonstrate how outstanding libraries are evolving their brands, their positioning strategies, and their promotional efforts. We offer these case examples not as recipes for success or solutions to the problems you may face, but rather as expressions of the concepts and principles we introduce throughout the book. From the Wyoming State Library serving fewer than six inhabitants per square mile, to Queens Library in New York serving over 20,000 per square mile, from the suburban Denver Front Range Library District of Adams County in search of a game-changing identity that became Anythink, to Columbus Metropolitan Library in Ohio that leverages and refines a well-established brand in service to its targeted customers—all provide exceptional models for breakthrough branding.

It is not our intent to convey a single set of answers befitting the needs of all libraries. In fact, you will observe that we focus a lot more on the questions you need to ask yourself than on the answers you will derive. The authors ascribe to the views of Margaret J. Wheatley: "We inhabit a world that co-evolves as we interact with it. This world [including libraries] is impossible to pin down, constantly changing, and infinitely more interesting than anything we ever imagined" (Wheatley 2006, 9). Libraries contribute to and concurrently experience this co-evolution. Marketing— including an intentional approach to branding, positioning, and promotion—is a process and a means of influencing this co-evolution.

Extending this idea to customers and broader markets that libraries serve, the authors also believe that branding, positioning, and promotion are less about directing your message *at* a target audience and more about leveraging all of your resources to *engage* the target audiences you serve—to be culturally relevant. This is arguably true of any product or service being offered today—and especially true for libraries. Here is how Faith Popcorn, futurist, founder/CEO, and author of *Faith Popcorn's BrainReserve*, sums it up:

> Simply put, in the new marketing landscape, culture is the new media. For marketing purposes [branding, positioning, and promotion], the old media channels no longer work. It is through culture, and only culture, that companies will reach customers in the post-advertising future. What is culture? It's what people are passionate about. It's the music, the fashions, the language, the technology, the spirituality of generations. (Popcorn 2005)

Reflecting briefly on the ancient though contemporary roles of libraries, there are three constants that seem to embrace this idea of *cultural relevancy*:

- Sustaining trustworthiness in the quality of cultural knowledge
- Propelling social and cultural interests from the basics of literacy to intellectual, creative, and spiritual enlightenment
- Supporting a public commitment to education for all and the attendant implications for self-governance and a civil and just society

With this very bold sense of mission for libraries in general, the authors have set out to offer you a path to follow—one that begins with the big idea of branding, then focuses on the strategic notion of positioning, and concludes with practical applications for promotion. Along the way, and lending clarity and credibility while breathing life into these concepts, we explore outstanding case examples of different kinds of library systems.

Chapters 1, 2, and 3 introduce you to the concept of branding, how to assess your brand, and the process for developing your brand—either from the ground up or by leveraging the brand asset you have. Chapters 4, 5, and 6 address the concept of positioning and how you can leverage your positioning strategy to address specific audiences and to promote your unique value as a library. Chapters 7 and 8 guide you in applying your positioning strategy to take the best advantage of your marketing mix—including product, place, price, promotion, and people—and the importance of doing so within the framework of a brand architecture that ensures consistency, continuity, and cumulative impact of your promotional efforts. Chapter 9 serves to summarize the preceding chapters with a focus on the overriding goal of advocating on behalf of libraries and the importance of leadership in support of advocacy and transformation. Throughout, examples are drawn from the extraordinary and courageous work of libraries across the country to stimulate your thinking, stir the imagination, and encourage creative action.

Mindful of the uniqueness, richness, and capacity of the library culture, we propose a brave new approach to marketing that is

- More reliant on the clarity of purpose and strategy, and less reliant on recipes and borrowing the tactics of others;
- More reliant on your culture as it is and the resources you have, and less reliant on the need for outside forces to come to your rescue; and
- More reliant on your willingness to understand your markets and prioritize your efforts to effect the transformational change to which you aspire, and less reliant on the circumstances of scarcity and competition to define your future.

In the final analysis, this book seeks to enable you to develop, position, and promote your brand to achieve meaningful and sustainable outcomes. As expressed by Jim Collins in his book *Good to Great*, "When you have disciplined people you don't need hierarchy. When you have disciplined thought, you don't need bureaucracy" (Collins 2001). We agree with Mr. Collins. When it comes to marketing resourcefulness, libraries and librarians can get the job done, can communicate their transformative value, can engage their audiences in a balanced exchange of that value, and can *survive* and *thrive* in the process.

REFERENCES

Collins, Jim. 2001. *Good to Great: Why Some Companies Make the Leap . . . and Others Don't.* New York: HarperBusiness.

DeRosa, Cathy, and Jenny Johnson. 2008. *From Awareness to Funding: A Study of Library Support in America.* Dublin, OH: Online Computer Library Center.

Popcorn, Faith. 2005. *Faith Popcorn's BrainReserve.* www.faithpopcorn.com.

Public Agenda. 2006. *Long Overdue: A Fresh Look at Public Attitudes about Libraries in the 21st Century.* www.publicagenda.org/reports/long-overdue.

Wheatley, Margaret J. 2006. *Leadership and the New Science: Discovering Order in a Chaotic World.* San Francisco: Berrett-Koehler.

acknowledgments

HIS BOOK COULD NOT HAVE BEEN WRITTEN WITHOUT the significant contributions made by other people. Individuals from Anythink Libraries, Queens Library, Columbus Metropolitan Library, and the Wyoming State Library have contributed their time, energy, expertise, and experience, as well as their written and graphic materials. They have all spent hours reviewing copy as well as holding us accountable and challenging us to create a final manuscript that met their standards. It is their stories that we have been proud to share and to illuminate for libraries everywhere.

Specifically, Pam Sandlian-Smith, director of Anythink Libraries, has been most gracious in sharing her knowledge gained through the evolution of the Anythink Libraries. Pam is the recipient of the 2012 Charlie Robinson Award for her "transformative vision and leadership in reinventing the Rangeview Library District." She was also named the Colorado Librarian of the Year in 2010. We were so fortunate to have the opportunity to share this story. Anythink Communications Manager Stacie Ledden has provided materials and brand standards guidebooks, as well as graphics. Steve Hansen gave us great insight, while John Bellina of Ricochet Ideas was helpful in providing graphics and copy.

We are indebted to Queens Library's Director of Communication Joanne King, whose assistance was invaluable in this process. James Keller, former director of marketing for Queens Library, spent hours reviewing copy and assisting us in the development of the Queens stories. His experience in developing the branding process within commercial ventures brought a great deal of knowledge and skill to Queens Library.

What would we have done without Alison Circle, director of marketing and strategic planning at Columbus Metropolitan Library? Alison has been selected by *Library Journal* as one of two "Movers & Shakers" in marketing for 2011. She regularly shares her marketing expertise via her *Bubble Room* blog, at LibraryJournal.com. She was kind enough to share room on her blog for our initial research that contributed to this publication. Alison invested hours in reading drafts of the manuscript, as well as Columbus Metropolitan Library stories, and her input was invaluable.

Wyoming's State Librarian Lesley Boughton and Tina Lyles, the publications and marketing manager for the Wyoming State Library, provided great insight, creativity, knowledge, humor, graphics, and incredible assistance. The Wyoming story provides a unique prospective, and we are very grateful to have had their enthusiastic assistance. State Librarian Lesley Boughton was awarded the "Unsung Hero/Heroine" award for 2009.

We were very fortunate to have the endorsement and the participation of several library executives. Tom Galante, president and chief executive officer, and Patrick Losinski, chief executive officer, of Columbus Metropolitan Library offered their support and encouragement for this publication.

Our graphic artist also deserves a round of applause, as she accurately translated marketing concepts to delightful graphic interpretation. We are grateful to Sandy Smith of Alexander Smith Design (www.alexandersmithdesign.net) for her talent, timeliness, and beautiful work.

The publication includes many smaller vignettes of various libraries. Even these examples required interviews, research, reviewing copy, and assistance. We enjoyed working with the University of Denver, Dean Emeritus R. Bruce Hutton, PhD, and Nancy Allen, dean and director of the Penrose Library. Mary Anne Hanson-Wilcox, executive director of the Grand County Library District, and Andra Addison of the Seattle Public Library provided valuable stories from their institutions. Eliose May, executive director of the Arapahoe Library District, provided us with assistance, insight, and recommendations. Robert Murphy, manager of OCLC public relations, was helpful, too. Our copy of the OCLC study, *From Awareness to Funding: A Study of Library Support in America,* is tattered from use. We also want to extend our gratitude to our editor at Neal-Schuman, Sandy Wood. Sandy encouraged, corrected, suggested changes and edits, and worked with us throughout this process, including the transition of the book to the caring hands of the ALA publications staff, Alison Elms and Jack Kiburz, and especially Senior Editor Patrick Hogan.

Suzanne so appreciated the encouragement and support of her two children, Laura and Robert. Their shared love of books, libraries, and adventures far and wide served as a constant reminder of the transformative power of libraries in our lives.

Kent thanks the love of his life, Donna, for always encouraging him to "be the truth," and his children, Janelle and Jeremy, their spouses, Kevin and Adrianne, and his five grandchildren, Hayden, Lizzie, Ava, Zoe, and Dakota for demonstrating what it means to find one's own truth.

We hope that libraries everywhere use this publication as a guide to create powerful branding and positioning programs. It has been written to offer insight and encouragement for libraries in their quest to survive, thrive, and be true to the premise and promise of the library brand.

SECTION I

BRANDING

What Is a Brand?

SCHOOL WAS OUT AND IT WAS AN EARLY SUMMER MORN-ing in 1952 when a seven-year-old boy and his mother walked up the steps of their neighborhood library, just blocks from the apartment they had recently moved into and the new school the boy would attend in the fall. It was his first trip to a library, a real library, and one that would define his emotional connection to libraries for the rest of his life—a castle of magic, filled with books, and just for him.

Some sixty years later the little boy, now a man of maturity, can still remember a redbrick V-shaped English cottage featuring a green tiled roof, raised courtyard, chimneys at both ends, ornate concrete trims around leaded-glass windows, and a gabled entry with two large oak doors. What he remembers most, though, was walking up the steps, holding his mother's hand, and being greeted by festive banners and booths in the courtyard, promoting summer reading as well as all sorts of programs of arts, crafts, and play to be held during the summer.

In the shadows of his memory he recalls walking through those doors and seeing the welcoming smile of a librarian—a lady like his mom, and with an authority about her. She was the keeper of the castle and all within. And there were books everywhere, from floor to ceiling, sitting on tables, stacked on carts, and bundled in the arms of children and adults. Looking up he remembered seeing ornate beams crisscrossing the ceiling. On every wall were bookshelves, and above hung murals depicting knights, princesses, and dragons suggesting mysteries to be revealed in the books below. And with the sights were hushed sounds and new smells that he would forever associate with places of books, knowledge, mystery, and magic. This place had the patina of time, including the rich scent of aging wood, stone, and paper, and the echoing of footsteps, muffled chatter of adults, and unbridled excitement of children.

As this lady, the librarian, welcomed him, she ushered him to a wing where other children where gathering in front of the stately fireplace, over which was a huge wall mural depicting the Pied Piper surrounded by dancing children and next to which stood a curious-looking man costumed in black mustache, tuxedo, and top hat and holding a wand. And next to him, with curtains closed, was a puppet stage—just like the one he remembered seeing on his parents new black-and-white TV at home. A show was about to begin, and he noticed that his mom had stepped away—standing now with other mothers in the background.

And what a show it was! A real magician with magic tricks and a puppet show better even than anything he had seen on TV. And then there was storytime—that librarian lady sat down and read one of those books from the shelves—giving it a life he had never imagined possible and signaling his first choice of the book he wanted to take home. He left that day with an armful of books, a mind full of wonder and promise, and something else—*an enduring memory of a magic castle, filled with books, all for him.*

Knowing a Brand Means Experiencing a Brand

What this little boy experienced that day, in that library, was the power of branding and the power of "library" as a brand. To this day, whenever he experiences a library anew, those memories and sensations come back to him, are integrated and mixed with his latest experience, and together either strengthen and enrich his brand associations with the idea of "library," or, with anything less than a good experience, confuse, diffuse, and maybe even disappoint and weaken his associations. There is little room in between—the experience of a brand is never neutral.

Another way to understand brands and branding is to look outside the unique realm of the library experience. Unless you have been living under the proverbial rock, these are brands you will recognize and may even own—State Farm, Nike, and Apple. State Farm is the leading property and casualty insurer in the United States, boasting a stable market share of nearly one in five households, with a brand that has survived and thrived for nearly ninety years. Nike, a global multinational brand squarely in the arena of athletic shoes and apparel, has been around for forty-eight years and boasts the industry's leading market share of over 40 percent in their product sector. And then there is Apple, a brand that started in a garage in 1976 and now competes with over 12 percent of the PC market, 17 percent of the burgeoning smartphone market, and an aggressive but fragile 50 percent of the tablet market (IDC 2012).

However, market share is just one way to express the perceived value of brand, that is, by the number of people within a market who own one. There is also what is called "mind share," which embraces two big ideas: the share of the market that expresses some form of awareness of the brand and the share of the market that demonstrates some form of affinity or allegiance to the brand—an experiential connection like that of the little boy.

WHAT GOOD BRANDS HAVE IN COMMON

What do State Farm, Nike, and Apple all have in common? First, you recognize each one of them right away. They own nearly 100 percent of mind share in the markets they serve—you would be hard-pressed to find anyone who does not immediately recognize their brand. And what else do they have in common? Consider this: nearly 40 percent of all companies, and thus company brands, last fewer than ten years. These companies are beating the odds by four, five, and ten times over. What else? They have the ability to price their products and services at levels that set benchmarks for the industry, and when you experience their names, logos, or unique value propositions, you recognize them immediately, know what they do and offer, and relate to them on a personal level—perhaps through an agent in your neighborhood, with a celebrated athlete and a favorite pair of running shoes, or by browsing products in their store, utilizing Apple's Genius Bar, or savoring the joy of opening artfully designed packaging delivered to your home. Finally, you have a clear sense of their image—where they are in the pecking order of competition, how their products and services compare in value for price, and how you feel about their brand. This is what a brand and good branding is all about—an object choice, an enterprise and its offerings, about which you and the marketplace forge an emotional and intellectual relationship.

THE CONCEPT OF BRANDS AND BRANDING IS EVOLVING

The idea of branding and the branding process keeps evolving. Consider that just a few decades ago the word *brand* would have conjured up a clear definition like this one found in a 1984 edition of *Funk & Wagnalls New International Dictionary of the English Language:*

> **Brand** *(brand)* v.t. 1. To mark with or as with a hot iron. 2. To stigmatize; mark as infamous. [<n.] 1. A burning stick: *firebrand.* 2. A mark burned with a hot iron. 3. A name or trademark used to identify a product or group of products of a particular owner or manufacturer.

Notice that the ripple of meaning begins with the simple idea that brand is something you do to something or to someone—to mark or identify it with a degree of permanence, implied goodness or perhaps badness, and ownership. Now consider a more contemporary definition—one found in Wikipedia that represents a collective mashup of ideas about brands and branding in today's world:

> A *brand* is the identity of a specific product, service or business. A brand can take many forms including a name, sign, symbol, color combination

or slogan. The word *brand* began simply as a way to tell one person's cattle from another by means of a hot iron stamp. A legally protected *brand name* is called a trademark. The word *brand* has continued to evolve to encompass identity—it affects the personality of a product, company or service.

Once mostly about an outward appearance or an application to something of value left to the marketing department, the concept of brands and branding has evolved to a complex process, engaging the entire organization and extending to the entire range of markets and publics it services. Branding today is more akin to the broad concept of organizational development—guiding not just how the organization looks and feels to its public but also how it *lives as a culture.*

Branding—An Idea Whose Time Has Come

While the Wikipedia definition of brand has broadened the idea substantially, those who have studied the concept for years give it even more legs and increasingly a living persona or personality—extending brand to embrace the entire enterprise, the entire culture within and outside of it. In his book *Understanding Brands: By 10 People Who Do,* Don Cowley described the brand concept in 1982 as "probably the most powerful idea in the commercial world" (Cowley 1989, 11). By 2002, Mark Earls observed that the concept of brand had become a "ubiquitous" part of everyday conversation extending well beyond commercial enterprise to all aspects of organizational behavior, including the world of politics (Baskin and Earls 2002, 7–8). He further notes, referring to remarks by an executive of Coca-Cola, that were Coke to lose all of its physical assets, including its proprietary recipe, but still retain its brand awareness with the public, it could remain in business.

Branding Inspires Action

According to Tom Asacker in his book *A Clear Eye for Branding,* by focusing on its brand an organization is forced to understand itself, its place in the world, and the markets it serves. Going beyond "understanding," Asacker further asserts that by attending to your organization's brand, ". . . you'll be driven to do something to both improve it and to improve people's lives" (Asacker 2005, 5).

In the experience of the authors, the concept and process of branding are also unifying forces within an organization. By the very act of engaging in a process to understand the brand, the organization's culture of people tends to renew its appreciation for and adherence to the driving mission and orienting values that brought them together in the first place. And as understanding evolves to aspiration, a vision for the brand comes into play, affirming the culture's commitment to the future. In this way, the concept becomes a unifying framework to guide the basics of near-term business planning, longer-term strategic planning, and externally focused market planning.

In summary, a brand is an indentifying mark and an encompassing idea that captures the essence of the enterprise. It is an asset of substantial value and a clarifying, focusing, and motivational force. Brands and the process of branding are an idea whose time has come—an idea distinctive in its own right and pivotal to an organization's development.

It Begins with the Basics

With all of the power of branding in mind, it's important to remember that a brand is not a thing. It is a metaphor for a thing, or more correctly for many things that make up a brand. Those many things generally consist of the *readily observable,* the *tangible,* the *experiential,* and the *intentional.*

THE READILY OBSERVABLE ELEMENTS OF A BRAND

When encountering and describing a brand, people often think in terms of at least three distinguishing elements—a name, an aesthetic, and a value proposition. These elements convey a brand through effective marketing that pairs each element in close temporal contiguity, or time and place, with the other elements. By experiencing the elements together, they take on a combined sensory quality greater than the elements alone. Assuming that the experience is both frequent and consistent over time, and done in a manner that attracts and holds attention, the association of the elements becomes so strong that any one element will prompt recall of the missing elements. For example, when facilitating graduate-level marketing classes, the authors will often use the example of Nike by presenting just one element, say the swoosh graphic, and then ask class members to provide the name that aligns with the swoosh, and perhaps the value proposition or tagline that goes with both. *Swoosh* prompts recall of the name, Nike. Nike and the swoosh graphic prompt recall of the value proposition—"Just do it." Here you have the most common triad of memorable and powerfully associated brand elements:

- **A name**—Includes the formal, legal, or public name of the enterprise, organization, product, service, or person. It may be a proper name, a noun, a contrived or nonsensical name, or an acronym.
- **An aesthetic**—The graphic treatment, font, color pallet, or graphic element(s) that includes and/or aligns with the name, including logos. Aesthetics can readily extend to environmental brand expressions including décor, sounds, and smells—stimulating a consistent sensory experience.
- **A unique selling or value proposition**—A word or phrase that expresses a premise (a reason to be) and/or a promise (an implied commitment to deliver a future benefit or value). Sometimes the selling or value proposition is expressed in a slogan or perhaps a composite of message points, or sometimes it can be implied in the name itself or an extremely well-established name for which the value is well understood.

By employing these simple elements together in context to the power brands discussed, you immediately recognize what they represent and appreciate them for their elegant simplicity, consistent presentation, and communications utility. Whether you use their products or services, or consider them good alternatives to the choices you make, you have some sense for what they offer in goods, services, price, value, personality, and perhaps even such esoteric qualities as aspiration and inspiration.

THE TANGIBLE ELEMENTS OF A BRAND

Beyond these most basic of brand expressions, however, are the tangibles that actually make up a brand. Tangibles include the products and services identified with the brand; the attitudes, personalities, and performance of people, stakeholders, and customers who affectively align with the brand; and the image a brand conveys, including the quality of its offerings and the reputation of those who deliver the brand or align or partner with and even use the brand. Tangibles can extend as well to environments where the brand is created, promoted, and delivered—from physical plants to offices, from retail and service environments to marketing venues real and virtual. These are all tangible expressions of the brand.

EXPERIENTIAL ELEMENTS OF A BRAND

Closely associated with the tangible elements of a brand is the intentional process of experiencing the brand. By "intentional" we mean that the organization representing the brand intends for the market or the audience to experience the brand in a certain way, in a certain order or sequence, and with certain milestones and decision points. Conversely, the consumer approaches the brand with intentions born of some combination of "need" and "want," and with some preconceived expectation of what they are about to experience.

Just as the basic elements of a brand are integrated—a name, an aesthetic, and a unique selling proposition—so are the more complex and tangible elements of the brand and related brand experiences. Consider, for example, the buying experience in an Apple Store, either live or virtual. The visual experience, the interactive experience, and the transactional experience (whether sales or service) are carefully orchestrated, highly personalized, obsessively consistent, and readily adaptive to change. Following is a characterization of the Apple Experience expressed in "Six Design Lessons from the Apple Store," an online article by Jesse James Grant (2004), author of *Elements of User Experience:*

- **Create an experience, not an artifact.** Emphasize the importance of an environment that sweeps you in and focuses your attention on what the entire brand has to offer, enabling you to then focus on what you want.
- **Honor context.** Organize products and services by the context in which customers are likely to use or live with them, rather than by category. This includes the important relational context of the purchase—where the customer is when ready to buy.

- **Prioritize your messages.** Focus on a limited number of messages and make sure they are presented in relative order of importance. Limit messages related to specific products and services to areas/opportunities/moments where and when the customer would expect to focus on them.
- **Institute consistency.** Make sure the customer experiences the brand consistently no matter the venue. This requires a rigorous commitment to designed consistency through all channels of communications.
- **Design for change.** Brand offerings and customers are in a constant state of change, and so too, therefore, are the environments in which they come together, which must also change and anticipate the changes to come. Communications platforms, including social media and research-related customer tracking and feedback, play a key role in staying with and ahead of the customer.
- **Don't forget the human element.** Brands and the products and services they represent are more than objects, ideas, graphics, environments, and even the sensations they produce. They also include the people involved—those who represent the brand and those who engage with the brand, including employers, customers, volunteers, donors, and so on.

THE ORIGIN OF INTENTIONAL ELEMENTS OF A BRAND

Beneath these complex expressions of a brand that translate into palpable and memorable experiences reside the *origins of intent* that extend internal meaning to the brand—intentions expressed in mission, values, and vision. While the literature in business and organizational development is replete with references to the importance of the customer experience, there is often a practical disconnect when it comes to creating a customer experience that is truly brand aligned. In an effort to land on a cool marketing idea, to craft a great marketing message, or attract a new market, enterprises often make the mistake of overlooking the fundamentals of branding by simply using or employing a tactical approach they experienced elsewhere. Whether refreshing, updating, or aligning with an existing brand or creating a new brand, it becomes critical as a first step to revisit and thoroughly understand the organization's mission, values, and vision. Chapter 2 will examine the brand process—beginning with this first step. For now, let's consider an even more advanced way to think about brands and their relationship to libraries.

Advanced Branding and the World of Libraries

As the conversation about branding has expanded, so has the necessity for all entities, including commercial enterprises, governmental agencies, and nonprofits and libraries, to leverage the science and art of branding. We increasingly live in a "brand world" in which the sheer complexity of choice requires a shorthand way to determine which among many choices should be made. This is true when looking through the internal lens of the organization that is seeking better ways to reach those customers who can benefit most by what it has to offer. At the same time (and being totally respectful of the customer's perspective), it is increasingly incumbent on organizations—especially those serving a social purpose—to find better ways to enable customers to make good choices. Effective branding, positioning, and promotion serve the enterprise and the customer. A well-developed brand provides a shorthand—a trusted point of reference to guide decisions and a mutual exchange of benefit—whether the decisions and exchanges involve a transaction of services, a vote, an investment of personal energy, or a contribution of time or resources.

How do we use the principles of branding to at once serve the interests of the organization and the customer? First, we need to conceptualize the concept of brand considering all of the dimensions that apply.

THE THREE DIMENSIONS OF BRANDING

The literature frequently references three words when discussing the concept of brands and branding—*identity, personality,* and *image.* In fact, these three words are often used interchangeably, implying that a brand is a blend of all three but without clarifying how they differ. More than an academic discussion, separating these three dimensions is an important step in understanding how brands work and especially in evaluating how your brand is working for you (see figure 1.1).

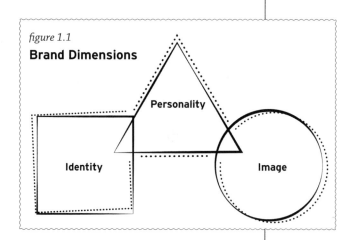

figure 1.1
Brand Dimensions

While each will be examined in much greater detail in the chapters that follow, here are working definitions for each:

- **Identity**—Clarity about who you are, what you do, and who benefits—largely premised on past tense: evidence
- **Personality**—Affinity with your personal features, characteristics, and attributes—largely premised on present tense: experience
- **Image**—Aspiration to associate with your standards, qualities, and vision—largely premised on future tense: possibility

APPLICATION TO LIBRARIES

The 2008 OCLC report *From Awareness to Funding: A Study of Library Support in America* reveals a very favorable public perception of the collective library "brand," and yet those perceptions are substantially limited by the prevailing view of the library as a traditional information source. In effect, the general public does not identify with the library as a venue for transformation and value-added programs and services—there is disconnect between how libraries see themselves and how they want the marketplace to see them. Furthermore, there is a distinct disconnect between the perceived brand value of libraries and the public's understanding and support of libraries when it comes to funding (DeRosa and Johnson 2008). This situation represents a kind of brand crisis for libraries in general—as an institution and certainly for individual library organizations regardless of setting.

In the spring of 2011 the authors, while interviewing Alison Circle of Columbus Metropolitan Library, became aware of her marketing blog called the *Bubble Room* at www.libraryjournal.com. Dropping in on the *Bubble Room* conversations, the authors saw an opportunity to engage blog participants in a discussion about their library brands—to examine more carefully how this brand crisis may be expressing itself on a more local level. At Alison's suggestion, the authors took the conversation one step further by approaching those most active in the *Bubble Room* blog, through a survey titled *Library Branding: A Garden Party Conversation* (Jackson 2011). From her list of over thirty active bloggers, nineteen responded to the initial survey, representing libraries from various types and settings across the country. Here is how they responded to questions pertaining to the three dimensions of their brand.

Library Identity

Question: Do most of our customers have a reasonably good understanding of what our library is about and what we have to offer?

This question goes to the heart of library "identity"—the extent to which the marketplace understands what the library is and has to offer. In the brand development process, identity is the first ingredient to consider. In order for a market, any market, to have reason to engage, the market must first have sufficient understanding of what it is the organization represents—and therefore a sense for the range of possibility it represents. Interestingly, of the nineteen library professionals who answered this question, only two, or just over 10 percent, answered with a strong affirmative "Yes," while fourteen, or nearly 75 percent, reported a more tentative "Somewhat," and three, or 16 percent, answered with a definitive "No." It is also important to note, however, that most of the follow-on comments suggested that the problem of library identity was not so much one of misunderstanding by the marketplace, but rather one of incomplete understanding of what the library actually and potentially has to offer (see figure 1.2).

Those who answered "No" to this question asserted reasons having to do with a lack of marketing communications and/or a commitment on the part of the organization to actively engage in marketing communications. No surprise here. Organizations, no matter how well their collective industry or sector brands are understood by the marketplace, must continually promote themselves to make certain the marketplace has a contemporary, complete, accurate, and confident view of what they have to offer.

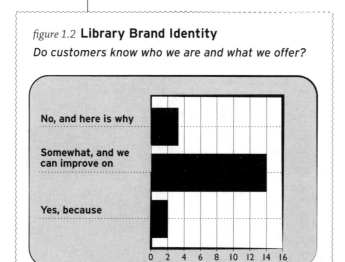

figure 1.2 **Library Brand Identity**

Do customers know who we are and what we offer?

When examining the "Somewhat" responses, reasons varied substantially and offered interesting insights. Several referenced the concern that they were not getting the word out in one form or another. Two noted that they struggle to reach their markets at times when the markets most need, want, and are ready to consider what they have to offer. Most addressed the challenge of expanding the customer's view beyond what customers *expect* to find at the library, particularly those in the programmatic and digital arenas. One mentioned the challenge of reaching a growing Hispanic audience, and another addressed the challenge of communicating the idea that what libraries offer may not be perceived as truly valuable because they are available free to the public. This comment relates in a meaningful way to the exchange theory, which postulates the importance of a mutual exchange of benefit (value) as essential to the perception of true value in an exchange (Bagozzi 1975).

Those who responded with an affirmative "Yes" cited their library's brand strength as a reason and bottom-line results combined with measures of market penetration and engagement as compelling evidence. Here are a couple of direct quotes from the Garden Party survey:

> We see a return on our investment in marketing and public relations: in our door counts, circulation figures, program attendance and fund-raising. We have a strong brand that is instantly recognizable and a catch phrase that has entered the lexicon in town: the community's living room.

> We have about 80% penetration of Library cards and integrate ourselves into the community through programming and outreach to effectively engage our patrons so that they have recently experienced the library and know it is more than books. So yes our customers know what we offer. However, those who are not our customers—haven't set foot in a Library in 10 years—don't know this. So, if you changed the question and asked does the entire community know . . . then I would choose somewhat. (Jackson 2011)

Library Personality

Question: Do we offer our customers an experience that conveys a personality they can relate to, trust, and enjoy?

For a brand to resonate, there must be personal *touch points* that express the personality of the brand while creating a relationship with the customer. Even in a digital world the personality of a brand is important. Interestingly, there was less unanimity of response to this question, with seven of seventeen answering affirmatively and five of seven negatively, and five in the middle range of "Somewhat." Overall, these results suggest that libraries do somewhat better in the dimension of personality than they do with identity, in part because a key differentiator for libraries as sources for information and hopefully for transformation are the librarians themselves. The results reflect a broader view of library branding that recognizes the importance of the total environment (facilities, programs, informational resources, technology, and librarians) leading to the total library experience (see figure 1.3).

Those who answered "No" to this question took a broad approach in identifying the need for organizational commitment to the user experience, to improving physical and virtual environments, and to creating a friendly attitude expressive of the organization's "brand values and brand identity," in the words of one respondent. Lack of staff and leader buy-in were also emphasized. The more tepid "Somewhat" responders noted a great deal of variability from branch to branch, and staff member to staff member, and an inclination among staff to focus on making the task easier rather than enhancing the customer experience. Those responding with a strong "Yes" emphasized the importance given to a "premium customer experience," scoring well on the measure of "helpfulness," and meeting every customer's needs. Following are two anonymous responses that capture how these libraries seek to align their "brand personality" with the most basic needs of their customers:

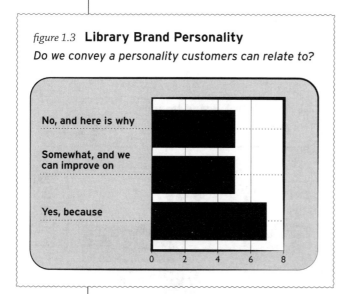

figure 1.3 **Library Brand Personality**

Do we convey a personality customers can relate to?

> Every public service person is given training on how to meet patron's needs. Every staff person is given an orientation on our brand. We run surveys and review comment cards and the feedback confirms that we are delivering on our brand.

> Because we survey our customers to ensure they get what they want. And if it's clear we need to up the ante or make changes, we do so based on their input and the availability of additional resources. However, we are also concerned about the folks who don't necessarily respond but have needs that the library may be able to meet. (Jackson 2011)

Library Image

Question: Do we have an image in the community that sets achievable expectations while inspiring confidence in what we offer?

The idea of "inspiration" is one that permeates discussion about branding and brands. Beyond being clear about what you offer and expressing a personality through good service touch points along the way and an exceptional experience, good brands are expressive of lofty and inspiring goals—increasingly associated with the social good. Respondents captured this concept in their remarks. It would seem that libraries as institutions have an inherent image to uphold, a clear commitment to the most lofty of goals—an informed and civil society. Yet among these respondents, libraries are challenged with understanding, clarifying, and expressing a lofty image internally and externally (see figure 1.4). Here is a sampling of comments that put the brand image challenge in perspective:

> Beyond being a proprietor of information many people don't understand the value that an academic library can offer to campus and to the community. I alluded to this earlier. I'm convinced, however, that our wonderful library staff—including librarians—also doesn't understand the real value-add benefit that an academic library can deliver to campus and the community.
>
> Among non-customers in the community, we are still working on increasing their understanding of today's libraries, and of how relevant libraries are in the 21st century. Some people who don't use the library don't think they should pay the taxes for it. We need to do a better job showing the public how public libraries strengthen communities through contributing to greater school success, job hunting, and business information needs, leading to greater economic stability and a reduction in crime—which everyone benefits from, not just those who use the library. (Jackson 2011)

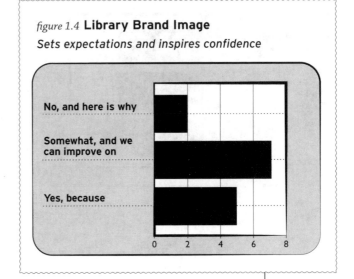

figure 1.4 **Library Brand Image**
Sets expectations and inspires confidence

This very simple survey, while limited to an insider's view of libraries, reveals much brand work to be done in all three areas of identity, personality, and image. If we go back to the story of that little boy at the beginning of the chapter (the author of this chapter by the way), we will recall the extent to which his experience captured all three. He came at an early age to appreciate the library brand for all that it represented within his range of youthful need and interest. It conveyed a personality that was friendly, approachable, and embracing in place and in people. And it was a place of magic, mystery, and inspiration. This was his foundational brand experience that, though modified and enhanced over many years, remains core to the meaning he associates with libraries in general and with specific libraries with which he engages to this day.

Summary

In this chapter, we introduced the concept of brand, beginning with a personal story and introducing how brands and the branding process are designed to forge emotional and intellectual relationships between organizations, customers, and constituents. Branding is a concept that has evolved from a largely external advertising or marketing idea to one more akin to organizational and cultural development. The branding process stimulates and guides improvement, serves to unify and align, and acts as a motive force for change.

We explored the elements of brand in-depth, including *identity, personality,* and *image.* In the final analysis, brands are always experienced by the user, internal and external to the organization, beginning with the origins of organizational intent—what you want the customer to feel, know, believe, and ultimately do. The challenges of library branding were introduced in context to the three elements and examined in the *Bubble Room* blog with inputs from a variety of library professionals.

REFERENCES

Asacker, Tom. 2005. *A Clear Eye for Branding.* Ithaca, NY: Paramount Market Publishing.

Bagozzi, Richard P. 1975. "Marketing as Exchange." *Journal of Marketing* 33 (January): 32–39.

Baskin, Mary, and Mark Earls. 2002. *Brand New Brand Thinking: Brought to Life by 11 Experts Who Do.* Sterling, VA: Kogan Page.

"Brand." 1984. *Funk & Wagnalls New International Dictionary of the English Language.* Comprehensive ed. Newark, NJ: Publishers International Press, 162.

"Brand." n.d. In Wikipedia. http://en.wikipedia.org/wiki/Brand (accessed January 2011).

Cowley, Don, ed. 1989. *Understanding Brands: By 10 People Who Do.* Sterling, VA: Kogan Page.

DeRosa, Cathy, and Jenny Johnson. 2008. *From Awareness to Funding: A Study of Library Support in America.* Dublin, OH: Online Computer Library Center.

Garrett, Jesse James. 2004. "Six Design Lessons from the Apple Store." *Adaptive Path,* July 9. http://adaptivepath.com/ideas/e000331.

IDC. 2012. "Androids Tablets Gain Momentum in the Third Quarter, Expectations Remain High for the Holiday Quarter." Press release, November 5. www.idc.com/getdoc.jsp ?containerId=prUS23772412.

Jackson, Kent L. 2011. *Library Branding: A Garden Party Conversation.* http://dl.dropbox .com/u/31044078/Library%20Branding-Garden%20Party%20Report.pdf.

Assessing Your Library Brand

YOUR LIBRARY HAS A BRAND BY VIRTUE OF ITS name, its history, and how it is perceived internally and externally. Brands comprise a *brand premise*—what a "library" is understood to be as a place of informational resources and service—and a *brand promise*—a declared or implied commitment to a certain level of quality or uniqueness in offerings, conveniently available at little or no cost and supported by services tailored to the customers' needs and wants. Generally, libraries are well understood in our society for what they are, treasured within their communities, neighborhoods, universities, and schools, and considered so important for the public good that they have been publicly funded for years. Libraries are viewed as essential to the communities they serve as keepers of the past and transformational influences for the future. "The library is not about 'information'; it is about 'transformation.' The library is not an outdated institution. It is a vital part of community infrastructure, it is not simply a 'nice to have' service—it is a necessity" (DeRosa and Johnson 2008, 6-12).

This chapter deals with assessing your current brand. The first step is to realize that you already have a brand, you have a brand story, and you have the data and information that can be very helpful as you begin this process. Often, the use of outside consultants can provide assistance to quantify information, help you develop your vision, and assist you in boldly addressing your need for an organizational, strategic, or marketing plan. This chapter specifically deals with the first steps in formally assessing your current brand, of conducting a SWOT analysis that will provide you with both internal and external analysis of your strengths, weaknesses, opportunities, and threats. The SWOT analysis provides opportunities for growth and insights in new areas. The development of strategic initiatives enhances the power of your brand development and will serve to guide your planning process, whether to address an overall strategy or a specific opportunity.

It is imperative to conduct a thoughtful, quantitative, and qualitative look at your current brand in order to embrace the changes and programs that will allow you to become *transformative,* to develop a current, relevant, and resonant brand premise and brand promise.

Start with Your Own Intuition

Remember that little boy and his first encounter with a library? Had that been his only experience, then his understanding and appreciation for the meaning of "library" would have been limited and quickly eroded over time. But it didn't stop there. Libraries, and the meaning behind libraries, were a part of every milestone of his life, and as it was in his seminal experience, the library was ever branded as a place, a source, a resource, a refuge, and a castle of magic. For this little boy, the power of the library brand would impact his entire life and would ultimately give him reason to participate in the authoring of this book.

This is where intuitive "good sense" about brands begins—by examining your own relationship with a brand, its objective, and its emotional dimensions and

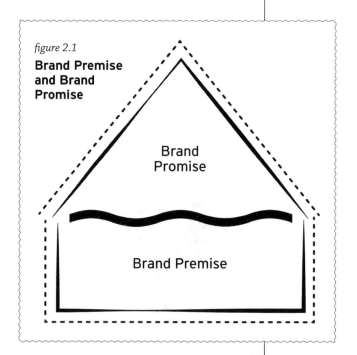

figure 2.1
Brand Premise and Brand Promise

Brand Promise

Brand Premise

meaning. Then and only then are you primed to extend your thinking to the perspectives of the many audiences you serve. What are your customers' presenting life experiences when they cross the library threshold, and what impression do you intend for them—to shape their experience and to evolve their relationship with you over time? When did they or might they have their first experience, what can and should it be for them, and where might and should it lead next? These are "brand questions" that go to the very heart of *premise* and *promise* (figure 2.1).

POWER OF THE BRAND STORY

To further appreciate the power of one person's "library story" and where it can lead, consider an article from *Time* magazine in December 2011, titled "The Little State That Could." Gina Raimondo, the treasurer of Rhode Island, in her first year in office and in the midst of a statewide crisis over a broken pension system and reduced funding of libraries, boldly took the reins by moving the general assembly to actually "fix" the problem. In the article, the author skillfully connects the dots of Raimondo's experiences as a child with her local library, taking a city bus to school, attending the local college, winning a Rhodes scholarship, graduating from Harvard, and succeeding in business. When asked to explain what attracted her, this is the story she shared (see figure 2.2):

> I was reading a story about budget cuts in the *Providence Journal*. The story talked about libraries closing and bus service budget cuts. I had an image of a kid like me trying to get into the library and it's closed. The public bus is how I got to school every day. The public library is where I studied. It's where my grandfather taught himself English. (Von Drehle 2011)

As someone intimately involved with libraries, you no doubt have your own story and an exceptionally accurate intuition about what brought you to your first library and keeps you engaged in the cause of libraries today. That you are reading this book suggests that you have a sense that branding and related ideas like positioning and promotion of libraries are important subjects for libraries and librarians to consider. And we're betting that's why you picked up and are reading this book. Malcolm Gladwell, author of *Blink*, reminds us of the power of rapid cognition, when seasoned by preparation and experience, in rendering insightful observations and arriving at good decisions about what we already know and understand in a deep and personal way (Gladwell 2011). The late Steve Jobs, founder and strategy genius behind the Apple brand, reminds us of the power of intuiting what customers will want in the future based in part on what it is we want. Both would likely agree that you need to prepare yourself, to inform and nurture an intellectual and emotional understanding of what it is and who will care, in order to truly impact the future or "put a dent in the universe," as Jobs was fond of saying (Editors of *Fortune* magazine 2011). So, ready yourself for the process of "rapid cognition" as we take you through three intuition-prompting questions to begin assessing your brand.

figure 2.2 **Brand Story**

REVISIT THE *BUBBLE ROOM*

The Garden Party survey discussed in the first chapter offered several deep insights from individuals like you—based on quick intuitive insights about their library's identity, personality, and image. Like them, you can begin by simply asking yourself the same three questions:

- Do most of our customers have a reasonably good understanding of what our library is about and what we have to offer?
- Do we offer our customers an experience that conveys a personality they can relate to, trust, and enjoy?
- Do we have an image in the community that sets achievable expectations while inspiring confidence in what we offer?

Based on how you answer these questions, you can widen the process by engaging others in the conversation, internally and externally, colleagues and customers alike—expanding, refining, and validating your intuitive sense for the way things are now and where you need to focus your brand for the future.

ASK CUSTOMERS, COLLEAGUES, AND COMMUNITY LEADERS

Once you have given yourself permission to thoughtfully explore these questions, many more will be begin to surface. Do you know who most of your customers are, and as important, what do you know about their perceptions of your library, of what your library offers, and of how they experience the library in their interactions and exchanges? As more and more questions emerge beyond the reach of your own informed intuition, it's time to expand your company of conversation to selectively include colleagues, customers, and community leaders with whom you have a confident relationship. It is typically in this stage, as you are engaged in this process, that the seeds of brand change are born. And if those seeds take hold, you are ready to move to a more formal assessment.

The Nexus—Forging a Purpose and Focusing Your Library

There are a host of paths you may take to discover or rediscover a need and desire to focus on branding, positioning, and promotion. The path may have been one marked by a drumbeat of incremental change over time—within the organization itself and/or within the market area it serves—the sum of which ultimately reached a critical mass requiring a new purpose and focus. On the other hand, the path may be the result of

Taking a Brand Leap—From County Library to Anythink

THE ADAMS COUNTY Library System, with a collection geared more to reference than popular materials and small, musty branches and a dwindling patronage, had been mired in a vicious cycle for years. In 2006, the voters approved a mill levy increase after a grassroots campaign led by the library board, staff, and a few loyal customers. With the advantage of a good economic climate timed with a midterm election that would produce a high voter turnout, the board and leadership tapped a unique opportunity to rebuild the library system as they crafted a new and courageous brand that was relevant, future focused, and inspired toward innovation. It no doubt began with one person asking a few questions and then by the engagement of many gave purpose and focus to an undertaking that was to change everything.

dramatic shifts within the organization or community—a sudden economic down-turn, the arrival of a major new employer, a natural disaster, or severe budget cuts owing to problems outside the control of the library. More likely your situation is a bit of all of these in an era marked by uncertain economic and political landscapes, and with communities that our libraries serve being buffeted by changes that are often more chaotic than the incremental or progressive change we plan for (see figure 2.3).

Libraries large and small, independent, part of a network, or embedded in another institution are resourceful and transformational learning enterprises closely woven into the complex fabric of the communities they serve. Libraries are not just complicated institutions staffed by professional libraries, but also they are complex institutions influenced by a multiplicity of programs and services, changing patterns of interaction and interdependence, and the diversity of those they serve. This inherent complexity can mask and sometimes confuse how change is perceived, leading to inaction or adherence to dated and limited modes of thinking about how to address the library's brand, positioning, and promotion. Accordingly, it behooves those within the library community to be open to palpable changes in their communities and institutions and to vigilantly prepare the library to address those changes. For more on the subject of managing complexity, review a series of articles appearing in the September 2011 issue of *Harvard Business Review* (Sargut and McGrath 2011; Morieuz 2011; Sullivan 2011).

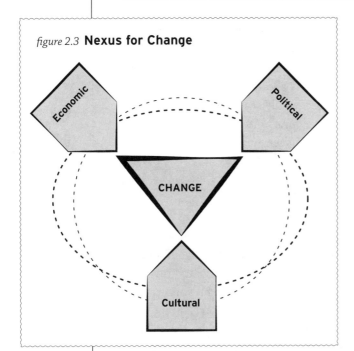

figure 2.3 **Nexus for Change**

It is in this convergence of awareness—of change, the interactions of change, your own readiness for change, and even your acceptance of chaos born of observation, questioning, and engagement with others—that you will find the motivation and basis for taking next steps. What are these next steps—the formal first steps you should take? They may include development of a business plan, with a holistic enterprise focus on the immediate challenges of the present and near term. Perhaps a more long-term strategic plan is in order, one that addresses present realities and emerging trends and opportunities. Or your focus may be more specific to the development of a marketing initiative, communications strategy for a new service or program, or a fund-raising campaign.

Taking Stock of Your Library Brand

In their professional work with organizational branding and positioning, the authors are accustomed to coming into the conversation at about this stage—when someone or a group has concluded that an organization needs to address matters of branding or positioning and has decided to seek outside help. What happens next may sound simple, but it is a process that requires a guiding framework, can take time, and may be aided by involving others who can provide an objective perspective.

Taking stock is not new to libraries or to librarians, as they have demonstrated the ability to adapt to incredible changes over time. Libraries and librarians have prided themselves on the ability to accommodate needs as they emerge and to anticipate changes on the horizon, and through it all they have sustained a relatively clear and favorable brand premise in the mind of the public and those who make decisions about the place and role of libraries. Even today in arguably the most complex of times we have ever faced, libraries as institutions are viewed favorably, and their premise is relatively intact. Yet today's fierce competition for our attention challenges the very premise of libraries—raising questions about the role they play in a world abundant in immediate information and increasingly scarce in resources. And so it may be time for you to thoroughly reexamine your library's brand—starting with its premise or very reason to be. Then and only then will you be prepared to address the promise of the brand—its reason to become.

START WITH MISSION AND VALUES— WHY YOU ARE HERE

The process of brand assessment begins by assessing your mission—your premise—that which declares what it is you do best for whom, and predicated on your core competencies, assets, and resources. In this world of diminishing resources and increasing technological sophistication, libraries must be more succinct, direct, and clear about their mission. Review your mission and examine as you do the underlying values that serve to anchor that mission—providing the framework for guiding principles and precepts that define why and how your library works, interacts, performs, and evolves as it does. Consider how your values serve as attractors and solidifiers of your library culture—the "sticky" substance that causes people—staff, volunteers, customers, and the community—to attach and stay. Consider also how your values serve your organization operationally, providing guidance when faced with difficult choices and shaping standards for performance and measures for success. Force yourself to write a clear and concise mission statement, or review and carefully consider the one you have. Do the same with your value statement. If you can't capture your mission and values in writing, they are probably no longer in effect. If they do not testify to what you do now, they are probably not accurate.

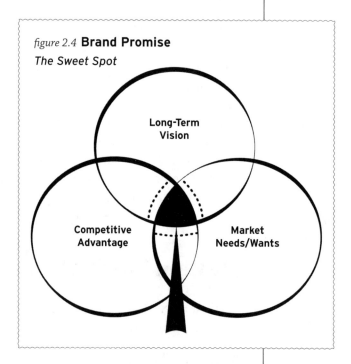

figure 2.4 **Brand Promise**
The Sweet Spot

Long-Term Vision

Competitive Advantage

Market Needs/Wants

CONSIDER YOUR VISION—WHERE YOU ARE GOING

> "If you don't know where you are going, any road will take you there."
>
> —Cheshire cat to Alice in Lewis Carroll's *Alice in Wonderland*

Now you are ready to examine your vision. With mission defined, you have a clear sense of what you are doing. With values clear, you know why you are doing what you do. And with vision, you are ready to declare what you intend to do in the future. A vision statement should provide a vivid and compelling picture of a future that is rationally tied to your mission, emotionally tied to your values, and inspirationally tied to the future of your organization. The stirring nature of an effective vision statement becomes a powerful motivational tool for your staff and stakeholders. A strategic vision charts a path to the future while building the commitment of the board, staff, and community. And a strategic long-term vision ultimately provides a creative springboard for development of your brand, your brand aesthetic, and the unique value proposition as discussed in Chapter 1, an articulation of a "sweet spot" for your brand promise that will resonate with your customer and differentiate you from the competition (see figure 2.4).

Assessing Your Situation with SWOT

Now that you have assessed your mission, values, and vision, the purpose of your brand should be clear—you know what you are about, what you believe, and what you envision for the future. You've clarified your purpose and focus. Now you are ready to assess that purpose and focus with a clear-headed and realistic look at

Creating a New Library—A New Library Brand

GUIDED BY THE landmark OCLC study *From Awareness to Funding,* the Rangeview Library District (RLD) leadership knew that they had a choice. They could either replicate existing libraries or create a unique library system that examined and met critical community needs, designing an organization with the flexibility to grow into a library that meets the needs of twenty-first century learning. The OCLC study said, "The information landscape is anything but stable. The knowledge landscape is expanding rapidly and the library's once unique position as the place that provides books and information is increasingly crowded. Without action, it is almost certain that the library's brand will continue to be seen as a legacy service, a 'nice to have,' but not critical institution, more relevant in the past than for the future" (DeRosa and Johnson 2008, 7-1).

Before any branding discussions could occur, district leadership needed to define what type of library system they wanted to become. Rather than let tradition dictate their direction, the RLD board and administration developed their own visioning process and examined an "experience model" that focuses on the experience of each customer who visits the libraries. This new service philosophy guided each decision made, from designing spaces and programming to the development of the Anythink brand.

Director Pam Sandlian-Smith employed the consulting firm of Mildly Delirious Design and Peter Robinson to work with the library. Robinson had created the GASP process to assist in creating brands and identities for hotels, restaurants, and events and said that it could be adapted for the library. He explains that the GASP process he worked on at the West Palm Beach Public Library indicated "a welcoming, contemporary library that merges innovation with tradition." GASP stands for Graphics, the image of the project; Ambience, the feeling in the air; Style, the service approach; and Personality and Programs.

Anythink libraries needed to clarify their vision before they could move forward, and this project was the first collective visioning of the future library.

the library's present situation. A SWOT analysis (Strengths, Weaknesses, Opportunities, and Threats) provides an excellent framework to guide situational assessment (see figure 2.5). Although the true origins of SWOT are unclear, the technique is generally credited to Stanford University's Albert Humphrey, who as part of a research project completed in the 1960s set out to identify ways to improve the effectiveness of the corporate planning process. This project and the research studies that followed pointed to the need for a

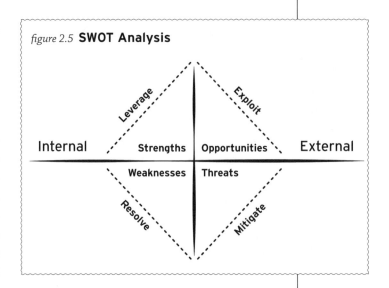

figure 2.5 **SWOT Analysis**

logical appraisal process that would enable organizations to establish a consensus understanding of their present situation in order to plan effectively for the future (Friesner n.d.).

A SWOT analysis is often referred to as a situation analysis because it provides a general examination of both the internal and external situation in which your library operates and addresses both present realities and anticipated future realities. Demonstrated capabilities of your library are considered *strengths,* while capabilities to address anticipated future realities are considered *opportunities.* Conversely, inabilities of your library to address present realities are considered *weaknesses,* while inabilities or potential inabilities to address anticipated future realities are considered *threats.*

INTERNAL STRENGTHS AND WEAKNESSES

The first step in a SWOT analysis is the close examination of the library's present strengths and weaknesses—from the inside out. Three key dimensions should be considered in arriving at this assessment, beginning with considerations of the library's *depth* in terms of existing resources, capacities, and core competencies. The second is the library's *demand* in terms of current customers being served and new customers to be served. The third dimension is the motive force that moves the library, or its *desire,* in terms of the relevancy of the library's mission, values, and vision. Kent Jackson has applied this "3D" model to isolate the very essence of a brand in the context of a SWOT analysis for a variety of organizations from start-up businesses to large corporations, and from nonprofits to government-supported institutions (see figure 2.6). He was first introduced to the 3D model while working with his brother's firm, Lance Jackson and Associates, Inc., a Denver-based brand marketing firm now doing business as Art + Business One.

Focus First on Your Strengths

Beginning with the first "D," or *depth,* consider the inherent strengths of your organization and summarize or create bullet points for each of them. For example, perhaps you have substantial strength in the location of your library or libraries or in the quality and functionality of the design of your facilities. Or maybe your collections in essential content areas and related resourcing services are especially strong—something you have carefully developed over time. Or your library staff, board, or even volunteers may reflect exceptional competencies in certain areas, including customer service. Your financial structure may also reveal certain areas of strengths, solidity, and resourcefulness important to factor into your analysis.

Moving to the second "D," or *demand,* consider how your library serves customers as measured by your penetration of cardholders within the market(s) you serve, and extend your analysis to measures of usage (such as frequency of visit, items accesses or checked out, and so on) and customer satisfaction. Consider programs and services that have been especially successful in addressing certain customer groups and perhaps new customers you have been seeking to serve. Extend your *demand* assessment to include the identification of other audiences you may want to serve, including community organizations, other governmental or institutional groups, or business interests.

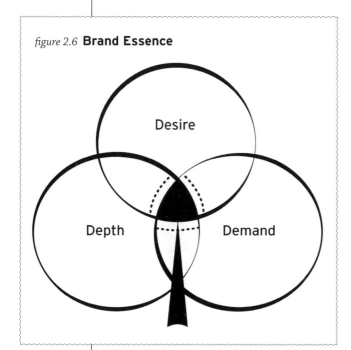

figure 2.6 **Brand Essence**

You have already explored your mission, values, and vision—the essential components of the third "D," *desire.* Combining depth, demand, and desire, finally consider the history of your library—the story of why and how it was established, how it has evolved over the years, the changes and challenges it has faced, who it has served and continues to serve, and the enduring qualities and characteristics for which it has come to be known. As you review the history of your library and highlight its strengths, you may also be reminded of times and circumstances where the organization faltered, failed to deliver, or encountered difficulties. Keep these in mind, but first give yourself and your colleagues the opportunity to account for and sum your strengths—to capture all of the positives before you turn a critical eye on the negatives. This is important because you build, position, and promote your brand from a foundation of strength, maintaining and leveraging all that is right, working, extendable, and promising about your organization. Once you feel confident that you have accounted for and given historical perspective to the strengths of your library brand, you are attitudinally and objectively ready to pursue the subject of weaknesses.

Keep Your Weaknesses in Perspective

The subject of weakness is an interesting one. Often a weakness is considered something you simply have not chosen to do in the past as an organization, or perhaps something you tried but executed poorly. Such weaknesses tend to come to mind first because they are so vivid in memory and/or are painful reminders of failures and faults. However, having fully assessed your strengths as a first step, you may discover that what you are good at in some instances, you may not be so good at in others. For example, your facilities—given their locations, designs, and interiors—

may be serving certain customers, staff, and volunteers extremely well but failing to meet the needs of others seeking you out or those you have set out to serve. Similarly, your special collections may represent a point of pride for your brand among a limited segment of your community, yet be viewed as an excessive investment compared to the unmet needs of other constituents. Or your customer service model may be performing extremely well with young families and seniors, but faltering when addressing the teen population or perhaps adults seeking employment. This is the territory you want to explore first—strengths of your brand that under scrutiny also reveal areas of weakness. Weaknesses that are closely allied with strengths are the areas you can likely address most readily and in ways that align best with your brand. Weaknesses that fall historically out of your realm of strengths will require the most investment from your organization—perhaps more than you can or should give—and will be very challenging to address with your brand.

EXTERNAL OPPORTUNITIES AND THREATS

Your strengths and weaknesses are primarily internal dimensions you want to evaluate first. On that foundation, the SWOT process then guides you to more carefully assess the external environment, including present realities and signals of future trends. The main purpose for scanning the external environment is to discover opportunities that you are well positioned to address, and to anticipate areas of external (present and future) threat that you should consider. As with internal strengths and weaknesses, opportunities and threats can be closely linked. Start with the exploration of your opportunities. Next, being mindful of your relative strengths and weaknesses, consider threats. For example, the problems of declining economics and unemployment create an opportunity for libraries as they seek to serve their customer base. Assuming you are well positioned by current strengths, you may be in an advantageous position to address this situation as an opportunity to serve the local interests of business development and the needs of the underemployed or unemployed. At the same time, this situation may contribute to a declining tax base and/or level of community support for your library—posing a threat to your ability to maintain your current levels of service or to expand your offerings.

Team Involvement

The processes we have just described, forging a purpose and a strategic focus for your brand through thoughtful and comprehensive assessment, is a corporate matter involving all major constituents with a stake in your brand (see figure 2.7). Your major constituents certainly include

figure 2.7 **Strategic Purpose and Focus**

Organizational Development & Communications

Environments & Resources

Services & Convenience

customers—present and future library users—as well as people and organizations that provide monetary and voluntary support, essential resources and capabilities, and strategic partnership that in combination bring value to the marketplace. Your board, executive leadership, and marketing team must be involved, and there can be great value in extending participation to friends groups, supporting foundations, and government representatives (town, city, county, state, and federal), as well as allied and local institutions and business/industry partners. Their participation can be scaled depending on their level of involvement, availability, and expertise—from direct hands-on participation, to arm's-length survey involvement, to oversight and final review, and perhaps to endorsement or approval of assessment outcomes and recommendations. There is no single "right" way to engage constituents in arriving at your strategic purpose and focus for developing your brand. Consider all the people, processes, and protocols that best fit your situation and develop a participation plan accordingly.

From Strategic Plan to Brand Development

COLUMBUS METROPOLITAN LIBRARY developed its strategic plan in 2004 with guidance from the members of the community, library, staff, Friends of the Library, and the board of trustees. The strategic planning process identified measurable objectives, clear initiatives, and a purposeful mission that focused on helping customers in their pursuit of information, knowledge, and wisdom. Leadership clearly identified the need for marketing expertise within the organization as well as careful examination of its customer base. The library began its marketing plan process in 2005.

Using Market Research

Up to now we have described processes that represent a combination of informal and anecdotal information-gathering and evaluation. These processes may involve the use of existing statistical data and financial data, and perhaps extend to local or regional demographic and economic trend data, including census-based information. To the extent that this information is useful for the purposes of assessing your brand, positioning, and promotional strategies, it all contributes to and represents a form of market research. What defines market research is not just the information involved, nor the methods used to gather and analyze the information, but rather the purposes to which the information is being applied. Therefore, market research will be introduced first as it applies to brand assessment and to how it informs the branding process. In Chapter 5, the discussion will focus more on market research as applied to positioning and targeting of specific markets. And again in Chapter 8, market research is addressed under the heading "Evaluation—You Get What You Measure" in relationship to the implementation and assessment of promotional strategies and tactics. Here is a simple definition of market research that aligns well with the experience of the authors and the purposes of this book:

> Market research is the systematic and objective planning, gathering, recording and analyzing of information to enhance the decision making of marketing managers. (Shao 2002)

As you reread this definition, consider the key qualifier "systematic," implying an organized, integrated, and, where possible, automated process. This definition also recognizes the two-dimensional meaning of "objective" as having one or more objectives in mind as a reason for conducting research and doing so in a manner that is reasonably independent and free of contaminating or misleading bias or error in measurement. The core of this definition is "to enhance the decision making" of those assuming responsibility for any and all aspects of library branding, positioning, and/or promotion.

WHAT CONSTITUTES MARKET RESEARCH?

When applied to branding, market research is invaluable in understanding how your library brand is perceived internally and externally, and can be extremely useful in guiding brand assessment and development—whether it be with a focus on branding from scratch, rebranding, brand refinement, or updating your brand. Types of market research are best understood in terms of their sequence and application within the brand assessment process, by the sources of information used in the assessment process, and by the methods employed to analyze that information.

By Sequence and Application

There are basically three kinds of market research as defined by the intended applications or objectives of the research, typically falling in an order or sequence that begins with exploratory research, followed by descriptive research, and ending with conclusive or causal research (see figure 2.8).

Exploratory research, as the name implies, captures information described in early parts of this chapter, including intuitive, informal, tangential, observational, and anecdotal information that is gathered along the way. This is typically where you begin in the process to initially identify the brand problem or problems to be addressed, to formulate initial hypotheses or informed guesses about how to address the problem, and to gain insights on matters surrounding the problem that may later be helpful in formulating new insights—connecting the dots of information in new ways. There is both a tentative and empowering quality to exploratory market research—tentative in recognition that such research is by definition preliminary and based on high degrees of uncertainty and empowering given the freedom to explore the problem both wide and deep—to go where the information leads. Exploratory research tends to be small scale, requires the direct involvement of only a few people, and is relatively inexpensive—sometimes aided by but seldom requiring the costly involvement of outside experts or resources.

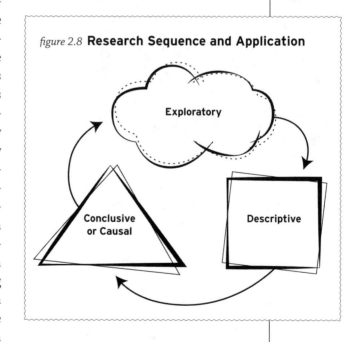

figure 2.8 **Research Sequence and Application**

Descriptive research is useful in painting a true picture of the brand situation, the customers served or to be served by the brand, and perceptions toward and behavioral interactions with the brand. Different from exploratory research, descriptive research is guided by clearly stated objectives and based on carefully formulated questions related to what you want to know and understand about the subjects of your research. Descriptive studies comparing the demographic, psychographic, and geographic characteristics of your cardholders to better understand their lifestyles and consumer preferences is a good example of descriptive market research. Descriptive research is useful in framing decisions and can serve to guide decision making but is seldom the exclusive basis or source for making final decisions about the brand, its positioning, or promotion. More time-consuming than exploratory research, descriptive research can be costly, often requiring the informed assistance of outside expertise and the analytic merger of multiple data sources.

Conclusive or causal research is where the "rubber meets the road" in market research—providing the basis for rendering decisions and predicting outcomes or effects. Conclusive research is designed to lead the organization to conclusive decisions about its brand, its brand positioning, and promotional strategies. A survey of carefully segmented customers, based first on an exploratory investigation of those who utilize the library and descriptive research that provides a wealth of insights regarding their demographics and lifestyle characteristics, might yield conclusive data within a reasonable level of confidence and range of error about how customers perceive the library brand and what products and services they associate most favorably with the brand. Based on this data, your library might then decide on the best ways to enhance the brand (identity, personality, or image) with similar customers and the products and services they are most likely to favorably associate with your brand. Most conclusive research is reliant on correlated data—data that signal associated relationships between two or more data points, say gender status and library usage patterns. While the correlated data may strongly support an association between female gender status and high library usage, for example, it does not necessarily suggest that being female is causal to library usage. Though not rising to the causal level, conclusive research is valuable in guiding best-bet decision making about whom your brand is reaching and how your brand is perceived. Conclusive research is very focused, is clearly defined by objectives and methodologies, and relies heavily on expertise in areas of basic research design, data collection, and analysis.

Causal research, the crème de la crème of market research, is often used in brand development to test conceptual alternatives, to assess alignment of brand attributes with characteristics of the library culture—including staff, volunteers, and customers—and to measure the efficacy of branding, positioning, and promotional strategies—including calls to action. Causal research, like descriptive and conclusive research, requires careful delineation of research objectives, sophisticated research design, and rigorous control of variables and outcomes to be measured, tracked, and analyzed. It can be difficult and costly to acquire the expertise necessary to effectively and efficiently design meaningful causal research.

Decisions about the use of conclusive and/or causal research in the branding process should be weighed carefully, considering the extent to which your library feels it can and must invest in the branding effort. If the exploratory and descriptive research efforts used to assess the brand reveal the need for substantial rebranding, the costs of which can also be substantial, then it will make sense to factor in a reasoned level of conclusive and perhaps causal research to guide crucial decisions. As discussed in Chapters 5 and 8, these more advanced research methods (conclusive and causal) are more commonly used to guide and assess positioning strategies and to evaluate promotional strategies and tactics over time, providing a means of amortizing the costs of such research over a range of initiatives and activities.

By Source of Information—Primary and Secondary

Research can all also be defined by source of information and by type of information (see figure 2.9). Source of information is discussed in this section, while type of information is covered in the next section. There are essentially only two sources for you to consider—information you acquire directly or indirectly and information that comes in the form of numeric, or quantitative, data or in the form of narrative, or qualitative, data.

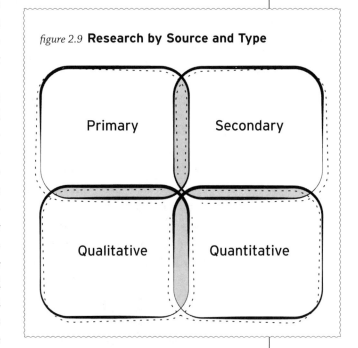

figure 2.9 **Research by Source and Type**

Primary market research, as the name implies, derives from prime or original data generated by you or your organization. For example, your cardholder database that descriptively defines the geographic reach (by street address or zip code) of your customers is primary market data. If you were using this primary data, sourced by your library, in combination with census data made publicly available to perhaps identify underserved geographic markets, the census data you employed is secondary information that is sourced from a secondary provider. There are important benefits and limitations to each that will factor into your decisions about sourcing research information.

Libraries carefully and routinely capture information about users and usage patterns, and thus have tremendous primary and secondary data that can be applied to marketing. The authors are well aware of reasons why you might overlook or be disinclined to tap these sources—because you may not have realized how valuable it can be in branding, positioning, and promotion or perhaps because you perceive an ethical problem in using it. The answer to ethical concerns resides in developing a sensible approach that aggregates and integrates data in ways that are fully respectful of the interests of cardholders and library users and that protect their identity and the confidentially of data associated with their identity.

By Types of Information

At the most basic level, market research information can be categorized as either something you can count, as in numbers, and therefore objective and quantitative, or something from which you can derive subjective meaning, as in words, symbols, and other forms of human expression, and therefore subjective and qualitative. Numerical data, perhaps related to descriptive demographics, or behavioral data related to purchasing behaviors are examples of pure quantitative information. Generally, results from surveys or tracking data on how people are engaging with a website or responding to e-mails or QR codes are expressed in numbers and are therefore quantitative measures. On the other hand, much of the information derived from a focus group, the recorded emotional expressions of customers engaging with a product or service, and the narratives found in blogs or on Twitter and other forms of postings and collaborative interactions, fall primarily in the domain of qualitative information. Keep in mind, however, that virtually all research methods can yield a blend of both quantitative and qualitative insights and information. For example, in a typical survey primarily comprised of quantitative response modes, such as multiple choice, Likert scale, or ranking options, you might add several open-ended questions. Thus, you are deriving both forms of data—quantitative in terms of numerical measures of choice selections, rank orders, and so on, and qualitative in terms of word-based responses to open-ended questions. Likewise, in a focus group you might precede an open-ended question or prompt by asking participants to rank-order their choice and then ask them to explain why. So again, you are collecting both forms of research data. Each affords and requires very different forms of data collection and analysis, and there can be crossover methods that integrate the two. For example, in analyzing subjective responses to an open-ended question, analysis of the meaning of responses can be accompanied by analysis of the frequency (counting) of similar or dissimilar responses. To measure the relative intensity of response, perhaps a word count might be used or a frequency count of meaning-packed words might be included. Often words and their meanings are analyzed using a quantitatively scaled semantic differential (Osgood et al. 1957).

Generally speaking, good market research is going to include a balanced combination of quantitative and qualitative data. Also generally speaking, quantitative data are more efficiently obtained and analyzed across a larger sample size, using generalized and often anonymous methods and lending reliability to the information obtained—the degree of certainty that if you asked the same question again of a similar audience under similar circumstances you would get the same or similar results. On the other hand, sound qualitative research, assuming you asked the same questions of similar but typically smaller audiences in a more personal and engaging environment and in a manner that allows for additional probing for clarification and elaboration, yields a result often more logically related to the subject and criteria you have in mind—to the degree of certainty that the answers you derive are a true and valid reflection of the perspective of the subject with regard to the questions posed.

In short, you might use a quantitative measure to gauge the relative strength of emotion or conviction customers have toward your library brand, and then use a more qualitative approach to find out how to express that emotion. Quantitative research, properly done, is more cost and time efficient than qualitative research and should generally precede more costly and time-consuming qualitative research.

Research Focused on External Markets and Internal Markets

When you commonly think of market research, particularly as it relates to branding, positioning, and promotion, you are inclined to focus only on the external customer—the donor, volunteer, or strategic partner. Yes, the demand dimension of a good brand always requires willing and engaged customers who reside primarily outside of or external to the organization. And, a good brand requires a committed, well-trained, and capable staff; volunteers; and invested board members to ensure its success over time—the more internal customers. Therefore, a complete market research program, especially one designed to address branding, accounts for the internal market as well as the external market. The reason is simple—it is the internal market that will ultimately translate the brand to external markets. Even in these times of substantial customer interaction occurring online—over the Internet or via websites and automated customer service and transaction management systems—the persona of the brand is ultimately expressed by the people behind those transactions. This is especially true when the transaction or the customer demands a face-to-face interaction. And to a great extent, the internal market also "wears the hat" of external markets, living and interacting in both worlds.

OCLC Study

ACCORDING TO THE OCLC study *From Awareness to Funding:* "Current associations and perceptions of the public library reveal that the imprint left by early memories of the library still affects a deeply held, lasting belief that the library is a transformative place where anyone can realize their potential. ... Many described the ability to expand their horizons as the heart of the library's value." One Super Supporter described it this way: "People who've been exposed to libraries realize that there are a lot of other cultures and things out there that a small town of 4,000 doesn't provide access to. The library is literally a window on the world." (DeRosa and Johnson 2008, 5-6-5-7)

UNDERSTANDING THE COMPETITIVE MARKET

Many libraries may not feel they have competition or need to compete, but in many ways they do. They compete for funding resources within a community, university, or corporation. They compete for private funding with individuals, foundations, and corporations. They compete for volunteers and staff. They compete with other institutions for bond elections. They compete with the Internet, television, and leisure activities.

Competition has its positive side in that it challenges you to deliver customer service equal to or better than your competitors—by focusing your attention on what good service means to customers. It encourages libraries to deliver services more efficiently and also to learn from the example of good competitors. Often your competitors can become partners in collaborative ventures, willingly sharing their service strategies and tactics in trade for valuable cobrand association with your library.

The primary competitors to consider are those that represent the emerging choices that consumers have. In the funding arena, they might choose to save the pension funds of those engaged in emergency services, such as police and firefighters, over the library you represent. In the consumer arena, it may be Google or Barnes & Noble, or the Nook or iPad. In the professional arena, it may be firms offering specialized databases and research expertise. It all depends on context and whom the library seeks to serve.

Market research should therefore factor in and use effective qualitative and quantitative means to assess the competitive landscape and to inform the process of evaluating competition. To find out who it is you truly compete with, just ask your customers. Ask them where else they go for many of the resources and services you have to offer, and ask them why. You will discover that in the "mind" of the marketplace you may have some interesting and perhaps opportune bedfellows you have never considered.

ASSESSING MARKET SHARE AND MIND SHARE

Especially important to the subject of brand assessment are measuring and understanding how your brand not only interacts with the market, as measured by the transactions (market share), but also the extent to which markets are aware of and have formed impressions or perceptions of your brand (mind share). Mind share is defined as "the level of awareness in the minds of consumers that a particular product commands," according to the *Collins English Dictionary* (2009). So market share and mind share involve looking at your market by looking through the same lens but from two different perspectives.

You are likely familiar with the notion of market share based on measures, such as the number of households in your service areas that have one or more library cards. Let's assume that in your community of 50,000 households, you have issued one or more library cards to 20,000 of those household addresses. Arguably, then you can declare that you have penetrated 40 percent of the market, or that you have a market share of 40 percent. Sounds good, doesn't it? Yet perhaps you recognize that of those 20,000 households only 10,000 demonstrate regular transactions with your library, measured by visits, checkout of materials, logins to website, and so

Rangeview Library "on the Map"

THE RANGEVIEW LIBRARY District (RLD) is very much on the national map, after perhaps the most dramatic turnaround in the nation following a *Denver Post* article naming it one of the worst in the state.

Yes, the library needed to focus on its internal markets. It had to examine its structure within the county, look at its collections, facilities, and services, as well as the Adams County community. RLD was guided by the landmark OCLC study *From Awareness to Funding*. The library examined the way it classified material and switched from the Dewey Decimal system to a word-based system. It eliminated overdue fines. By analyzing internal research, it was able to remove the barriers and shift to a customer service model.

From the OCLC study: "The information landscape is anything but stable. The knowledge landscape is expanding rapidly and the library's once unique position as the place that provides books and information is increasingly crowded.... Without action, it is almost certain that the library's brand will continue to be seen as a legacy service, a 'nice to have' but not critical institution, more relevant in the past than for the future." (DeRosa and Johnson 2008, 7-4)

Yes, Anythink had to really conduct internal examinations of its services, staffing levels, facilities, and collections in order to take the next step.

on, suggesting a more refined measure of market share closer to 20 percent of all households. You have sharpened the focus of the lens you are using to assess your market share—from penetration of households with a library card to penetration of households with both a library care and demonstrating "active" engagement with the library.

Now let's reverse the lens. Looking back at the number of households with a library card we can reasonably assume that at least those households are aware of what your library has to offer . . . so your "mind share" is no less than 40 percent. At the same time, perhaps you have recently conducted a community survey that reveals another 10,000 households without a current library card and reporting no current or recent use of the library but are generally aware of library services in your community and can relate to or have an expressed interest in one or more services you have to offer. By adding this household measure your "mind share" calculation is now reaching 60 percent of households.

Your "mind share" will and should exceed your "market share," depending on how focused your lens is from each perspective. But let's consider the exceptions that occur when we narrow the lens. Let's say that your library has recently developed a new business initiative in response to local economic trends. Upon initial introduction, because the program is new and represents a program not previously associated with the library, you may be starting a program with very little "mind share" from which to attract "market share" in support of the program. Thus, your marketing focus will need to address the creation of awareness or "mind share" early on.

As you contemplate your market research efforts, especially those associated with assessing your brand, become familiar with recognizing the similarities and differences between these two measures—market share is transaction-driven while mind share is awareness-driven.

ASSESSING BRAND EQUITY

Brand equity refers to the distinguishing qualities of a brand that result in a personal commitment to the brand, beginning with level of awareness that extends to the associated good will and recognition of the brand. Ultimately, brand equity is measured by a combination of market share and mind share and is expressed in higher usage volumes and public support in all forms. Libraries that are able to build strong positive brand equity have greater capacity to maintain and grow and to withstand pressures, manage risks, forge strategic partnerships, and address the challenges of change. As previously discussed, the generic library brand tends to be imprinted early, providing the potential for building powerful equity over time.

Brand equity refers to the essential value of your brand. Is your library viewed as a historical institution nice to have? Or is it viewed as a vital part of the community infrastructure—a must to have?

Implications for Planning and the Formulation of Strategy

The entire process of assessing your brand—beginning with careful examination of your mission, values, and vision and extending to market share, mind share, and brand equity—provides a sound basis for and contributes to the development of a clear and robust positioning strategy, including a framework for strategic planning. It may be that your library has initiated a strategic planning process that prompted a focus on branding, positioning, and promotion. If so, the assessment processes described in this chapter will complement and contribute to the planning process. Conversely, it may be that by focusing on your library's brand, the need for a comprehensive planning process emerges. Either way, the processes are much the same.

Columbus Metropolitan Library—A Transformational Agency

COLUMBUS METROPOLITAN LIBRARY (CML) represents the energy and passion of a dedicated team and their marketing and branding program, which has resulted in significant financial and political support for the library. Columbus Metropolitan Library is one of seven library systems serving Franklin County in central Ohio. There are twenty-one branches and one operations center within the system. In 2011, the library circulated fifteen million items and served seven million visitors.

Columbus Metropolitan Library has always viewed its role as a *transformational agency* in the community. Chief Executive Officer Patrick Losinski says, "Marketing is the last profession to be welcomed into libraries. It has made all of the difference at Columbus Metropolitan Library." The marketing plan and the development of the CML branding effort continue to be the rudder that has helped guide the library.

The first step of the marketing plan for Columbus Metropolitan Library was research. They reaffirmed their mission, vision, and values and developed a strategic plan, utilizing a SWOT analysis.

Summary

Your brand has a past, present, and future, and periodically assessing your brand with all of these dimensions in mind is critical. Your brand is evolving, constantly reinventing and anticipating a new future. It lives with and on behalf of the life of the community it serves. It is dynamic, changing, and transformational. According to the OCLC study *From Awareness to Funding,* "The library occupies a very clear position in people's minds as a provider of practical answers and information. This is a very crowded space, and to remain relevant in today's information landscape, repositioning will be required." (DeRosa and Johnson 2008, 4-9)

In this chapter the authors introduced you to the process and research methods to employ in assessing your brand, from informed intuition to understanding the brand story. From forging a clear purpose and focus for brand assessment to taking stock of your mission, values, and vision. We explored the use of a SWOT analysis— the assessment of internal strengths and weaknesses and external opportunities and threats—that involves your team in the entire assessment process. We described market research, along with the importance of assessing your competition, market share and mind share, and brand equity. Finally, we briefly explained the relationship between brand assessment and organizational and strategic planning.

Assessment of your brand will guide determination of what is needed to develop your brand. Is it a matter of revisiting and making sure you are staying on your brand message? Or does it mean updating the brand to make it more relevant for your customers? Or does it mean changing the brand—to leave behind one that is not viable or to move toward a whole new market or purpose? Here is a sampling of declarative outcomes that may derive from this process, paraphrased from *Designing Brand Identity* by Alina Wheeler (2009, 7):

- **New library, new offerings, new markets, new services**—therefore a new brand
- **Brand name change**—for a host of reasons from legal to competitive, to addressing an outdated, outmoded or troubled brand
- **Brand refinement or revitalization**—an opportunity to focus on strengthening brand identity, personality, or image
- **Brand integration**—tying separate parts, facilities, branches, and programs together under one integrated brand architecture
- **Brand mergers**—tying together previously separate entities or parts into one, a merger of library districts, of a state with county libraries, or of one or more companion institutions, including universities, colleges, and research institutes

Strategic Initiatives

RANGEVIEW LIBRARY DISTRICT (RLD) identified six strategic initiatives with related goals. Those strategic initiatives enabled them to achieve their strategic outcome for improving the quality of life in Adams County:

1. Deliver superb customer service, products, and programs.
2. Build beautiful and inspiring environments.
3. Deliver convenience and innovation through technology.
4. Provide meaningful communications.
5. Provide highly effective organizational development.
6. Create financial sustainability for the future of RLD.

These strategic initiatives were integral to and supported by the development of the Anythink brand.

REFERENCES

DeRosa, Cathy, and Jenny Johnson. 2008. *From Awareness to Funding: A Study of Library Support in America.* Dublin, OH: Online Computer Library Center.

Editors of *Fortune* magazine. 2011. *The Legacy of Steve Jobs 1955–2011—A Tribute from the Pages of Fortune Magazine.* New York: Time Home Entertainment.

Friesner, Tim. n.d. "History of SWOT Analysis." *Marketing Teacher.com.* www.marketing teacher.com/swot/history-of-swot.html.

Gladwell, Malcolm. 2011. *Blink: The Power of Thinking without Thinking.* New York: Little Brown.

"Mind share." 2009. In *Collins English Dictionary—Complete & Unabridged.* 10th ed. New York: HarperCollins.

Morieuz, Yves. 2011. "Smart Rules: Six Ways to Get People to Solve Problems Without You." *Harvard Business Review* 89, no. 9 (September), 78.

Osgood, C. E., G. Suci, and P. Tannenbaum. 1957. *The Measurement of Meaning.* Urbana, IL: University of Illinois Press.

Sargut, Gokce, and Rita Gunther McGrath. 2011. "Learning to Live with Complexity." *Harvard Business Review* 89, no. 9 (September), 68.

Shao, Alan T. 2002. *Instructor's Manual for Marketing Research: An Aid to Decision Making.* Cincinnati, OH: South-Western.

Sullivan, Tim. 2011. "Embracing Complexity: An Interview with Legg Mason Chief Investment Strategist Michael J. Mauboussin." *Harvard Business Review* 89, no. 9 (September), 88.

Von Drehle, David. 2011. "The Little State That Could." *Time,* December 5, 30–36.

Wheeler, Alina. 2009. *Designing Brand Identity: An Essential Guide for the Entire Branding Team.* 3rd ed. Hoboken, NJ: Wiley.

Developing Your Library Brand

THE PROCESS OF DEVELOPING YOUR LIBRARY BRAND requires a yeasty blend of research and introspection. The process also requires imaginative and visionary thinking, coupled with a strategic orientation and decisive leadership at all levels of the organization. Your brand is your external face that you present to the world. It also touches everything within your library, including customer service and employee relations, teamwork, and training. Your brand affects all of your services, collections and materials, displays, facilities, and distribution channels, including online distribution as well as physical delivery systems. Your brand is reflected in your communication pieces and your website. Your brand influences your relationships with suppliers, the media, donors, and stakeholders. Your brand represents your true identity—who you are and what you do, your personality as an organizational culture, what you value and how you express that value, and your image, all reflective of your vision for a future. Tackling brand development is a serious undertaking and one that you and your entire organization must address with care and commitment.

This chapter addresses the basic steps in the process of brand development. You have already been introduced to the process in Chapter 2 by taking the first serious step of assessing your brand. You have learned how to inform and apply your intuitive sense for what your brand is and needs to be, how to objectively assess your brand using SWOT analysis, and how to describe your brand platform—the foundation of your brand past, present, and future. Fortified with this information, you are now prepared to develop your brand—to clarify and enhance your brand's identity, personality, and image.

Your Brand Is a Living Thing

Your library brand has a *living* past, present, and future. It is evolving and constantly anticipating and reinventing a new future. It lives with and on behalf of the life of the community it serves. It is dynamic, changing, and transformational. Thus, your brand is not something you consider on occasion or periodically. As a living thing, it requires constant nourishment and attention—and discipline. The processes outlined in this chapter are intended to guide you down a path that can and should become a regular journey for your organization—a way for you to "check in" and prompt reassessment whenever internal and/or external dynamics suggest. Sometimes the brand development journey will be major, calling on resources and participation of the entire library, while at other times it may be short and focused, addressing only limited aspects of the brand and requiring select resources and a few key players in the process. Regardless of the causal reasons for brand development and the extent of direct involvement of resources and people, the entire organization should be privy to the process, the outcomes of the process, and certainly the implications for positioning and promotion. As you consider the purpose and focus of your brand development effort, think of all perspectives, internal and external, that relate to and contribute to your brand—people, collections, programs, and facilities (see figure 3.1).

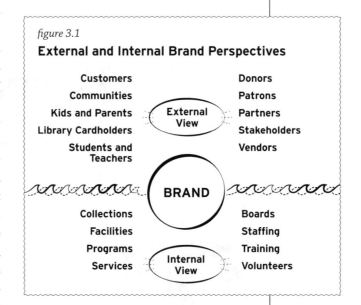

figure 3.1

External and Internal Brand Perspectives

A Path to Follow

Brand building is a process and thus requires a path to follow. There are a variety of ways in which organizations can approach this process, often influenced by the guidance of those in leadership. Regardless of the specifics, the process to build a brand should always begin with a thorough understanding of your library, your customers, your community, the current situation, and your vision for the future. Leadership is essential, from key staff to the executive office, to the board and volunteers. This process goes well beyond simply updating the look and feel of your brand, your website, or the signage or décor of your facilities. It is a process, done properly, that serves to realign, redirect, refresh, and energize the entire organization, providing an opportunity to bring new attention to what your library is and seeks to be.

WHO SHOULD BE INVOLVED IN THE PROCESS?

Most libraries have found that a team approach is optimal in order to build the necessary support and unity. Included on the team should be representation from the executive level of your organization, marketing, public relations, and human resources staff primarily responsible for external and internal library communications, leadership representing branch or satellite operations, facilities managers, board and volunteer representation, and representation from key strategic partners such as community organizations or agencies and corporate partners. It can be very helpful to include individuals, typically external to the library, who have experience or expertise in the areas of branding and marketing. Look to your board, community volunteers, and strategic partners for this kind of expertise. Keep in mind that this is a process, one that begins with a concentrated focus on assessment but expands to embrace a range of planning considerations and ultimately the successful execution of those plans (see figure 3.2). Consider early on everyone who should be "on the bus" to ensure the process is successful to completion and generates a dynamic momentum for change throughout the organization (Collins 2001).

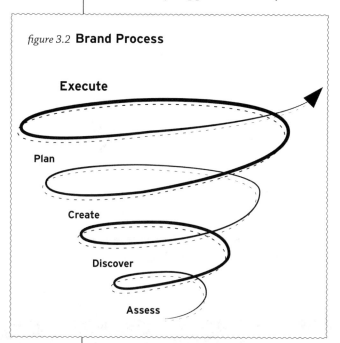

figure 3.2 **Brand Process**

Execute

Plan

Create

Discover

Assess

USE OF OUTSIDE EXPERTS

Once you have determined who should be part of the team, consider what additional or complementary expertise you might need. You may find it valuable to engage outside expertise, perhaps from another library that has recently undergone a successful branding process or a branding or marketing consultant with experience in library branding and marketing strategy. Depending on the nature of the effort you have in mind, other more specialized resources may be helpful, including market researchers, strategic planning and visioning experts, graphic designers and creative copywriters, web designers, public relations professionals, and social media experts. They can bring invaluable and selective expertise, objectivity, and experience to the process. Often these specialized experts can be found within your community or a nearby community, contributing perspective based on work in a variety of business and organizational settings. Because of their marketing orientation they will bring a sensitivity to the principles of marketing consistency, continuity, and tempo—all essential dimensions when it comes to creating and sustaining momentum, and with a clear focus on milestones for measuring progress and success.

Relating the Branding Process to Planning

There is an obvious and close connection between branding and organizational planning processes, focused on the basics of business planning for the present and near term, strategic planning for the projected or envisioned future, or market planning to address specific market challenges and oportunities. The need for a branding process may emerge from or develop concurrently with the organization's focus on any or a combination of these planning activities. Conversely, the branding process my stimulate interest in and create demand for a new look at the business, strategic, or marketing objectives of the organization. However your library has arrived at a need to engage in a branding process, the process itself should

figure 3.3 **Strategic Brand Planning**

The Process at Anythink Libraries

PAM SANDLIAN-SMITH, MEMBERS of her staff, the board of trustees, and community stakeholders joined together as a group of ninety participants to develop a new vision for the library system. The visioning process was to address all aspects of the library system, including ambience, style, personality, and graphics. Words such as *creative, timeless, Colorado, new, soaring, majestic, whimsical, magical, pioneering, vibrant,* and *intriguing* emerged from the process. The OCLC study *From Awareness to Funding* served to guide the library in its decision to become an experience library.

Following the visioning process, Sandlian-Smith initiated a creative team and an RFP to hire a marketing/branding/advertising firm. John Bellina and Tasso Stathopoulos, cofounders of Ricochet Ideas, were two of the creative consultants who helped the district develop the Anythink brand.

District leadership knew that they had to change the identity of the library district and that brand naming was a powerful tool to consider. They wanted to create a challenger brand, one that would resonate with the young demographics of the county. It had to be something playful and friendly—just as the library Anythink was becoming. The "doodle" logo came next, and the creative team pondered the value of a special visual element to go with the name Anythink. They thought that to do something as important as changing the name of the library, they wanted to make sure they got it right. This was a

time to take a big risk. The doodle could be anything, any idea, anything they wanted it to become. "It represents the most democratic concept of a library" noted Library Director Sandlian-Smith. "Everybody sees something a little different in it," suggests Susan Dobbs, the library's human resources director.

For Anythink, the secret of developing the process was first the creative team of library staff members, board members, and community representatives. The work of the committee was reinforced through the creative and expressive efforts of Ricochet Ideas. Board support was crucial. The board knew this was a bold move for the district, and they assembled the collective courage to move forward.

Every step in brand development and implementation has been guided by a group of individuals representing different areas within the library. Sandlian-Smith at Anythink says, "I am often asked how we engaged the team or have changed the culture. Our approach was very much like the old-fashioned barn raising. At many of our junctions, we had so much work to accomplish and a compelling sense of urgency. We had to weed the collection, we had to RFID the collection, we had to relabel and reorganize every collection to accomplish our transition to WordThink™.

"The only way we accomplished this was to work together as a team. When we began weeding, this was a very sensitive issue and staff was very worried about this project. Our approach was to close each branch for a day or two and ask for volunteers, including most of build on current business, strategic, or marketing plans in place. As deemed necessary, the process should also provide the framework and context for developing a strategic brand plan that embraces the essential goals and objectives of a sound business plan, while positioning the library strategically for the future to address the specific needs and wants of target markets (see figure 3.3).

People, Protocol, and Process

Beyond the core branding team, who else should be involved in the process and how should they be involved? The answer is simple—everyone in the library that touches a customer. Arguably, this translates to everyone employed by, volunteering on behalf of, and partnering with the library in the delivery of value. In a fascinating and groundbreaking book titled *Brand Manners,* authors Hamish Pringle and William Gordon (2003, 11) assert, "The challenge for general management is to ensure that the whole [library], and in particular the customer-facing [volunteers and strategic partners], actually 'live their brand' and convey its essence in everything they do on its behalf for customers and other stakeholders." So people, as individuals and as a company, are the primary purveyors of the brand, and therefore it is essential they be involved in the branding process from beginning to end.

the administrative and support services staff. A team of twenty to thirty people spent the day working together, and at the end of the day we were all exhausted but could definitely see a huge success. Besides getting the work done and sharing expertise, we all got to know each other and trust each other. We turned it into a party of sorts, with lots of food, snacks, and music.

"One of my favorite quotes: 'To succeed you have to believe in something with such passion that it becomes a reality.' [from British business executive Anita Roddick] This describes our work at Anythink. We believed that we could recreate our library with such passion, with such a sense of imagination that we almost willed our success.

"Another thing that is critical is creating that philosophical why. Getting the heart and soul of the organization established and why we show up for work every day are essential to success. Once that core is established the details can always be worked out and changed as necessary and appropriate. Leadership is helping everyone get the why and then bringing it all back to that center when we begin to stray. For the team who worked on the transformation, we know that there were elements of magic and inspiration. There was a drive and a passion to create a library so special that it would be irresistible, a library that would become the heart and soul—the idea place—for our community.

"We also know that accomplishing this work required the creation of a common vision and philosophy. We were inventing a library that would create the foundation for learning in the twenty-first century: 'We open doors for curious minds.'

"It also required planning, collaborating, communicating, sharing ideas, and thousands and thousands of hours of work—some of it thrilling, some of it difficult, some of it just plain physical. Transforming an organization requires everyone's participation—everyone has a role. Some of our most difficult and challenging tasks were handled as if it were a barn raising. We formed teams, created plans, and did our 'winter work,' in accordance with barn-raising terminology. In the library world, that translated to creating lists of books that needed to have new spine labels with words instead of numbers, selecting the perfect collections, furnishings and equipment, and preparing all the details for our grand openings. This collaboration, with everyone rolling up their sleeves, getting dirty, and working diligently, helped us develop our team and a sense of *esprit de corps*.

"In any successful barn raising, there has to be attention to people's needs. There is sharing, a chance to get to know each other, a chance to form a common bond. Out of this comes a sense of reciprocity, a sense of mutual respect. There has to be fun, music, food, and frivolity. There has to be a party to celebrate the work. Anyone who knows Anythink knows we work hard, but we also love to have fun together. We celebrate our heroic barn-raising efforts!"

Because the branding process involves more than one person and ultimately extends to the entire organization, protocols for internal communications and involvement are essential to ensure that all perspectives are honored and given a voice (see figure 3.4). From the outset, the branding process should consider how and when individuals, teams, departments, branches, and partners should be involved, and what "rules of the road" should be established and adhered to in managing their involvement, including consideration of matters of etiquette and ceremony.

The first place to look is at how your library currently involves its employees, volunteers, board, friends groups, and other partners in planning, and organizational decisions and initiatives. Where possible and assuming current protocols are working well, stay with those that are understood and appreciated and build them into your branding process. At the same time, a branding process can provide an excellent opportunity to introduce new protocols you might want to consider—protocols that invite elevated interest and engagement in the organization's affairs and help to introduce and express the brand. Conducting an in-depth internal staff survey for the first time, engaging volunteers in up-close and personal focus groups, bringing your board and strategic partners together in a unique setting to reflect on and envision new strategies, or engaging the entire organization in the ceremonial introduction or reintroduction of the brand—all are ways in which you might introduce new protocols for interaction and participation. Critical, however, is making certain that the protocols employed are consistent with your brand—your identity as an organization, your personality as a culture, and your image as a library.

The protocols employed in the branding process provide a point of reference for participating employees as they begin to internalize the meaning of the brand in their lives and their behaviors toward and in interaction with customers.

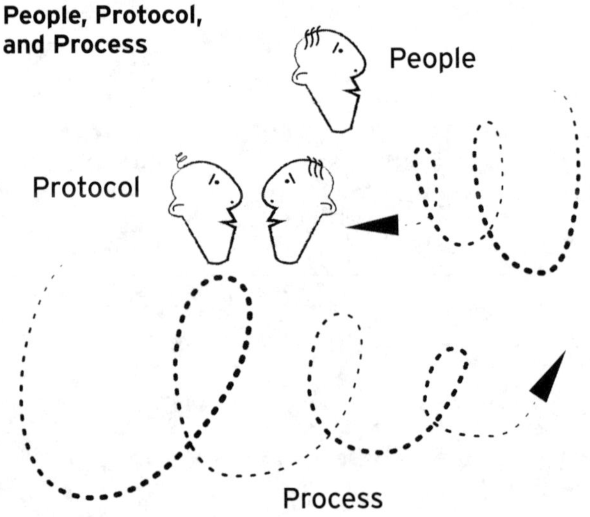

Beyond the people and the protocols, it is important to clearly define and lay out the process, including key decision points and milestones. To ensure that the entire library culture is on board, it is essential that everyone understand what the process will be and how the timing of decisions and initiatives is likely to impact them and the library's customers. Certainly, as the process evolves, decision points and milestones may change, and as they do there is opportunity to continually engage and reengage the culture in the process. Value your employees and they will value the brand. Teamwork is the secret to success in building the brand. You might consider a *brand team* that consists of representation from the staff, administration, board, and foundation. Teamwork will strengthen the brand, the brand concept, and the adoption of the branding process.

figure 3.4

People, Protocol, and Process

People

Protocol

Process

Grand County Library System

JIM COLLINS, IN his book *Good to Great* (2001), discusses the characteristics necessary to build a great company (or a great library). "The type of leaders [of great organizations] seems to have come from Mars. Self-effacing, quiet, reserved, even shy—these leaders are a paradoxical blend of personal humility and professional will." Next, those leaders "get the right people on the bus, the wrong people off the bus, and the right people in the right seats—and then they figured out where to drive it." The old adage, "People are your most important asset" is wrong, according to Collins. "People are not your most important asset. The *right* people are."

He goes on to add other characteristics, such as "confronting the Brutal Facts and never losing faith," "the Hedgehog Concept" (Collins's interpretation of consistency as relates to branding), and a culture of discipline and technology accelerators. (Collins 2001, 65, 90)

To Mary Anne Hanson-Wilcox, director of the Grand County Library District (GCLD), these directives are the key to a successful library district. Getting the right people on the bus, in the right seats, and the wrong people off of the bus has been a mandate for the GCLD. Having the destination in mind for the bus is essential. It has been the secret of building a team that expresses their excellence in every area.

A Disciplined Approach

The process of brand development reflects a logical and disciplined approach, sized and timed to fit the requirements, complexity, and constraints associated with the task. If the requirements suggest the need for a completely new brand or rebranding effort, the process may require months and can even extend to a year or more before a branding process culminates in implementation. On the other hand, if the requirements call for an updating, enhancement, or refinement of the brand, the effort may be accomplished over several weeks. While doing so can pose significant challenges, branding processes can be phased over time, addressing essential elements of the brand a step at a time, implementing according to resource limitations, and being mindful of the importance of sustaining consistency and continuity of brand messages the organization sends. Every branding process will reflect its own uniqueness influenced by a host of variables, including the very nature of the library culture and the circumstances of the times. Whatever the degree of complexity or the time frame involved, the following five steps typify the process (refer back to figure 3.2).

STEP 1—BRAND ASSESSMENT

As discussed in Chapter 2, this first step entails a comprehensive brand assessment to include consideration of your library's brand *depth, demand,* and *desire* by applying a SWOT analysis to each. The assessment process enables you to clarify the purpose and focus of your branding efforts, to engage the appropriate people in the process, and to set initial goals and objectives for the process. While this is largely an analytic process, it is also one that is aided by the collaborative sharing of perspectives and information and by synthesis of the information in ways that can shed new light on challenges and opportunities your brand represents.

STEP 2—BRAND DISCOVERY

With the brand assessment process complete, or at least well under way, you are ready to imaginatively explore and discover concepts that express what you are seeking to achieve with your brand. This step in the process requires a very different way of thinking—one that begins with the synthesis of information in step 1, prompting exploration of new possibilities, and that concludes with an objective assessment of those possibilities against present realities and resources. Brand discovery is often best facilitated by an outside expert who is skillful in posing questions and guiding a collaborative process. It is also helpful to have creative talent in the room (such as graphic designers, copywriters, web designers, and social media experts) to contribute to the process by sharing insights from their professional experience and rendering initial translations of ideas as they emerge into words and visuals. A very efficient version of this approach that can merge this step with the next one, and thus save time and perhaps resources, is a "design charrette" in which people of different perspectives and capabilities come together to address a design challenge in an intense period of time. Design charrettes are often associated with architectural or landscaping projects, though the principles and methods can be readily adapted to brand development. For more information about design charrettes, visit www.peopleandparticipation.net.

STEP 3—BRAND CREATIVE

The potent combination of exploring possibilities unbridled by imposed limitations, as in step 2, followed by a careful assessment of those possibilities, prompts the creative conceptualization of how the brand can be developed. It is during this step that the creative talent on the team becomes critical to the process—talent that renders loose ideas that emerged in step 2 into viable branding concepts for

Planning at Columbus Metropolitan Library

FOR OVER ONE hundred years, the phrase "open to all" has been etched over the front doors of the main library in Columbus, Ohio. For generations that concept, the idea that libraries were for everyone, was the driving principle behind their institutional decisions and it has and continues to serve the library well. At the same time, the implication that being open to all also meant seeking to serve everyone to the same degree became less and less realistic, especially amidst increasing demand and decreasing resources. It became clear that Columbus Metropolitan Library (CML), while remaining true to the principle of being open to all had to focus what precious resources it had. The answer was to focus on market research to identify their customers by segments. The library realized that fundamental to marketing is the notion of "exchange," in which all parties to a transaction expect to receive value greater than or equal to what they have to offer.

In the fall of 2011, Columbus Metropolitan Library initiated a new strategic planning process. A number of factors have influenced the strategic planning process for the library, including discussions with community leaders regarding the issues and challenges within the community. In addition, CML addressed issues of infrastructure, technology, and its website. With the passage of a significant levy, the library is once again able to reexamine how it provides the best in customer service. The library is assessing facilities and updating them and building new facilities, including a Technology branch that will focus on computers and will be 100 percent self-service. It will offer computer classes and technology training as well as access. CML will also be examining the development of an Express branch in leased space. It is redefining the traditional library.

Branding provides the foundation and the structure within which Columbus Metropolitan Library conducts its strategic planning processes every few years and lends focus to the analysis of those the library serves. The branding work provides the guidelines and the direction and unifies the board and staff as they develop specific strategic goals for the future.

organizational consideration in both graphic and word form. Creative concepts may be presented in board form or by electronic media to the branding team, and the organization can assess those concepts that work and eliminate those that do not. By definition, brand concepts are just that, trial ideas expressed in facsimile form sufficient for the organization to explore, test, assess, and refine before making commitments to implement. Developing the brand concepts includes extending applications to a variety of tactical forms to visualize how the brand can be expressed across a variety of mediums and media, from concepts for the home page of the website, to collections and services brochures, to building signage. In the process of testing brand concepts with various applications, some concepts will hold up better than others. Creative concept development also gives expression to the emerging positioning strategy—how the brand will relate to the target markets you are seeking to reach.

STEP 4—BRAND PLAN

With brand concepts in place, the process turns next to the analysis of how to plan the brand experience for the customer, including each customer segment. A useful tool to guide this process is a customer experience map that anticipates how the customer or the target market is likely to experience the brand in all of its expressions or touch points (see figure 3.5). Following is a brief discussion of the components of a complete customer experience.

The customer experience map includes the following stages and brand touch points as identified. The initial task in developing a brand experience map is to apply the brand concepts developed in the preceding step by visualizing how each brand concept should, most ideally, be experienced by the customer at each stage of his or her experience with the brand.

1. **Awareness stage**—The touch points include exterior building signage, directional signage, interior signage, and merchandising of materials, collections, and so on, and extend to ads, promotional e-mails, flyers, and

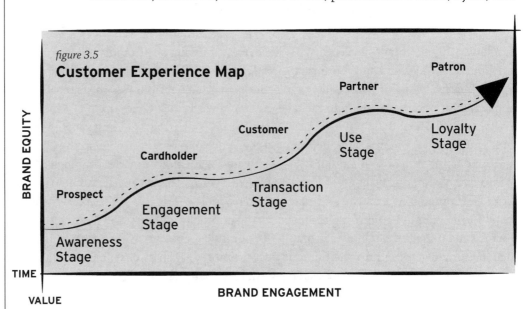

figure 3.5
Customer Experience Map

other communications mediums—including kiosks, external signage, bookmobiles, and other library vehicles.

2. **Engagement stage**—The points of entry at the website, the library entry and check-in/checkout kiosks, event or promotional displays, or registration tables—anywhere customers are intentionally crossing a library threshold and registering their presence. In so doing they are signaling an intention to engage with you.

3. **Transaction stage**—The points where an actual transaction occurs—signing up for a library card, checking out the first book, downloading the first document, signing up for the first program, and so on. The transaction stage will include sequential touch points—getting the card, checking out the first book, providing feedback on the experience, and so on. A transaction is an act of exchange involving something of value—a valid library card in exchange for the privilege to borrow a book and the responsibility to return it on time.

4. **Use stage**—The ongoing, expanding, and more intensified use touch points, including checkout of books, downloading of documents or use of databases, inquiry about programs and offerings, and signing up for new programs. The use stage of the customer experience is reflected in measurable, consistent, and evolving patterns of use over time.

5. **Loyalty stage**—The touch points that relate to the building, rewarding, and acknowledging of loyalty and create a heightened sense of partnership and a deep sense of ownership. The loyalty stage can extend to referral, volunteer, and donor programs, and applies equally to external and internal audiences.

STEP 5—BRAND IMPLEMENTATION

Implementing the brand, including the deployment of your positioning strategy as introduced in Chapter 4 and your promotional strategies discussed in Chapters 7 and 8, is a creative, dynamic process involving the entire organization. Key to successful implementation is your ability to manage the brand with consistency, market sensitivity, and efficiency. To maintain consistency, you will look to two guiding sources—first your brand standards or guidebook and then your implementation plan.

Brand standards or a brand guide is a published work that provides employees, board members, and Friends of the Library with all of the essentials about the brand—its premise, promise, and how the brand look and feel is to be expressed in all forms. A brand guide for a complex organization like a library will include the history and philosophy behind the brand—the brand story—as well as very specific instructions regarding how the brand is best promoted, such as customer interaction and suggestions for how to best engage library customers in a host of common

The Apple Brand

THINK OF THE Apple brand experience. Apple's core values include design and innovation, ease of use, simplicity, and quality. You can see that these core values drive the Apple brand and the Apple brand experience. The brand experience includes the look and feel of products, customer service, the environment and décor of store environments, packaging, and other elements of the Apple experience. Apple carefully considers how each customer is likely to experience its brand—at point of first awareness through actual use and formation of brand loyalty. Reflect on the experience of walking into an Apple Store, being greeted by a customer representative whose only task is to make you feel welcome and ensure that your needs are addressed, allowing you to explore products uninterrupted and to engage a salesperson at your signal that you would like assistance. Consider how the positioning of product, of signage and essential information, and of staff contributes to the total experience, and how the handling of furnishings, lighting, and graphics align with the Apple brand. None of this is by accident, and all is based on the development of a very carefully designed customer experience. For more on the Apple customer experience, read "You Had Me at Hello: Secrets of Apple's Customer Experience Exposed" by Mike Wittenstein (2011).

settings, including in person, by phone, and online. The brand guidebook raises the level of awareness with the view of improving how both individuals and the organization "live the promise" (Knapp 2000, 133). In very important ways, the guidebook also provides staff and volunteers with helpful tools and templates for use in development of promotional materials, signage, newsletters, and other forms of communications, relieving staff of the burden of having to design everything from scratch while ensuring brand consistency. Typically, the guidebook includes specifics on how the elements of the brand are to be presented in print and electronically, including templates, color pallets, and instructions for use. The guidebook will also identify the departments/people responsible for brand management, for guiding library staff with unique applications of the brand, and for providing ongoing support with development of new promotional initiatives and supporting materials.

Regardless of how well your plan is developed, there will always be a need to adjust and revise strategic and tactical elements in response to changing conditions internally and externally. Your implementation process will also include an evaluation component that will enable real-time assessment and adjustment in the deployment of specific strategies and tactics. For example, perhaps your brand plan calls for a positioning strategy to reach parents of young children using a combination of targeted direct mail and e-mail, a rotating website banner, and point-of-sale promotions at checkout kiosks. In the process of deploying all four tactics your response measures may tell you that the combination of e-mail and web banners is accomplishing your objectives. Accordingly, you might choose to drop the point-of-sale and direct-mail tactics early in the process, allowing you to conserve or redirect valuable resources.

Internalizing Your Brand

Conversations about branding, positioning, and promotion tend to focus primarily on how an organization relates to its external audiences. The reality, however, is that the internal culture of the organization is primarily responsible for delivering the brand experience. Just as you want to make sure your brand relates to and is positioned well for your target markets, it must also relate well to and be an honest expression of your internal audiences. It is for this reason that the branding process is an organic one, beginning with a clear and candid appreciation for what you do as an enterprise, the personality you express as an enterprise, and the image to which you aspire as an enterprise. The essentials of internalizing your brand include the following (Knapp 2000, 134):

- Creating the brand's guiding principles
- Establishing brand equity goals
- Outlining the brand communication plan
- Designing a culturalization plan

Each and every employee must understand the brand's premise—its raison d'être—as well as the brand promise to those it serves. The promise, encapsulating the core values of the library, provides the framework to guide every decision the library makes—from when to open to whom to hire. This is no simple task; it

Policies at Anythink

AT ANYTHINK, HUMAN Resource Director Susan Dobbs and Public Services Director Ronnie Storey-Ewoldt helped to organize staff teams to rethink and standardize policies in a system where some branches were quite distant and operated as individual entities.

Job descriptions were revised. The library moved from a skills-based organization to a competency-based organization, from very traditional job descriptions to new job descriptions and a performance review system. For staff, this better reflected the new direction and aspirations of the organization. All frontline staff were asked to apply for these new positions. There were three caveats: everyone would have a job, no one would see a decrease in salary, and everyone would have an opportunity to participate in the job decision. Some employees chose to take a step down, while others moved up. The new job roles included the role of guide, described as "part education, part reference advocate, and part event planning." Of the seventeen staffers working as guides, about half have their MLS and one has a master's in education. Adult, children's, teen, and tech guides design and deliver programs and what Anythink calls "experience zones." "Upon examining the role of the librarian, it became apparent to us that librarians are really guides to information, interactions, and experiences. That is an important shift in thinking about the relationships with customers and with information," noted Pam Sandlian-Smith.

Anythink's staff manifesto says: "You are not just an employee, volunteer or board member. You do not merely catalog books, organize periodicals and manage resources. You are the gateway into the mind of the idea people who come to our facilities to find or fuel a spark. Part WIZARD, Part GENIUS, Part EXPLORER. It is your calling to trespass into the unknown and come back with a concrete piece someone can hold onto, turn over, and use to fuel their mind and soul." "This manifesto redefined the way we look at our work. This statement created the impetus for the team to realize our work was about helping people find that fuel or spark that could transform their lives," says Sandlian-Smith.

The busywork of checking books in and out was replaced with the role of concierge: "You're the essence of the customer's experience at the library. You greet people with a smile and welcome them into our library. You enrich people's lives through meaningful dialogue and our products and services. You earn trust by being knowledgeable about our products and making recommendations that connect with the customer. You help our library customers find the fuel and the spark to unlimited ideas and opportunities."

Achieving the culture change is never simple.

requires persistence and passionate role modeling. It requires a comprehensive and multifaceted approach to influence employees at every level. Of course, it begins at the top. The CEO or director must create an atmosphere that encourages employees to participate, understand, and express the brand in the work they do and to provide them with the tools, discretion, and confidence to act on behalf of the brand.

It is the brand team's job to gather information, to support brand guidelines, and to monitor brand implementation. Customer service is one of the most powerful ways to differentiate a brand and build long-term brand equity. Initiating a program of customer service can be challenging, especially when it requires the changing of employee work patterns. You can invest significant dollars on tactics to reach and communicate with customers. However, if employees aren't aligned with the brand and enthusiastically rally around the brand, the delivery of the brand promise will be broken. Staff members are your ultimate channel to connect and build relationships with customers.

Employees who "live the brand" create the personal embodiment of the brand. How do you transform employees into brand advocates? It does not happen overnight, and it will not happen because of a few T-shirts and e-mails. It happens because you have developed a dynamic process that builds employee knowledge, shapes attitudes, and enables employee behavior to deliver on the brand promise. Not all employees are on the same page when it comes to being brand advocates. Nancy Lee and Philip Kotler, in their book *Social Marketing: Influencing Behaviors for Good* (Lee and Kotler 2011, 146), discuss the development of knowledge, belief, and behavior objectives. Those objectives apply to employees as you seek to enlist them as your brand advocates. Yes, you will have staff members who fall in different employee segments. Commander (2007, 3) identifies four different styles of employee expression that emerge in the process:

- Brand resisters
- Brand learners
- Brand believers
- Brand advocates

Brand advocates, of course, live the brand at work and in the community and model the behavior for others. In order to inspire and enable employees to become brand advocates, they must be involved in the process. There are a number of tools to be considered, including brand training and orientation, employee involvement in shaping the brand, peer-recognition programs, performance incentives, and brand events. Most employees will get on board with the brand; a few will not.

BRAND MANAGEMENT

Brand management is an assigned responsibility typically given to one or more staff members responsible for marketing, public and community relations, and perhaps internal relations. The responsibility of this role extends to all aspects of managing the brand, but with primary focus on ensuring that the brand is expressed correctly and consistently across the organization. Brand management includes all aspects of brand development, positioning, and promotion and requires both competent staff and systems support to ensure that brand-related communications are coordinated, integrated, and aligned with brand standards. Certainly having a well-developed and practical set of brand standards or guidelines is helpful, but even more important is having the right people involved who have been assigned the authority and responsibility to manage the brand to those standards. The libraries cited in this book provide good examples of sound approaches to brand management. Each decided how it would manage its brand—ensuring the ability to fully leverage its investment in the branding process.

BUILDING BRAND EQUITY

The investment that branding represents is obvious in the cost and effort that goes into it. Not so obvious is the importance of not only recovering the investment you put into building your library brand, but also the effort you expend to manage and build equity beyond the initial investment. There are basically three areas of effort involved in managing the brand's equity:

- **Brand impact**—What was your intended impact on customer behavior and engagement? What was your intended impact on organizational outcomes and goals? Measures of fulfillment of these intentions reflect realized equity in the brand.
- **Brand alignment**—It is essential that all brand expressions—formal and informal and reflecting both positioning and promotional strategies—must be aligned; that is, they work together in harmony and with consistency. Doing so increases the likelihood that the brand will connect with customers, and customers will increasingly understand, engage with, and appreciate the value of the brand. Misaligned brand expressions lead to marketplace confusion, raise levels of skepticism, and can contribute to the declination of perceived value.
- **Brand vision**—The vision for the brand must always maintain a forward motion as a dynamic and evolving identity, personality, and image. Sound brand management requires continuous commitment to improving the brand, repositioning the brand, and monitoring the public's perceptions of the brand.

Summary

In this chapter the authors introduced the branding process and concluded by emphasizing that your library brand is a living thing. Developing your brand begins by getting the right people involved from the start, including leadership and outside experts as needed. Brand development also ties directly to other planning activities, including those associated with the basics of business planning, strategic planning, or market planning. Because the process is so people intensive, we discussed the importance of who should be involved and the protocols and processes to use. We described the process in five steps, beginning with brand assessment and concluding with brand implementation. Finally, we explored the importance of internalizing the brand with a discussion about the basics of brand management and building brand equity.

REFERENCES

AllAboutBranding.com. 2007. "Brand Assessment Questionnaire." www.allaboutbranding .com/index.lasso?page=11,53,75.

Collins, Jim. 2001. *Good to Great: Why Some Companies Make the Leap . . . and Others Don't.* New York: HarperBusiness.

Commander, Cindy. 2007. *Report Brief: Transforming Employees into Brand Advocates.* Forrester Leadership Boards, The CMO Group. www.scribd.com/doc/36256382 /Transforming-Employees-Into-Brand-Advocates-Report-Brief.

Knapp, Duane E. 2000. *The Brand Mindset.* New York: McGraw-Hill.

Lee, Nancy R., and Philip Kotler. 2011. *Social Marketing: Influencing Behaviors for Good.* 4th ed. Los Angeles: Sage.

Park, C. Whan, Bernard J. Jaworski, and Deborah J. MacInnis. 1986. "Strategic Brand Concept-Image Management." *Journal of Marketing* 50 (October): 135–45. https:// msbfile03.usc.edu/digitalmeasures/macinnis/intellcont/strategic_brand86-1.pdf.

Pringle, Hamish, and William Gordon. 2003. *Brand Manners: How to Create the Self-Confident Organization to Build a Brand.* Chichester, NY: Wiley.

Wittenstein, Mike. 2011. "You Had Me at Hello: Secrets of Apple's Customer Experience Revealed." www.mikewittenstein.com/2011/07.

SECTION II

POSITIONING

Defining a Positioning Strategy

Why Is It Important to Your Library?

The purpose of a business [library] is to get and keep a customer. Without solvent customers in some reasonable proportion, there is no business. Customers are constantly presented with lots of options to help them solve their problems. The surviving and thriving [library] is a [library] that constantly seeks better ways to help people solve their problems. To create betterness requires knowing what customers think betterness to be. . . . The imagination that figures out what that is, imaginatively figures out what should be done, and does it with imagination and high spirits will drive the enterprise [library] forward.
—Theodore Levitt (1983, xii)

"**M**ARKETING IS NOT A STATIC DISCIPLINE. MAR**keting is a constantly changing discipline and positioning is one of those revolutionary changes that keep the marketing field alive, interesting, exciting, and fascinating. It is a powerful tool for creating and maintaining real differentiation in the market place" (Kotler 2001). This chapter discusses the following:

- The positioning strategy and why it is important to the library
- The secrets of positioning: target markets and identifying the competition
- Examples of positioning within the marketplace
- The evaluation of your library's position in the marketplace
- The integration of branding and positioning
- Branding as a prerequisite to positioning
- Strategic planning and strategic positioning

What Is Positioning?
What Is a Positioning Strategy?

How often have you heard, "If only people knew what we have at our library"? Librarians have sought ways to promote the library, to communicate in a media-obsessed world the uniqueness and opportunities to be found in the library. The secret of rising above the din and creating an awareness of products and services lies within *positioning.*

If you were going shopping to buy a pair of shoes, you would pick a store that was top of mind. If you were asked why you selected this store, you would probably either talk about the selection, low prices, or styles that the store carried. You are describing the store's positioning. Perhaps it has developed a positioning strategy based on price or on its variety of offerings. The store has given a lot of thought to its positioning and has spent money developing a positioning strategy.

How do you position a library so that it is top of a customer's mind? How do you create awareness that the library has what the customer needs and wants? How do you cut through the competing choices and make it easy for the customer to think of the library as his or her first and best option?

SECRETS OF POSITIONING: IDENTIFYING TARGET MARKETS AND THE COMPETITION

There is a secret to positioning, and that is targeting your market and refining your collections, products, services, and programs to meet the specific needs of that market. Libraries often say that they serve everyone; however, this is misleading. Positioning is being intentional, making deliberate decisions, and studying, understanding, and addressing the needs and wants of your target audience. Positioning means you meet the needs of specific target audiences. It means that you avoid dilution of your efforts by trying to meet the needs of all people in a generic way. Positioning requires passion, it means taking risks, and it demands creativity, sensitivity, and constant vigilance.

Positioning and Target Audiences

Libraries do have specific target audiences for their services. According to James Keller, the former chief marketing officer at the Queens Library, "Libraries have made the grave mistake of assuming everyone knows how important and relevant they are. Among the first steps, before developing a branding and marketing plan, is determining who you serve, who has a real stake in what you do."

Positioning and Marketing Mix

According to Alison Circle, director of marketing and strategic planning for Columbus Metropolitan Library, "Our positioning strategy addresses the target audiences. With them in mind, our task is to position the library to best serve their needs." The positioning strategy informs the strategies in the marketing mix of products, place, price, and promotion, the four Ps of marketing. The first step is to identify your target audiences, the focus of Chapter 5.

Positioning and Competition

Another secret of positioning is to identify the competition. Yes, libraries have competition. You have competition from information providers such as Amazon, Barnes & Noble, and Google. Even Starbucks provides competition as it seeks innovative ways to bring people together. Think of how many libraries have adopted Starbucks' concept of providing a coffee shop to bring people together? Consider the story of Netflix, a company that was started because of a $40 late fee for a video rental. Reed Hastings, founder of Netflix, knew that there had to be a better way of providing videos and movies to consumers. Netflix delivers "what you want, before you know you want it." There is also obvious competition like bookstores or museums. "Competition is everywhere," says Joyce Mestis of the Tattered Cover Bookstore. "Each Saturday morning I pray for rain. We compete even with the weather. People have time, leisure activity, and some money. The choices are myriad in our culture. Competition never lets you relax! However, rain makes a huge difference!" Yes, libraries need to understand that there is competition. With today's busy lifestyles, consumers are demanding value and more control. If they have to work to find what they need, there is no value. Libraries do operate in a competitive environment, and often those competitors can be the most stimulating educators in helping us understand our customers.

The secret of positioning is in understanding your target market, identifying the specific products and services to meet the wants and needs of that target audience, understanding and learning from the competition, and promoting or communicating the services available. Positioning requires a change for libraries that have served as a repository of information into one that provides convenient, pleasant, and friendly access to information sources for targeted audiences.

Anythink is a good example of a library that breaks conventions by taking an active role as a competitive brand. It moves its customers from the passive world of information into the eyeball-grabbing world of persuasion. It is not a standardized facility operated via bureaucracy. Anythink is anything—a poem, a sketch, an equation, musical history, cooking clubs, submarine architecture, community gardens, and even the lowly but invaluable e-mail. Anythink is where anyone's idea is made more possible.

Using Positioning to Differentiate Your Library in the Marketplace

Positioning differentiates your products and services from others in the marketplace. Positioning identifies your uniqueness and builds upon your brand, your essence, and your distinct offerings, especially to the target audiences you have selected. Positioning directs your message specifically to those who need and want to know about your services. Positioning develops a competitive advantage that elevates your library above any other choice. Positioning creates that "top of mind" experience that you desire for your library.

Positioning is about how you influence the mind of your customers and how they perceive your products and services. You probably know from experience that your mind screens and rejects much of the information presented at any given moment. There is simply too much information out there, and you are bombarded with a constant flow of messages. So, the ultimate task of positioning is one of cutting through the clutter from your customers' perspective—enabling them to know you for what you offer, for who you are, and for the credibility you represent when they need or want you most.

POSITIONING DIFFERENTIATES YOUR PRODUCTS AND SERVICES

Positioning ultimately differentiates your products and services from others in the marketplace, less by the specifics of what you do and more by the perceptions that your customers have of what you do. Effective positioning enables your customers to relate to your uniqueness as an institution and to the specifics of your service offerings. Positioning directs your message to those most likely and most ready to receive your message. Positioning delivers competitive advantage not because you focus on defeating competing messages, but because your customers are more likely to choose your message as more relevant to their needs and wants. And finally, effective positioning influences changes in the behavior of your customers, causing them to interact with you in ways and with frequencies more consistent with the brand you seek to express.

There are many examples of positioning that will instantly create awareness about positioning and positioning strategies. Think of positioning as it is used in political campaigns, product advertising, banks and financial institutions, resorts, airlines, retail organizations, social marketing campaigns, even churches and universities. Think how targeted these examples are and how effective they are for you as a consumer. Most organizations see their positioning strategy as the most important decision they will make. Positioning is the most crucial decision you make for your library, as it expresses your core values and identifies for whom those core values will make the greatest difference.

Al Ries and Jack Trout introduced the concept of positioning as primarily expressed through the power of words as the "first body of thought to come to grips with the problems of communicating in an overcommunicated society."

> You must understand how words affect people. Words are triggers. They trigger the meanings which are buried in the mind. Language is the currency of the mind. To think conceptually, you manipulate words. With the right choice of words, you can influence the thinking process itself. You need vision, you need courage, you need objectivity, you need simplicity, you need subtlety, you need patience and you need a global outlook. (Ries and Trout 2001, 202)

Ries and Trout were perhaps the first to realize that positioning comes well before other marketing communication strategies that focus on specific products or services, pricing or exchange rates, places for exchange, and suitable promotions (messengers and mediums) to the right audiences. Product, place, price, and promotion are what is commonly referred to as the marketing mix, or four Ps, of marketing. While Ries and Trout introduced the concept of positioning in the 1970s, positioning takes on an even deeper meaning when combined with branding.

EXAMPLES OF POSITIONING WITHIN THE COMMERCIAL MARKETPLACE

Let's explore some examples of positioning strategies within the for-profit arena, as this exercise will create an instant familiarity with the concept. Both Johnson and Johnson as well as Olay cosmetics use *age* to position their products. Johnson and Johnson baby products capture the market while Olay Regenerist products for women are best sellers. Gillette certainly positions shaving products for men and distinctly for women. Volvo uses *safety* to distinguish its automobiles, which is a good example of the use of an attribute to position a product. Walmart has built its positioning strategy on price, while Rolex watches are positioned on their premium value. Avis rental cars are positioned on being *better than the competition,* while Coca-Cola enjoys its positioning leadership within the soft drink category. You can see and are probably familiar with the various positioning strategies of these retail products. Can you detect the positioning strategies used by various airlines, or of political campaigns and social marketing campaigns? Universities have embraced positioning and branding to differentiate themselves and to secure their place in the marketplace for students and support. The University of Phoenix positions itself with the challenges to "Experience a Different Kind of Classroom," while stalwart Harvard University "is devoted to excellence in teaching, learning and research," and Regis University in Colorado has positioned itself as "Learners becoming leaders in the Jesuit Catholic tradition." You can see how positioning a product or a service identifies the unique differentiation of a product or an organization. You will also notice that products, services, and organizations are positioned in comparison to their competition. Recall how positioning is used with products, companies, and causes you value. Then consider your own experience with how targeted and effective they are for you as a consumer.

"Funding the collective library mission is a growing problem and without proactive and large-scale action, we can see no economic, social or political factors or events that will reverse the trends in library funding." The OCLC has set out to ask the question, "Is it possible to apply the latest marketing and advocacy techniques that are being so successfully used in other venues to create funding awareness, drive action and ultimately increase funding for public libraries? . . . Can libraries be more effectively positioned alongside other critical local services like fire, police, schools and public health?" (DeRosa and Johnson 2008, viii). (See figure 4.1.) DeRosa and Johnson offer this call to action:

figure 4.1 **OCLC Logo**

> Libraries have responded by launching marketing efforts to focus on increasing awareness of the library and its services. Yet, despite numerous marketing and communications efforts across the country, the

perception of the library as "a physical place offering traditional information services (books and information)" remains well-entrenched in the minds of library users. And while the perceptions of the library may remain fixed, the information landscape is anything but stable. The knowledge landscape is expanding rapidly and the library's once unique position as the "place that provides books and information" is increasingly crowded. Powerful rivals with deeper pockets—think Google and Barnes & Noble— are able to mount far stronger marketing initiatives in pursuit of the information consumer, claiming more of their mind share and redefining their expectations of information access. Without action, it is almost certain that the library's brand will continue to be seen as a legacy service, a "nice to have" but not critical institution, more relevant in the past than for the future. (DeRosa and Johnson 2008, 7-1)

Your Library Has a Position in the Marketplace

Your library currently occupies a position within the community, whether or not you have made a conscious effort to develop that position. How is your library perceived? Is it perceived as a dynamic, leading, vital, and significant institution providing important services to citizens? If all libraries have a position within the

Anythink

FOR LIBRARIANS, ANYTHINK is very much on the national map, after perhaps one of the most dramatic turnarounds in the nation. Rangeview Library District (RLD) and its Anythink brand transformed the mediocre Adams County Public Library into the snazzy Anythink—an anchor in a community with few cultural institutions. The Anythink story suggests that public libraries, given leadership, creativity, and careful allocations of resources, can foster a start-up culture and take a fresh look at almost anything.

Called one of the worst in the state by the *Denver Post*, the Adams County Public Library with old and crumbling materials and small, musty branches had been mired in a vicious cycle after many years of underfunding. A mill levy increase passed in 2006, and under the direction of Director Pam Sandlian-Smith, the library had the opportunity to create its own future. The board and leadership recognized that they had a unique opportunity to rebuild the library system from the ground up and create a new brand that is relevant, inspires innovation, and represents the future.

The first step for the district was a visioning process to address all aspects of the organization, including ambiance, style, personality, and graphics. Words such as *creative*, *whimsical*, and *intriguing* emerged from the process. Staff had the drive and the passion to become something wonderful. The OCLC study *From Awareness to Funding* asks, "How can the library be positioned as a 'transformational force'?" Anythink took on the challenge to become a transformative power within its community; because of this it also became a transformational force within libraries and cultural organizations everywhere.

Transforming from Adams County Public Library to Rangeview Library District and then into Anythink was a big decision for the board and staff of the library. They decided to position the library as big and bold, yet friendly and accessible. Anythink is really the *value proposition* for the RLD and was used to brand the library. The Anythink brand emerges from the essence of the organization's carefully developed and articulated vision, mission, values, and strategies.

community, how do you determine your current position? Just because you haven't consciously developed a position doesn't mean that you don't occupy one. Customers do think about the library, and they do have opinions. On what dimension would they rank your library "first" or "best" in class? And in what class would they put you?

CONDUCTING MARKET RESEARCH TO UNDERSTAND YOUR POSITION WITHIN THE COMMUNITY

Profile your community and identify the demographics, geographics, and lifestyles within your community. Understand the challenges and opportunities that individuals, organizations, and corporations face within your community. Evaluate your own strengths and weaknesses in meeting those challenges and opportunities. Use market research techniques to determine how you are currently perceived within your community. How are you viewed by elected officials? By board members? By neighborhoods, schools, and community organizations? You must develop a deep understanding of your current position before you can develop new or different positioning strategies for the future. You must move strategically from the position your brand currently occupies in the mind of your customer to where you want it to be in your customer's mind.

MARKET RESEARCH METHODOLOGY

Research methodology is discussed in the next chapter. The use of qualitative and quantitative data gives you the necessary information to evaluate your current position.

How did board members react to the new direction, new logo, and new positioning? Director Sandlian-Smith met with the RLD board members separately and was surprised by their reaction: "It's risky, it's radical, and it's revolutionary. Why wouldn't we do it?" (See figure 4.2.)

Market research indicates that 70 percent of the population in Adams County is younger than fifty years of age. Many people in the community grew up without a relationship with libraries, and those who were familiar had a limited sense of loyalty to the library. There is a substantial Spanish-speaking population in the county, as well as Asian and Indian populations, many of whom speak their native language. Of those residents, many had never had a library card. This all has changed since "A Rev-

figure 4.2 **Anythink Logo**

olution of Rangeview Libraries."

The OCLC study posed the question of how a library can be positioned as a transformational force, and Anythink set out to be that force in Adams County and grew to become a transformational force in the state of Colorado and across the United States.

John Bellina, cofounder of Ricochet Ideas and creative consultant behind the Anythink brand, says: "Research across the U.S. told us that libraries were becoming irrelevant. People saw dated municipal facilities with harsh lighting, nasty librarians, and rooms and rooms of books. Anythink is the first library to be launched as a competitive brand. It's the intersection between Barnes & Noble, Netflix, and a Virgin Megastore. And there's nothing 'shhh' about it!"

The Integration of Branding and Positioning

Your brand is the entire experience your customers and stakeholders have about the library. The brand is the promise you make and the personality you convey. While it does include your logo, color palette, and slogan, these represent the creative elements of your brand. You develop a positioning strategy that delivers the essence of what you represent to those who will value it the most. It helps you stand out from the competition and brings your competitive position and value proposition to life. Your brand consistently and repeatedly tells your customers why they should use your services. Successful branding creates "brand equity." In the commercial world, brand equity is the amount of money that customers are willing to pay just because it is your brand. Brand equity makes your library more valuable over the long term. Think of the brand equity of Coca-Cola or Tide detergent. You seek that kind of brand equity for libraries.

Branding develops a resonance with customers for whom the brand is well positioned. These customers identify with the brand. They are proud and excited to be associated with the brand. Their resonance is demonstrated through one of the following four categories:

- Brand loyalty
- Emotional attachment
- A sense of community with the brand
- Active personal engagement with the brand

BRAND LOYALTY

Brand loyalty is necessary but is not enough by itself. There also has to be a strong personal attachment. Customers should go beyond having just a positive attitude. They should view the brand as being something special to them. Creating greater loyalty is evident in their attitudes, excitement, and behavior, and can be generated by developing market-relevant programs, products, and services that fully satisfy consumer needs and aspirations.

Have you noticed how enthusiastic people can feel about their favorite brand and how they affiliate with their favorite brand? Does that identification with a brand community extend to libraries, too? The answer is yes, we seek a strong attitudinal attachment to libraries to the extent we have had a positive experience with libraries.

The iPhone— An Example of Brand Loyalty

YOU HAVE EXPERIENCED the passion, dedication, pride, and enthusiasm of iPhone users. You have seen their photos, experienced the apps, and seen the loyalty of iPhone users. Apple has intended to make a lasting impact on how we connect with each other. Their goal is to change the way we communicate with each other. Apple seeks ways to enable people to engage and to connect. This is the brand excitement that we seek for libraries.

BRANDS EVOKE FEELINGS AND EMOTIONAL ATTACHMENT

Customers react emotionally to brands. Those brands have a *social currency*. Good brands seek to develop brand feelings, including the following:

- Affection
- Fun, amusement, playfulness, cheerfulness, enthusiasm
- Excitement and creating an energetic feel that they are something special
- Security and safety
- Self-respect by making customers feel better about themselves for choosing the brand
- Social approval through positive feelings about the reaction of others

Brand communication does not rely on your message alone. It is the level of emotional feeling that is communicated to the client that can make a difference. Feelings must be a priority, especially if you want your library brand to develop a deep engagement with the customer. You strive to build a brand community that is defined as a group of people interacting based on their common love of your brand. You seek to build an active engagement with your brand.

Positioning and Branding

Successful positioning is built upon the foundation of the brand. Positioning is defined by how you differentiate your products and services and create a unique value. When the individuals in your target markets see that what you offer is different from the competition, they will choose to use your services and develop brand loyalty.

Queens Library

QUEENS LIBRARY HAS been one of the top public library systems by circulation worldwide for years. The factors responsible for this achievement include technological innovation, the use of merchandising techniques, strong outreach programs, and the development of community library collections relevant to the needs of individual neighborhoods. However, circulation is just one of several indicators of the quantity and quality of public library services.

According to James Keller, former chief marketing officer at Queens Library, "Libraries have made the grave mistake of assuming everyone knows how important and relevant they are. Administrators and librarians have failed to realize that they truly need to promote what they offer." Among the first steps before developing a branding and marketing plan, according to Keller, is determining who you serve, who has a real stake in what you do.

Queens is a major port of entry into this country. There is a constant shifting of the population, and Queens Library's impact on these populations and thus the rest of the country is huge. How should Queens Library communicate its relevance? Staff and customers thought of their libraries independently; there was no coherence to the brand, and cohesion is essential when it comes to communicating relevance. A first step in developing any marketing and branding campaign is to develop a thorough understanding of the audience. The library needs to focus on whom it serves best and most often, and then address the needs of that population.

Columbus Metropolitan Library

figure 4.3 **Columbus Metropolitan Library Logo**

AT A MEETING with the editorial board of The *Columbus Dispatch,* editor emeritus Mike Curtin referred to Columbus Metropolitan Library (CML) as "a world class library on a shoestring budget." CML won the 2010 Library of the Year from *Library Journal* and passed a significant levy that same year. In fact, CML has proudly celebrated its 5-Star Library selection by *Library Journal* and achieved Hennen's American Public Library Index #1 rating three times in the past ten years. The library has a reputation for innovation, creativity, and leading the profession (see figure 4.3). In 2011, CML also was awarded the National Medal for Community Service, the nation's highest honor for museums and libraries, issued by the Institute for Museum and Library Services.

The professionals at Columbus Metropolitan Library asked, "How do we balance and focus our resources, yet stay true to the fundamental tenet of universal access?" The answer was to build a positioning strategy. They realized that the library needed to position itself in the mind of the customer in the context of the myriad other choices customers have as well as to analyze the competition.

figure 4.4 **Purpose of Columbus Metropolitan Library**

figure 4.5 **Vision of Columbus Metropolitan Library**

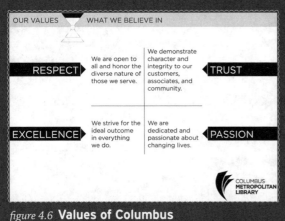

figure 4.6 **Values of Columbus Metropolitan Library**

figure 4.7 **External Audiences of Columbus Metropolitan Library**

IS THE BRANDING PROCESS NECESSARY TO POSITION THE LIBRARY?

Must a library go through a formal branding process in order to strategically position the organization? No—but the library must be clear about its essence, its values, vision, mission, and core objectives and must revisit its living brand with every positioning strategy. You already have a brand, whether it has been officially developed or not. You also have a current position within the community. It is important to understand your position, but you also need to reexamine your values, reaffirm your mission, and reassess your core competencies in order to effectively position your organization. You need to address your logo, signage, and buildings so that there is a consistency throughout the system and the brand. And, you need to be diligent in understanding the target audiences you serve.

Strategic Planning and Strategic Positioning

Libraries have engaged in strategic planning for decades. The strategic planning process forces organizations to define the mission and the vision and to set strategic

Arapahoe Library District

AT THE ARAPAHOE Library District located in Colorado, Executive Director Eloise May believes it is not always necessary to undergo a formal branding process. Although "positioning" is not what the library called it in the early 1990s, it sought to position itself as providing the very best in customer service. In other words, the library made customer service the "brand" around which everything else would revolve. Market research and strategic planning were seen as essential. The library knew that as partners the public must always be in the lead, with the library following so closely that both were seamlessly moving together. Its mission is: "We are dedicated to being the best public library for the communities we serve by providing outstanding and personalized service to everyone seeking access to the world of information and ideas." Its values are to "focus on our customers and anticipate their needs; live with integrity, inclusion, learning and fun; and act with courage, respect, empathy and passion." Its goal is to transform lives in two ways: (1) by empowering the community through preparing the youngest to learn to read and helping others learn to thrive, and (2) by building the community through connecting people with people and information, virtually and in person. These goals align well with the Arapahoe Library District brand.

Executive Director May participates directly in many community organizations, including the local chamber of commerce, and professional library staff members are placed on outside committees working on broader community issues. This integration positions the library within each of its communities and directly educates community decision makers on the value of library services. These decisions come because of the library's stated mission, values, and strategic goals—the essence of the library.

May and the Arapahoe Library District have not specifically invested in a distinct branding process; however, she, her administrative team, and her board of trustees have carefully developed the mission, values, and unique competencies as well as the specific target markets for their library system. Together they are positioning the library system according to their brand (see figure 4.8).

figure 4.8 **Arapahoe Library District Logo**

goals for the future. Strategic planning integrates the business planning, financial planning, and marketing planning for an organization. Marketing plans and positioning strategies often emerge from the strategic planning process. Strategic planning doesn't always capitalize on new opportunities or use the best leverage for an organization. Strategic positioning will often take sophisticated and successful libraries to the next level.

Strategic positioning recognizes the competitive and market environment in which the library operates. Positioning defines the library's specific niche within its sphere of influence. With a strong strategic position, the library obtains a distinct competitive advantage. Libraries often consider Google, Amazon, and other Internet delivery organizations as the competition. Positioning helps the library recognize its own unique qualities that separate it from the competition. Libraries can serve to

- Integrate service for information,
- Provide that human touch and personalized service,
- Localize information and provide relevancy, and
- Serve special groups, including children/ethnic groups/special demographics.

Strategic Planning and Strategic Positioning at Anythink

ANYTHINK CONDUCTED A strategic planning/positioning process that identified six strategic initiatives. These initiatives and their related goals enabled the district to achieve their strategic outcome of improving the quality of life in Adams County. Anythink's strategic initiatives from 2008 to 2010 were as follows:

1. Deliver superb customer service, products, and programs.
2. Build beautiful and inspiring environments.
3. Deliver convenience and innovation through technology.
4. Provide meaningful communications.
5. Provide highly effective organizational development.
6. Create financial sustainability for the future of RLD.

Libraries do occupy a special niche and have a competitive advantage. Positioning defines, creates, or re-creates the library's niche within the marketplace. Positioning is relative to the competition, and defines the library's identity and helps to create distinction in the competitive marketplace. It is very useful for an organization that needs to distinguish itself or to have a greater impact. Libraries clearly need to emerge from the shadows and create that greater impact if they are to survive.

Like the strategic planning process, strategic positioning is a systematic process based on information, deliberate decisions, and organizational alignment. It begins with a situation analysis that examines external and internal data as well as market information. Research identifies the potential target audiences to which the organization is to be positioned. Positioning does not take a library into totally new areas; however, it is based on the distinctive competence of the library and clarity about the brand and mission. Positioning is the key to rejuvenation. The positioning process is a tool that may uncover significant opportunities. The process involves developing a clear positioning statement along with succinct positioning strategies.

Summary

Positioning is a powerful tool for creating and maintaining differentiation in the marketplace. Most businesses and organizations believe that positioning is the most important strategy they have to promote and sell products and services. The secret of positioning is to understand your target markets, to identify the specific products and services to meet the wants and needs of that target audience, to learn from the competition, and to promote and communicate the available services.

Positioning identifies your uniqueness; builds upon your brand, your essence, and distinct offerings; and directs your message specifically to those who need and want to know about your services. Your library has a position in the marketplace, whether or not you have made a conscious effort to develop that position. To develop a positioning strategy for your library, you must first understand the current position. You must move strategically from the position your brand currently occupies in the minds of customers to where you want to be.

Your brand is the promise you make and the personality you convey. You develop a brand strategy that provides the essence of what you represent. Your brand consistently and repeatedly tells your customers why they should use your services. Successful branding creates brand equity. Successful positioning is built upon the foundation of the brand. Remember, if you don't consciously create a positioning strategy for the library, the community and your stakeholders will do it for you.

The strategic planning process forces libraries to define their mission and vision and to set strategic goals for the future. Strategic planning integrates the business planning, financial planning, and market planning for an organization. While strategic planning provides the foundation, strategic positioning and branding will often take sophisticated libraries to the next level. Traditionally, a strategic plan is built upon external and internal objective data and information. It involves a systematic and informed decision-making process. It leads to the development of decisions regarding positioning and market strategies as well as programs, operations, and resource development.

The process of developing the strategic plan gets all stakeholders on the same page. It enhances communication between the board and the staff, library customers, community organizations, and potential partners, as well as politicians. By working through difficult decisions, participants develop a greater understanding of each other, the library, and the brand of the library.

REFERENCES

DeRosa, Cathy, and Jenny Johnson. 2008. *From Awareness to Funding: A Study of Library Support in America.* Dublin, OH: Online Computer Library Center.

Kotler, Philip. 2001. *Foreword to Positioning: How to Be Seen and Heard in the Overcrowded Marketplace,* by Al Ries and Jack Trout. New York: McGraw-Hill.

Kotler, Philip, and Nancy R. Lee. 2008. *Social Marketing: Influencing Behaviors for Good.* 3rd ed. Los Angeles: Sage.

Levitt, Theodore. 1983. *The Marketing Imagination.* New York: Macmillan.

Ries, Al, and Jack Trout. 2001. *Positioning: How to Be Seen and Heard in the Overcrowded Marketplace.* New York: McGraw-Hill.

Understanding Segmentation

Selecting Your Target Markets

YOU POSITION THE LIBRARY TO BETTER ADDRESS your customers, potential customers, and stakeholders. Stakeholders include donors, elected officials, strategic partners, and other supporters and decision makers for the library. Your customers are unique to your library system. They differ in age, sex, geographical location, socioeconomics, education level, psychographic characteristics, behavior characteristics, beliefs, use of the library, as well as by the benefits they seek. A library cannot serve all segments (in spite of the optimistic expectation that libraries can be all things to all people). The library must choose which specific segments to consider a priority. Positioning identifies the target audience and the perceived state of the library relative to the competition for that target audience. The process of positioning builds on a unique set of attributes from which it creates a distinct position in the marketplace.

This chapter offers strategies to understand your target audiences. Those strategies include segmentation using demographics, geographic data, psychographics, and behavioral characteristics. It sounds simple to use these qualifiers to understand your customers; however, in order to segment your audience you must do some very thoughtful research/assessment and carefully consider the options for targeting your market.

The discussion in this chapter will focus on the assessment process to help you understand your target markets. The discussion includes:

- Understanding the library's current position
- Using primary and secondary resources
- Using quantitative and qualitative information
- Demographic, geographic, behavioral, and psychographic segmentation
- Cluster systems, such as PRIZM and VALS, that provide online assistance you can use
- Identifying and selecting your target audiences for your positioning strategy
- Criteria for evaluating segments/selection of target markets
- The relationship between strategic positioning and strategic planning

Using Market Research to Understand Target Markets

Do you really understand whom you are currently serving? It is very common to believe that you understand those whom you are serving; however, the results

Queens Library

STRATEGIC PLANNING AT Queens Library has incorporated staff from all levels of the library and is intended to drive operations in a concerted way across all levels, to analyze potential threats, and to maximize opportunities to serve customers, both present and future. At the same time, the strategy must be flexible enough to respond to quickly changing circumstances.

Every Friday, James Keller, former chief marketing officer, and the marketing staff visited four libraries like clockwork. They would sit in each library, observing customers and staff, and then ask questions. They would ask staff, "Tell me what's right and what's wrong with Queens Library? What is the best idea you can come up with? What needs to be done first, and where should we start?" Their credibility increased with each visit, taking ideas back, putting them through the system, and implementing them as fast as they could. In the process of learning, the marketing staff were engaging library staff, enabling them to grasp the big ideas behind marketing and how to ultimately promote the relevance and meaning of the Queens Library brand.

Marketing staff recognized the importance of understanding the publics they serve. To the marketing staff at Queens Library, the first step in developing any marketing and branding campaign was to develop a thorough understanding of the audience. The library needed to focus on whom it serves best and most often, and then address the needs of that population. They began by tapping the U.S. Census Bureau. By going to www.factfinder.census.gov they found a wealth of statistics on sex and age demographics, household relationships and types, housing and employment data, population characteristics associated with marital status, education, and income, and a host of other social and economic measures—and as localized as they wanted to make it. This was just the beginning; marketing staff also accessed and developed other research tools and measures that assessed the customer experience and engagement.

The first step was involvement with the staff. Staff engaged in chats throughout the system that were wide-ranging and covered all aspects of the organization. The meetings began to lay the foundation for the need for and importance of developing a Queens Library brand. Questions of staff members included:

What is Queens Library today?
What would you like to see Queens Library become?
What is the one thing you would like to keep about Queens Library going forward?

The questions were purposely left open-ended. The answers covered a broad range of thoughts, ideas, aspirations, and emotions. There were two common themes underlying a great number of the comments: many staffers indicated that Queens Library was a community center, a place where the diverse people of Queens could come together, and that the staff were committed to fulfilling customers' needs.

obtained through market research often vary from those perceptions. Although you can describe your customers, you need to undertake research to truly understand those whom you are currently serving and if you are meeting or not meeting their needs and wants. Market research is required to understand your customer base and to understand how your library is currently perceived.

GETTING THE MARKET RESEARCH ASSISTANCE YOU NEED

Some libraries will have sufficient budgets to develop a market research study to identify perceptions of the library within the community as well as identify the segments being served or to be potentially served. Professional firms are available to help in this area. For those libraries that need information but have a difficult time funding outside research services, research data is available using other means. Collaboration with a local university, community college, or research department from a corporation may provide the necessary help in developing a market research study. You can also hold community meetings, invite customers in to talk with you, or take the time to simply observe customers in the library. Remember not to be defensive or judgmental but simply to observe. Your website offers many opportunities to measure and track transactions. Your library card database offers opportunities for geographical penetration as well as information regarding segmentation of users. Look carefully at what information you have available to you.

Libraries can make good use of information from their own data. For example, computerized information from the online catalogue can be used to learn more about your customers. You can identify which materials have the highest circulation and which periodicals and databases have the greatest demand. You can use the computerized library card database system to identify the geographic areas from which your customers come. You can identify what we have described as "market share" or what is also referred to as "market penetration" within a specific geographic, perhaps defined by zip code, or within a specific demographic or psychographic, such as "seniors" or perhaps "boating enthusiasts," that you are seeking to serve.

As a customer, you have had experience with this kind of database market analysis. Every time you use a supermarket card or a credit card, your purchases are tracked. Ever wonder why you got on all of those mailing lists? The Internet has added another dimension to market research. Websites provide customers with remote access, and keep track of hits, page views, dwell times, etc. Technological advances have spurred the development of information systems, and those systems are at your fingertips (Walters 2004, 61).

You can see by the examples throughout the book that the methods and resulting segments differ; however, each library was able to obtain the information they needed. Your customers are unique to your library system and differ from other library systems. Your customers will differ in age, sex, geographical location, socioeconomics, education level, psychographic characteristics, behavior characteristics, beliefs, and use of the library, as well as by the benefits they seek. How do you obtain the information you need regarding your customers and stakeholders. Research is the basis of understanding of the various segments within reach of your library system. A library cannot serve all segments; it must choose which specific segments it considers a priority, its target market. The process of positioning builds on a unique set of target market attributes which you then set out to address in a very targeted way (see figure 5.1). Seattle Public Library provides an exhaustive example of how market research guides a targeting strategy (see figure 5.2).

figure 5.1 **Target Your Market**

USING PROFESSIONAL MARKET RESEARCH TEAMS

Professional market research firms design, administer, and analyze market research for you. Using professionals ensures that you get the information you need. Many libraries have worked with professional firms, and those libraries can assist you in identifying appropriate consultants.

Ask the various market research firms under consideration to provide you with a proposal that includes recommended methodologies to gain an understanding of your target markets. This proposal should also include time lines and expenses. Be wary of comparing market research firms on cost alone. Cost is certainly a factor; however, the quality and effectiveness of the work should be the first consideration.

USING PRIMARY AND SECONDARY RESOURCES

Primary resources for market information, as previously discussed, are those sources you control and from which you obtain market information. Libraries traditionally contain vast storehouses of primary information. This information might exist in your tracking of use and checkout of reference materials, periodicals, library cardholder information and transactions, and related information you obtain directly from or about your customers, your donors, your volunteers, and others. If you conduct surveys, gather satisfaction data, capture download requests, and so on, you are generating primary market information and your library is the primary source. Libraries can make good use of their primary sources of information for their own market research. For example, computerized information from the online catalogue can be used to learn more about your customers—who they are, how frequently they access information, how long they check out and/or dwell in reading online information, and so on. You can also identify which materials have the highest turnover and which periodicals and databases have the highest demand among selected target markets you have identified. You can use the computerized library card database system to identify the geographic areas from which your customers come. You can also identify how many customers there are in any given market you are currently reaching to estimate your market share or market penetration.

Let's pause here a moment to consider just how much powerful data you have on your customers related to market penetration. For example, the cardholder database gives you an initial understanding of where your current customers live. Now consider how much more you can learn by assessing how cardholders within certain geographical areas are using their cards.

Now let's turn to the subject of secondary sources of information. Libraries have access to many sources of secondary information, beginning with publicly available census data and even complex psychographic data that are made available through outside sources, some for free and others at a cost. In many instances, you will find useful secondary information about the markets you serve through other organizations in your community. For example, crime statistics related to a specific library service in which you are promoting informational sources on safety and home protection might be available through a local law enforcement agency. Attitudes toward early childhood education might be available through the local school district or perhaps a teacher's college in the area. If you are promoting library resources for starting a new business, you might turn to your local chamber of commerce or economic development agency for secondary information of value in designing your promotional strategy. The great benefit of secondary sourced market information is that it is often there just for the asking or at a reasonable cost. Furthermore, it is likely that if you have need for the information to guide the marketing efforts of the library, others in your community—from government agencies to nonprofits to local businesses—can use the information as well. It is likely that your reference area can guide you in identifying a vast array of secondary market information for which you are already the local repository.

UNDERSTANDING QUALITATIVE AND QUANTITATIVE RESEARCH

Market researchers typically distinguish two types of information based on the form it comes in—by the methods used to acquire it and by how it is analyzed and utilized. The first and most often used is quantitative information—information in the form of a measurement or value recorded from or by a measurement tool. For example, if you are counting the number of times a cardholder checks out a certain category of material, you are recording a quantitative measure. Generally, analyses of quantitative measures are conducted using basic arithmetic and/or advanced statistical methods. When you measure market share or market penetration, you are using quantitative measures and conducting a form of quantitative research.

Qualitative research, on the other hand, provides a combination of sensory and descriptive information—generally expressed in words, gestures, and emotional expressions. For example, if you are conducting research by stopping customers as they leave the library and asking them open-ended questions like "What brought you to the library today?" the information you capture will be expressed in the form of a statement and will include a mixture of thoughts and feelings. If you do nothing more than record the information and use it as is to better understand the subject, you are conducting qualitative research. Interviews, focus groups, direct observation of customer patterns and activities, and interpretations thereof are generally considered to be qualitative in form. Qualitative research is often more difficult to interpret and analyze but can be powerful in understanding how customers experience, process, and feel about the subject under consideration. Focus groups are often conducted with distinct groups of customers, including teens, seniors, or children, to develop an understanding about how they feel regarding policies or programs, procedures, or services. Qualitative market research can produce many "aha" moments, clarify customer perceptions, and provide valuable insight about how customers engage with your brand and the thought processes involved.

Now let's confuse things by pointing out that the line between quantitative and qualitative can blur in many instances and for good reason. Often data that are reported in quantitative terms are thought therefore to be purely quantitative, and thus more useful in terms of demonstrating a measurable value that can be evaluated using objective mathematical or statistical methods. For example, you might survey customers periodically to assess their relative satisfaction with the library, using questions that include a choice range from "very satisfied" to "very dissatisfied" and perhaps with two or three values in between. From your survey of one hundred customers your measurement of satisfaction reveals that most of them are "very satisfied" and you therefore feel confident that you are delivering

Seattle Public Library— A Case Study

IN 1998, VOTERS approved a $196.4 million bond measure to support the campaign for the Seattle Public Library to build a dramatic, new central library, as well as to renovate and build branches throughout the city (see figure 5.2). An additional $83 million was raised in private donations to support the public campaign, titled "Libraries for All." The staff asked, "Now that we have the buildings, what programs, materials, and services best meet the patron of the future? What do we do for whom?" they asked. "What kind of face do we put on it?" "Budget is certainly going to be a factor, as is technology. We need to reinvent using spaces and serving people!"

Assisted by consultants Berk and Associates, the library board of trustees launched a strategic planning process in early 2010 to chart a course that would meet twenty-first century information needs. The first stage of the strategic planning process was a comprehensive research project to identify and understand current customers. Many individuals and groups shared their ideas, insights, and passions in the development of this strategic plan. The Seattle Public Library is a public institution, funded by the public for the public, and so a great deal of effort went into consulting the public about the future of the library.

The research and planning process began in March 2010 with five community open houses held in libraries across the city. In May 2010, 32,893 people participated in the Seattle Public Library Community Survey, answering questions about their current use of the library's

figure 5.2 **Seattle Public Library**

resources and buildings and their engagement with library staff members. In addition to the community open houses and survey, the library hosted two public forums: "Technology and Its Impact on the Future of Libraries" and "User Experience in the 21st Century Library." Library staff also facilitated focus groups with service providers who work with children, teens, older adults, immigrants and refugees, and people who are homeless. The discussions focused on how the library can better serve these populations.

Library staff members were involved throughout the process. They provided valuable insight into the evolving usage patterns and preferences of Seattle residents. Staff members shared their ideas through an open-ended survey that asked about the future role of the library, trends and changes in how people use library resources, and suggestions for new or better ways to serve library customers.

high-quality service. However, when you use a measure like "satisfaction" you are effectively asking customers to give you an emotional indication of how they feel about something. You are asking a qualitative question but forcing your customer to respond within a quantitative framework that may be misleading. For example, if within your one hundred customers you have a mix of seasoned library users and first-time users, you would realize that the experience and expectations they bring to the library threshold are very different, and thus how they express their relative satisfaction with a specific experience can mean very different things.

Generally, quantitative forms of market research are most useful when seeking to generalize measurements or observations related to a specific market segment or group of market segments. There are simple guidelines for constructing quantitative research that are reasonably valid (measuring the right thing) and reasonably reliable (measuring the same thing in a consistent and repeatable manner). Included are sampling guidelines to ensure relative confidence in your ability to generalize results beyond those included in your sample. Similarly, there are also guidelines and methodologies for gathering and analyzing more qualitative forms

Throughout this planning process, an internal strategic plan project management team, an external eighteen-member strategic planning advisory committee, and the library board of trustees met regularly to review the results of these various inputs and to delve into the specifics of many topics, including the impact of digital media, community building, and effective partnering. The advisory committee served as a sounding board and source of inspiration, contributing thought-provoking and ambitious perspectives from academia, business, and the nonprofit sector. The library board, which is the library's governing body, was the steward of the plan, provided input at key junctures, and developed the statements of vision, mission, and guidance for the organization.

Pulling together the threads of this multilayered exploration, key themes emerged to guide development of the strategic plan. Supporting Seattle's devotion to reading and learning remains the core function of the library. The content of the library's collection is of paramount importance to customers. The library needs to aggressively expand digital resources while guaranteeing that customers would have access to material in formats with which they were comfortable.

The findings indicated that libraries play a central role in Seattle's communities and neighborhoods. Now more than ever, the library needs to strengthen our democracy by inviting civic engagement through discussion and dissemination of information. The Seattle Public Library should not wait for people to come through its doors but instead actively reach out to listen to people and connect them with library resources where they are.

The Seattle Public Library must team with public, community, and business organizations to expand its reach through strategic partnerships. Finally, the library's ability to actively enrich the lives of Seattle-ites requires creation of an organizational culture that encourages thoughtful innovation and experimentation.

Following is a summary of goals and objectives identified through the research:

Fuel Seattle's passion for reading, personal growth, and learning.

Expand Seattle's access to information, ideas, and stories.

Empower Seattle's distinctive communities and vibrant neighborhoods.

Build partnerships to make a difference in people's lives.

Foster an organizational culture of innovation.

The library sees itself as being a transformational organization, one that provides leadership within the community as well as within the library environment. It seeks to be in a leadership role, defining the library for the next generation of patrons as well as for the community. The library wants to be "out in front," innovating and exploring new ways to meet the needs and expectations of patrons. That means being flexible and able to adjust service models. It also strives to be the go-to place for information and resources in the community.

The Seattle Public Library has conducted both primary and secondary market research, engaging a wide audience. Through this research it has identified several strategic directions and initiatives to address the competitive market environment in which it operates. The library's goal is to become a transformative organization, one that provides leadership. This requires substantial market research to guide a positioning strategy for the library.

of information. Though beyond the scope of this book, it is important that you consider the sources, forms, methods, and applications of the research information you are using, and the limitations and advantages of each—and the extent to which the lines will blur. Consult your library holdings on the subject of market research.

Market research is used to help you make decisions. Some form of research is applicable in every decision you make. Traditionally, a research plan is developed to identify the purpose of the research and the informational objectives. Next, you discuss the audience that you are trying to reach and the technique that offers the most efficient and effective way to gather the information. Pretesting allows you to test the effectiveness of the research methodology and research questions. Finally, the data are analyzed. There are a variety of statistical procedures and qualitative methods that can be considered and applied.

UNDERSTANDING SEGMENTATION ANALYSIS AND TARGETING YOUR AUDIENCE

Targeting the market probably makes sense to you by now. It may create the greatest angst for many who feel that the library is a government agency and therefore expected to treat everyone the same. By targeting the primary audiences, you will be concentrating your resources in areas where you can have the greatest impact. While the library will still be available to all, the attention you focus on targeted audiences will produce the success you desire. You want to identify actual and potential customers, stakeholders, and donors who have the motivation, ability, and opportunity to use and support the library.

Market segmentation involves dividing the market into distinct groups that have similar needs, aspirations, and behaviors that require a similar marketing mix. Companies do not target everyone. Libraries, too, must select their primary segments. Those segments are identified by size, accessibility, and responsiveness. While libraries are open to all, there are particular segments whose needs and wants libraries can best try to serve. There are three steps to consider in selecting the target markets to serve. The first step is to identify the segments, the second step is to evaluate the viability of segments, and the third step is to choose one or more of the most viable segments for targeting. One way to determine the "viability" of a target market is to think of the target market as one you have the greatest ability/resources to reach. Consider time, money, staffing, and your ability to meet the needs and wants of the target market. There is a common adage in the world of market segmentation that places emphasis on first looking for the "low-hanging fruit" or those within your reach. There is a parallel notion that stresses the importance of "growing with those you know"—focusing first on customers already familiar to you and with what your library has to offer. See figure 5.3 as an excellent example of how Apple stepped through the process with the introduction of the iPhone.

Demographic Segmentation

Traditionally, libraries use demographic information to identify various groups of individuals within a library service or catchment area. Demographic information includes age, gender, ethnicity, occupation, income levels, and education levels. This is the most popular basis for segmenting markets and is most frequently

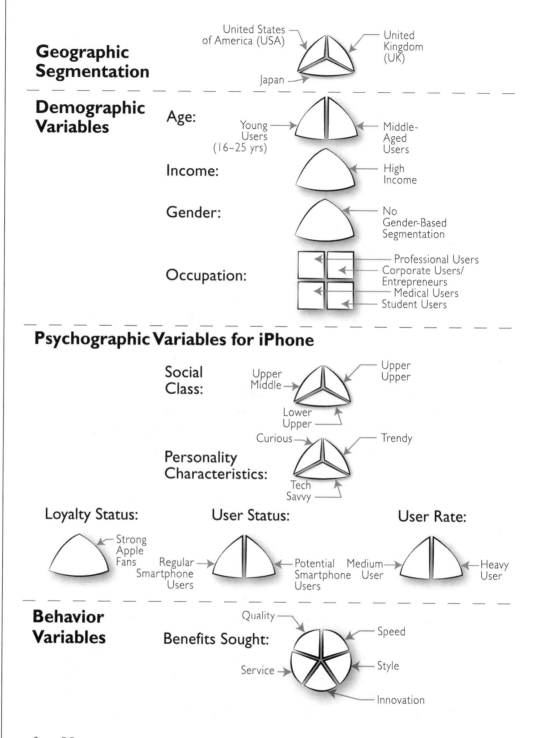

figure 5.3

Demographic, Geographic, and Behavioral Segmentation for the Apple iPhone

used within the library marketplace. Consider programs and services in libraries designed for children, teens, adults, and seniors based on the age demographic. Or perhaps you might focus on women, or like Wyoming has done, on men. You might combine age, gender, and household income—all basic demographics.

Geographic Segmentation

Libraries commonly identify their users using a geographical profile. Services are developed to meet the needs of users in various geographical locations. Librarians realize that the needs and wants in some geographical areas are different from others. Geographic segmentation divides a market according to geographical areas, such as continents, countries, states, regions, counties, cities, and neighborhoods. Geographic segmentation can also be based on such items as commuting patterns, places of work, and proximity to relevant landmarks. Branch libraries already employ geographic segmentation as managers develop collections and service plans to serve their neighborhoods.

Psychographic Segmentation

A logical extension of geographic segmentation based on "where" people live is psychographic segmentation. It is based on "how" people live. Libraries use psychographic segmentation in the development of their services and collection. Psychographic segmentation divides the market into different groups on the basis of life stage, lifestyle, and life value characteristics and behaviors. Life stage segmentation recognizes that individuals, family units, and even neighborhoods and whole communities reflect predictable life stage characteristics, including preferences and behaviors based on where they are in the aging process. Libraries seeking to serve a neighborhood primarily comprised of young families will consider a very different approach to marketing than one that is serving a neighborhood dominated by aging seniors. Lifestyle segmentation focuses on how individuals and households choose to spend their discretionary resources, whether expressed in the kinds of stores they frequent, the publications to which they subscribe, the destinations and means by which they choose to travel, or the athletics shoes and cars they choose to drive. A good example of successful segmentation marketing is Harley-Davidson. The segmentation paradigm for Harley-Davidson is about selling a lifestyle—complete with the emotional appeal of feeling the wind in your hair, the rumble in your bones, and the perfect tattoo. Life values expression is an increasingly powerful tool for segmenting markets. Political parties spend fortunes segmenting and targeting markets based on shared value orientations—expressed via opinion, attitudes, and beliefs associated with social, moral, cultural, and economic considerations. Cobranding strategies of corporate entities seeking to express their deep commitment to a social cause by sponsoring or supporting a nonprofit serving that cause, are often based on market research that indicates that their best customers share values associated with that same cause. Consider Whole Foods and its emphasis on supporting local growers and causes important to each of the neighborhoods in which they locate.

Libraries are in an especially good position to access and leverage psychographic research to ascertain the deeply held and enduring value orientations of the customers they serve. More than a high-sounding term, psychographics represents a high ground of market research.

Behavior Segmentation

Behavioral segmentation divides the market on the pure basis of observable and measurable behaviors specific to how customers interact with the library. How do they use the library? Are they using the library from remote locations? Are they using databases and reserve systems? Are they downloading books and materials? How frequently are they using the library? Are customers using electronic equipment like computers and not checking out materials? By analyzing behavioral patterns of your customers you can infer demographic, geographic, and psychographic characteristics.

You want to understand the needs, wants, motivations, values, behaviors, and lifestyles of your customers in order to serve them better. While libraries have traditionally developed profiles of their users by using demographic, geographic, or psychographic characteristics, behavior segmentation is relatively new in usage at the library and serves to bring all of these elements together. It does require more sophisticated research and a disciplined commitment to continuous and consistent observation to understand customers beyond the demographic, geographic, and psychographic characteristics. Only when you understand your customers behaviorally are you sure you have a good fix on the segments you can serve the best, with the most frequency, and with the highest return on your investment.

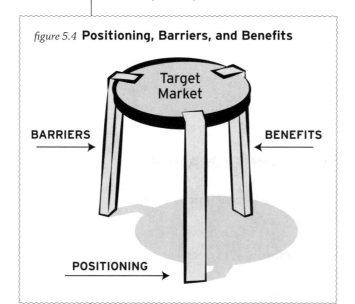

figure 5.4 **Positioning, Barriers, and Benefits**

For each segment you focus on, regardless of the methods you use, it is critical that you assess each segment in terms of positioning, barriers, and benefits (see figure 5.4). How can you position the library to promote behavioral engagement of each segment? What barriers exist that you must overcome to promote engagement of each segment? What benefit will each segment derive from this engagement? This is the "three-legged stool" of segmentation marketing—like a three-legged stool that is evenly balanced, you will have an approach that is strong, stable, and very cost efficient.

CLUSTER SYSTEMS: PRIZM AND VALS

There are several well-known commercial models used to group consumer markets into homogeneous segments, often referred to as clusters. PRIZM NE is a geo-demographic and psychographic classification system developed by Claritas and offered by the Nielsen Company that describes every U.S. neighborhood in terms of sixty-six distinct social group types called segments (www.claritas.com/MyBest Segments/Default.jsp). Each zip code is assigned one or several of the sixty-six clusters based on the shared socioeconomic characteristics of the area. It is based on the fundamental premise that "birds of a feather flock together," and that when choosing a place to live people tend to seek out neighborhoods compatible with their lifestyles, where they find others in similar circumstances with similar consumer behavior patterns. Segments are given snappy and immediately informative names like "God's Country," "Red, White & Blues," "Kids & Cul-de-Sacs," and "Blue

Blood Estates." Each segment is then described, providing demographic as well as lifestyle-related behaviors. There are other sources for this information, including Esri/Tapestry (www.esri.com/data) or Scan/US (www.scanus.com).

The VALS segmentation categorizes U.S. adult consumers into one of eight segments, indicative of personality traits considered to be determinants (drivers) of buying behaviors (www.strategicbusinessinsights.com/VALS/about.shtml). You can explore all of these commercial models of segmentation by going to their websites.

Selecting Your Target Markets

In choosing the best segments to pursue, libraries are encouraged to consider a variety of variables that include but go beyond the basics of low-hanging fruit and growing with those you know, including the criteria that follow (see figure 5.5).

CRITERIA FOR EVALUATING YOUR TARGET MARKET

Once you group the marketplace into viable segments for consideration, the next task is to evaluate each segment as follows:

- **Segment size**—How many people are in this segment? What percent of the population do they represent?
- **Potential for growth**—Does this segment represent a growing market?
- **Competition**—Who else is serving this segment? Is their potential for partnering with other providers turning competitors into partners?
- **Brand loyalty**—Are customers in this segment passionate and committed to the library? Do they have loyalty potential if their needs are addressed?
- **Potential to offer superior value**—What are the unique offerings that the library can provide for this segment?
- **Brand image**—What is the impact on the library's brand image?
- **Relevance of resources**—Does the library have access to resources, materials, facilities, equipment, staff, and a distribution network to meet segment needs and wants?

figure 5.5 **Selecting Your Target Audience**

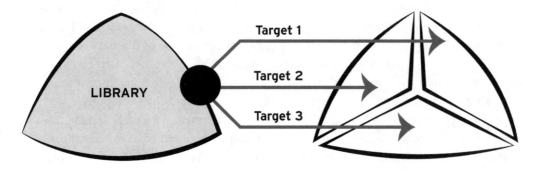

Wyoming State Library

WYOMING LIBRARY DIRECTORS and decision makers across the state had decided as a group that marketing the libraries to Wyoming residents would help in raising awareness of what libraries have to offer and what services residents can find at Wyoming libraries (see figure 5.6). The Wyoming State Library (WSL) was committed to this campaign and designated the funds necessary for this campaign. Wyoming residents were also not aware that Wyoming libraries work together, and that their local library card was really a card for any library in the state. As a result of raising awareness, there was a goal of increasing the number of library cardholders throughout Wyoming.

Research was done through the University of Wyoming Survey and Analysis Center, which conducted surveys and assisted in the planning and implementation of research. Over 1,500 postcards were sent to library cardholders with directions to an online survey. There were 442 respondents to the survey, which the UW Survey and Analysis Center said was an outstanding response. The responses to the survey questions were not surprising; women made up 81 percent of respondents, although there were an equal amount of men and women who received postcards. The WSL found that men did not find libraries as relevant to their lives as women and yet made up 51 percent of the population. They therefore represent a sizable market opportunity.

Wyoming libraries work together using their integrated library system, with one hundred libraries, including all public, community college, and most schools, as well as special libraries such as the Yellowstone Research Library and the Buffalo Bill Historical Center. Although Wyoming libraries are strong community centers and the residents who use the libraries are faithful and devoted users, there was a lack of knowledge and understanding by a large group in the state that libraries are also relevant to their lives: young to middle-aged

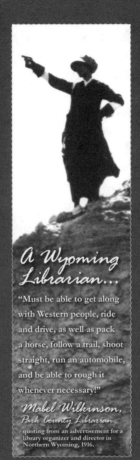

A Wyoming Librarian...

"Must be able to get along with Western people, ride and drive, as well as pack a horse, follow a trail, shoot straight, run an automobile, and be able to rough it whenever necessary!"

Mabel Wilkinson,
Park County Librarian
quoting from an advertisement for a library organizer and director in Northern Wyoming, 1916.

figure 5.6 **Wyoming Librarian**

men. Since this group makes up a large portion of the decision makers in the state, the targeting of this audience was imperative.

The WSL works diligently with elected officials within the state. State legislators and state funding are extremely important, as well as are elected officials in each community. Elected officials are a consistent target audience for the WSL. A campaign targeting the men in every community also serves to create awareness among elected officials.

The state of Wyoming is well known for its incredible natural beauty as well as its long distances and limited population. Communities are small and located some distance from each other. One of the primary needs of families and men is information on automobile repair, as commercial garages are few and far between. The WSL subscribed to the Chilton Auto Repair database to provide online auto repair information throughout the state. This database was just the tool and the service to appeal to the segment of young and middle-aged men that the library sought to reach. The library built partnerships with auto parts stores throughout the state and developed the Mudflap Girl campaign to meet the specific needs of this target audience (see figure 5.7).

The mudflap girl is the silhouette of a woman you have often seen on the mudflaps of large trucks. Ed Allen claims that the image was designed by his father, a long-haul truck driver who always decorated his truck with an image of his wife. The image has been trademarked and is now a popular symbol on the mudflaps of large trucks (Barry 2011).

WE'RE SHIFTING GEARS!

wyominglibraries.org

figure 5.7 **Wyoming Mudflap Girl**

SELECTING YOUR TARGET MARKETS (MARKET SEGMENTATION)

Selecting and focusing on specific markets is both effective and efficient. Targeting a specific market does not mean that you have to exclude people that do not fit your criteria. Targeting simply allows you to focus your resources and your brand message on a specific market that is more likely to use your services. It allows you to get a "bigger bang for your buck." If you develop strong programs for your target market, your success will become measurable and demonstrable.

Steps in Selecting Target Markets

The four steps involved in selecting your target markets are as follows:

1. **Segment the market**—Understand and divide the larger population into smaller groups that require unique but similar strategies in order to reach and to engage.

2. **Evaluate the segments**—Each segment is then evaluated based on the criteria and factors described previously in this chapter. These criteria will assist you in prioritizing segments.

3. **Choose one to three segments for targeting**—Develop a rich, descriptive profile of their unique characteristics.

Library Branding and Positioning—A Garden Party Conversation

IN THE SUMMER of 2011, the authors conducted a limited survey through the *Library Journal's Bubble Room* blog titled *Library Branding: A Garden Party Conversation*. The objective was how library staff with an interest in marketing view positioning within their organizations.

Positioning is based on a distinct knowledge of the target market, the value you deliver to that market, and the competition for that market. It is not possible to really target the market if you have not done the research to understand who your customers are and how they value your service.

Many times professionals within the library field indicated that libraries are in competition with Google, Starbucks, and Barnes & Noble. These are the obvious choices, but if libraries really knew what customers value about their services, they might list other competitors.

The first question of the Garden Party survey asked, "Does the library have a clear idea of the customers we are trying to target and serve?" Here is a sampling of verbatim responses:

"Somewhat, and we can improve. We have a lot of cardholders, but our door counts are off recently and we don't seem to be attracting new people of certain demographics."

"Somewhat, and we can improve. There is much discussion about who we need to target, but when it comes to implementation there is a lack of commitment, possibly due to fear of change."

"Somewhat, and we can improve . . . We have a good idea about our existing/current customers, but could better understand our potential customers. We are planning surveys and data collection to assess target markets." (Jackson 2011)

While a few replied that they have done substantial market research and truly understood who their customers are, the majority were less than confident about this important first step. Without good-quality information beyond door counts and library card usage, it is impossible to really understand who your customers are, what they do when they use the library, and what benefits they are seeking. Knowing your customers is the basic requirement for positioning the services to target markets.

4. **Choose segments that have a unique appeal and that are inspiring to you**—Keep in mind that you will need a different marketing mix strategy for each segment.

The segmentation process is often tedious and complex, but you will find that you can "slice and dice" groups of people in numerous ways. By targeting your audiences you will increase your effectiveness and efficiencies. You will also benefit by being able to make decisions on resource allocation as well as new strategies.

You can begin with one variable—the one considered most important—as a primary way to group a market and then further refine your segment definition by adding additional variables. Geographic segmentation is the typical beginning point considering the legal/political boundaries that are likely to define your service area.

Undifferentiated Marketing versus Differentiated Marketing

Undifferentiated marketing refers to the use of the same basic strategy to address a variety of segments, focusing on what is common in the needs of all rather the differentiated needs of each. It is sometimes referred to as mass marketing and is often employed because it seems to be the easiest approach. However, the downside is generally expressed in an overall high cost of sales and low return for dollars invested.

Differentiated marketing refers to identifying different strategies for different market segments, and orchestrating your promotional strategies and tactics to harmoniously address all segments in a differentiated manner. This requires both an

---

The second question for discussion in the Garden Party survey was, "Do the customers we are targeting or currently serving understand the unique value and benefits we offer as a library?" The generally affirmative responses included:

"Yes, because our fans know and understand . . ."

"Yes, because we can help in more ways than a person understands. We have access to so many resources that a single person may not have considered in helping themselves . . . and we have the community connections to either assist in solving their issue or enhance their experience."

"Yes, because each customer using our libraries does so because of the benefit they receive, or the improvement to his/her quality of life. Some customers value the free Internet access. Some appreciate the books, movies, materials, and databases that they couldn't otherwise afford. Some value the free family programs that entertain and educate. You may receive a different answer from each customer because of the variety of ways that libraries improve life for the residents we serve."

"Yes, because our strategy is focused on three customer segments, which drives all our tactics and strategic partnerships, it is easy for staff to understand and articulate."

"Yes, because choices include Google, cell phone, social media, which means we need to make our services easy to use and more user friendly."

"Somewhat, because customers who use the library understand the value; however, many potential customers don't even know we exist."

"Somewhat, because the library role is shifting and we continue to work on this changing perception by continuing to offer additional services." (Jackson 2011)

The responses indicated that these marketing-oriented staff appreciate the challenges and opportunities of positioning. While several focus more on what the library offers than what good market intelligence tells them customers want, there is an overall appreciation for the both sides of the question.

intelligent segmentation approach and disciplined execution. The advantages are many, including lower cost of sales and higher return for dollars invested.

Concentrated marketing refers to marketing strategies in which some segments are eliminated altogether and resources and efforts often are concentrated on developing and executing the ideal strategies for one or only a few key segments (Kotler and Lee 2008, 130). This approach requires a commitment to serve the few in lieu of the many and generally produces the most cost-efficient outcome.

CHOOSING THE APPROACH FOR YOUR LIBRARY

Most libraries are faced with limited budgets; therefore, the segments they serve will need to be prioritized. Librarians should choose where to allocate funds to the segments and services that will affect the most people and be the most cost effective.

Selected target markets are those that should represent the greatest opportunity for marketing success. They emerge as the markets with the greatest need, and they are the most ready to react, easiest to reach, and the best match for the goals and aspirations of the library. As a rule, libraries should seldom if ever focus resources on undifferentiated strategies, except those already in place. Most often libraries should focus on differentiated strategies based on clearly defined and selected target markets. Where given a community mandate to serve specific market segments or to seize opportunities to serve new or emerging markets, concentrated strategies will be in order.

Market segmentation is a key component of strategic positioning. Columbus Metropolitan Library provides an excellent example of how advanced segmentation methods are applied to strategic positioning.

SUCCESSFUL MARKET SEGMENTATION RESEARCH— COLUMBUS METROPOLITAN LIBRARY

Columbus Metropolitan Library (CML) demonstrates the successful use of a market research strategy. The library used both primary and secondary resources as well as a variety of market research techniques to guide a marketing plan that was "focused, consistent, cumulative, and impactful."

Columbus Metropolitan Library asked, "How do we balance and focus our resources, yet stay true to the fundamental tenet of universal access?" The answer was to build a strategy based on market research. The library began with the common understanding that marketing comprises a wide range of activities to meet the needs of its customers. Next, the library focused on those customers who represented the greatest need and likelihood of benefitting from the resources of the library. So, while the library is and will remain open to all, the staff focused the marketing and service efforts on those who represent the greatest need and opportunity to serve.

Columbus Metropolitan Library demonstrates the value of analyzing the competition and positioning the library in the mind of customers in the context of all the other choices they have. So, this is where it began—with an overriding strategy premised on research to guide a marketing plan that is focused, consistent, cumulative, and impactful.

First, Columbus Metropolitan Library adopted a rigorous, professionally led planning process directed by its newly hired team that began with research. The first and perhaps most critical step was knowing all about the library's customers. Not just demographic profiles, but how they live, how they behave, and how they express their values and aspirations. While the library had conducted some general customer feedback in the past, the responses provided little information about the customers themselves and seldom went beyond the basics of demographics and problem identification.

Columbus Metropolitan Library engaged a consulting firm in 2006 and embarked on a research process that examined customer engagement using five different methods:

- A cardholder database analysis across all branches
- Ethnographic observation studies conducted in various branches
- A customer intercept survey conducted in various branches
- An online customer survey
- Staff surveys and interviews to glean perspectives on customers' needs and wants

The library put together a cross-departmental team to analyze the information. Together with the consulting firm, the CML marketing staff and internal team began to study the library's customer database in-depth. Beginning with the cardholder database, they plotted gender, age, addresses, and zip codes against service districts and created specific profiles for each branch. This information included growth projections, racial/ethnic breakdown, household income levels and projected change over the next five years, education levels, and penetration levels. A penetration level is the percentage of cardholders within a specific radius of a branch. They then established penetration rates as a baseline for each of the branches with rates varying from 20 to 53 percent.

Next, they observed the customers ethnographically and behaviorally by asking, "Where do customers go when they walk in the door? How long do they stay? What do they do while they are here?"

Surveys in the form of personal interviews were the next step. The researchers used a technique called "Mall Intercept Interviews." Originally designed for use in shopping malls, they found this technique very well suited to the library setting (Kaden 2008, 178). Going beyond observation, the researchers intercepted customers during their visits, clipboards in hand, and asked them a series of interview questions. By intercepting customers in sixteen of the twenty-one branches and over twenty-five different shifts, they were able to conduct interviews with over 500 customers, all within an eleven-day period.

Next, they developed an online survey that included the same questions as posed in the intercepts, plus a host of questions pertaining to online services. Another 1,300 surveys were generated, providing a very complete picture based on a confident sampling of active library users.

Staff surveys and interviews came next. Staff shared their perceptions about customers—who they are and how they use the library. The staff analysis was conducted in two parts: an online survey to all staff members and direct interviews with key staff members, board members, and Friends of the Library. There were some surprising differences in how staff perceived customers and what the more direct customer surveys revealed.

Using this comprehensive and disciplined approach to research, Columbus Metropolitan Library began to change how it traditionally looked at customers, moving from a demographic to a behavioral viewpoint. Using the Claritas PRIZM clusters analysis (www.claritas.com/MyBestSegments), the library segmented customers into fourteen behavior clusters. PRIZM combines demographic, consumer behavior, and geographic data to help marketers identify, understand, and target customers.

Applying this combination of methods, Columbus Metropolitan Library uncovered a number of important insights to guide its marketing plan, including branding and positioning strategies. For example, the library identified these characteristics regarding dominant user groups:

- Age groups were 25–34 and 35–44. A large drop-off was seen after age 55.
- Families with children under the age 18 accounted for 34–39 percent of all adult CML customers. This statistic held true across branch survey responses and the web-based surveys.
- Primary usage within the library focused on borrowing books and printed materials for adults. Borrowing A/V materials garnered second highest use. This finding held consistent across age groups, with the exception of the 18–21 group of customers from the branch surveys, who listed "use computer/Internet" as the primary use of the library.

The library also observed how customers viewed the library and the extent to which the overall market of potential customers actually utilized the library. For example, customers viewed the role of the library as primarily a place to browse and borrow materials, and secondarily as a community service organization to promote learning opportunities and resources. And based on penetration measures, branches ranged from 20 to 53 percent within their defined service areas, while the Columbus Metropolitan Library system overall represented a penetration rate closer to 60 percent of all households when considering the entire Greater Columbus market area.

Income was not a driving factor in library usage, according to the analysis. Although fluctuations occurred, audiovisual usage fluctuated only mildly based on income. Gender and education level had some effect. Interestingly, website usage was strongly related to visitation, and primary website activities were reserving and renewing materials.

Customers were asked in the online survey to identify unmet or future needs that the library should address. In summary, they expressed interest in having services and resources convenient to them, in physical locations where they spend their time, including such places as the post office, cafés, and daycare centers. In the process, Columbus Metropolitan Library was able to identify clusters of customers that fit a combination of demographic and usage characteristics. Fourteen separate target groups emerged, each labeled according to its usage profile, including Media Hounds, Socialites, Bookworms, Power Users, Drive-Throughs, Virtual Users, Young Minds, and Lightweights. Following is a more detailed description of one of these clusters:

> *Power Users:* A key constituency that accounts for most of the circulation. They take advantage of reserve services, are active browsers, and check out six-plus items per visit. They range in age from 18 to 45, are balanced male/female, and vary ethnically by region.

Evaluating all the research as a whole, the Columbus Metropolitan Library team synthesized key findings, many of which aligned with the OCLC study *From Awareness to Funding.* Here are a few of the surprises that emerged:

- Visitors and cardholders were much younger than anticipated—25–34 and 35–44, respectively.
- Contrary to staff perceptions, 60 percent of visitors and cardholders did not have children at home.
- Income, ethnicity, and geography did not account for much difference, with only minor variations noted as related to gender and age.
- Behavior patterns were significantly related. Those who checked out books frequently (Power Users) also tended to check out large quantities of materials. In contrast, Browsers as a group tended not to check out books. Computer users devoted large blocks of time to computer usage and seldom ventured into other sections of the library.

The Columbus Metropolitan Library team vigorously debated each of these findings, addressing strategic questions about the primary focus of the library: how to measure penetration and value received, and how to define service areas. Each of the fourteen original clusters or segments was carefully evaluated through an assessment matrix to determine the extent to which CML should devote resources to address each of these target market segments. After careful study, the leadership team selected Young Minds as the top segment to promote, followed by Power Users to serve and Virtual Users to maintain. These groups emerged as the library's most important customer base and the ones whose needs and values most closely reflected the charter of the library.

Next, Columbus Metropolitan Library sought to make this commitment come alive in the strategic and tactical plans of the library. For each of these segments, the library has developed five- to ten-year strategic goals. Each year they build a tactical plan, identifying new opportunities to pursue within that year. Only those initiatives tied to priority segments received funding. Using the strategic filter, now staff understand how decisions get made and how priorities are determined.

In 2011, Columbus Metropolitan Library revisited its strategic plan, conducted additional research, evaluated trends and the environmental situation, and reexamined its target audiences. Changes in areas of technology, employment, and the economy required reexamination of target markets and a new strategic plan.

The Power User target audience selected in 2006 morphed into the new target audience titled My Library user. Young Minds, the second target audience, remains a major focus, while the third target audience has been identified as Life Skills user. The Life Skills target audience focuses on career literacy, financial literacy, health literacy, and technology literacy. The library will be developing community partnerships to serve this target audience. The library has done most of the heavy lifting regarding the Young Minds target audience, and has developed extensive products, programs, and services, as well as facilities and delivery systems, to serve this audience.

The My Library target audience will be a primary focus in the new strategic plan. Technology, social media, e-books, and exceptional customer service will be the hallmarks of new and enhanced service to meet the identified needs and wants for this target audience. The library launched a new website that allows its customers to personalize the website for themselves.

Summary

Defining the target audience is the first step in developing the positioning strategy. Libraries have specific target audiences for their services. Selecting target markets is a process involving several steps. The first step is to understand who you are currently serving and then to develop an understanding of the market segments you want to serve. Traditional variables used to describe the various market segments include demographics, geographic location, psychographics, and behavioral variables. There also may be segments who might not be the direct beneficiaries of your service but who should be targeted in your marketing mix. Those segments may include elected officials, board members, donors, and community activists, as well as your staff.

Libraries do have substantial research data available to them. There are also professional market research consultants to assist in identifying target audiences. Professional firms are skilled in obtaining and organizing data for descriptive and decision-making purposes. Market research is also available through partnerships with universities, community colleges, and corporations that have a market research department and source substantial primary and secondary data, including both quantitative and qualitative information.

Target markets are evaluated based on size, ease of reach, relevancy of offerings, resources of the library, and potential influence of certain segments over other segments. It is recommended that the market segments of greatest opportunity be selected as they will be the most responsive and the best match for the library. Success in serving these markets will encourage the development of additional segments at a later date.

REFERENCES

Barry, Keith. 2011. "'Mudflap Girl' Was This Guy's Mom." *Wired Autopia,* April 29. www.wired.com/autopia/2011/04/mudflap-girl-was-this-guys-mom.

Jackson, Kent L. 2011. *Library Branding: A Garden Party Conversation.* http://dl.dropbox .com/u/31044078/Library%20Branding-Garden%20Party%20Report.pdf.

Kaden, Robert. 2008. *Guerrilla Marketing Research.* Philadelphia: Kogan Page.

Kotler, Philip, and Nancy R. Lee. 2008. *Social Marketing: Influencing Behaviors for Good.* 3rd ed. Los Angeles: Sage.

Walters, Suzanne. 2004. *Library Marketing That Works.* New York: Neal-Schuman.

Crafting a Desired Positioning Strategy

Achieving a Distinctive Difference

NOW THAT YOU HAVE CONDUCTED THE RESEARCH and developed an understanding of your target markets, select three of those target markets and develop in-depth positioning strategies for each. You can transform your library by carefully targeting a few audiences with communications efforts, rather trying to address many audiences with limited resources. In so doing, you can create a remarkable experience for the customer by meeting and exceeding their expectations—by being remarkable. In his book *The Purple Cow*, Seth Godin (2003) writes how to "transform your business by being remarkable." He builds his case based on his family adventures in France as they were driving through pastures of cows:

> Cows, after you've seen one or two or ten, are boring. A Purple Cow, though—now that would be interesting. A Purple Cow describes something phenomenal, something counterintuitive and exciting and flat out unbelievable. Every day, consumers come face-to-face with a lot of boring stuff—a lot of brown cows—but you can bet they won't forget a Purple Cow. (Godin 2003, 2)

By effectively branding and positioning your services, you will be developing a purple cow (see figure 6.1) and creating something truly notable and worth talking about.

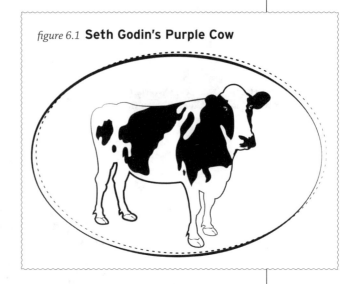

figure 6.1 **Seth Godin's Purple Cow**

You are now ready to develop your positioning strategy. You have identified a target market and developed rich descriptions using demographic, geographic, psychographic, and behavioral variables. You understand that different markets have different needs. And you have accepted the challenge to position your library strategically in the mind of your desired target market.

This chapter will address how to understand needs and wants of target audiences and how to develop a positioning strategy. It will also examine the process to understand the construction of a positioning statement and consider the difference between a *value proposition,* a *positioning statement,* and a *tagline.*

There is a strong relationship between a successful library and an effective goal-setting process. By setting goals, you will engage the staff and encourage employees across the library to focus and successfully achieve the goals together. This chapter also will address this important area.

Market Research at Anythink

MARKET RESEARCH STUDIES in the Rangeview Library District indicated that 70 percent of the population in Adams County is less than fifty years of age. It is a community in which many individuals grew up without establishing a relationship with libraries. There is a substantial Spanish-speaking population as well as Asian and Indian populations, many of whom speak their native language. Many individuals had never had a library card, and those who did had a very limited sense of loyalty to the library.

Knowing that its target market comprised primarily young families with little or no loyalty to traditional libraries, Anythink examined positioning strategies to meet this target audience. Beginning with the products they offered, they realized that their target audience gravitated more toward popular browsing and would be more comfortable having books arranged like a bookstore rather than by the Dewey Decimal system. With this change, Any-

think addressed a perceived barrier in its positioning strategy.

The staff and organizational culture also reflect the positioning strategy of Anythink. By addressing the "I'm busy" perception some customers have of librarians when seeking assistance, staff members called *concierges*—Anythink's version of library assistants—spend nearly all of their work time on the floor greeting customers and assessing their needs.

Previous market research indicated that library fines were barriers for many people, especially for parents of young children. Anythink has eliminated overdue fines to help enhance the user's experience. Customers no longer have any guilt or embarrassment associated with the libraries because of overdue fines. No matter where or how customers encounter Anythink, the library has worked to break down perceived barriers everywhere.

Understanding Positioning as It Relates to the Brand

Your brand is your essence, your identity, personality, and image. The brand reflects your values, premise, promise, and core uniqueness. The positioning process identifies the specific target audience that will be the most responsive to your brand and most likely to develop brand loyalty. It is appropriate to choose positioning strategies "that drive home specific *behaviors,* highlight *benefits,* overcome *barriers* and upstage the *competition* or *reposition* an 'old brand'" (Kotler and Lee 2008, 187–188).

BEHAVIOR-FOCUSED POSITIONING

Many libraries will have a very specific behavior in mind and may benefit from behavior-focused positioning. Columbus Metropolitan Library gives us an example of behavior-focused positioning in its selection of the target audience Power Users, as discussed in the previous chapter. This segment is selected based on how they use the library, accessing collections and materials through the Internet, utilizing databases and electronic searches, and downloading e-books and materials. These are observable and measurable behaviors for which a strategy can be designed and by which the strategy can be evaluated.

BARRIER-FOCUSED POSITIONING

With this type of focus, it is the goal in the library's positioning to overcome or at least minimize perceived barriers. The market research process will help identify those perceived barriers. Some of those barriers could include objective considerations, such as hours of service, location of facilities, overdue fines, or access to materials. Or, the barriers may be subjective and reside largely in the customer's mind as fear, a sense of intimidation, or confusion. A barrier-focused strategy addresses those factors that "get in the way" of specific target markets, making it difficult to access or optimize the benefits available. Queens Library offers a great example of barrier-focused positioning.

BENEFIT-FOCUSED POSITIONING

What's in it for me? Benefit-focused positioning focuses on the benefits the target audience wants and believes it can experience. As Kotler says, "When the

Queens Library

QUEENS IS THE easternmost of the five boroughs of New York City. The largest borough by area and second-largest in population, it has a population of over 2.3 million. Immigrants are 47.6 percent of Queens residents, many of whom have never been involved with a library. Queens residents are transient and often move on after they are established. Therefore, there is a constant churning of potential customers for Queens Library and a challenge to educate and inform new residents of the library and its services.

Marketing staff at the library sought to identify and remove barriers throughout the system. One of those barriers was the requirement that customers provide a Social Security number in order to obtain a library card. Customers were asked instead to provide some proof of residence, eliminating a barrier that was both objective and subjective.

The staff also found that by using their photographs reflecting the diversity of the public they serve, the library was able to convey to its customers that all were welcome. With a transient population, many of whom had never been exposed to a library previously, it was key to present the image of the library as a place for people as diverse as the staff.

best hook seems to be related to the WIFM ("what's in it for me") factor, the perceived benefits become the focus of positioning" (Lee and Kotler 2011, 224).

COMPETITION-FOCUSED POSITIONING

Can you create *competition superiority*? Can you employ tactics that focus on the benefits of using the library? Yes, the library has competition from the Internet, Google, Barnes & Noble, Amazon, and Netflix, as well as many others. Can you focus on the added value that the library provides that goes beyond what the competition has to offer, including highly professional personalized service, accuracy and relevance of information, and learning/living environments that are dynamic and inviting?

FOCUS ON REPOSITIONING

In marketing, repositioning involves changing or strengthening the image in the minds of a target audience. If you are considering repositioning, it is likely because your current brand is inadequate, inaccurate, or out of sync with the current marketplace.

Anythink

"RESEARCH ACROSS THE U.S. told us that libraries were becoming irrelevant. People saw dated municipal facilities with harsh lighting, nasty librarians, and rows and rows of books. Anythink is the first library to be launched as a competitive brand—it's the intersection of Barnes & Noble, Netflix, and a Virgin Megastore. And there's nothing 'shhh' about it," according to John Bellina of Ricochet Ideas.

Wyoming State Library and the Mudflap Girl Campaign

WYOMING IS A state of great distances, low population, and challenging weather patterns. Auto maintenance can be a difficult proposition in Wyoming, and there is a preponderance of auto parts stores within the state that reflects the population's tendency to repair their own vehicles. Thus, libraries partnered with auto parts stores throughout the state as they developed this Mudflap Girl campaign (see figure 6.2). Tied to the campaign was an integrated promotional and database collections strategy that focused on making the Chilton Auto Repair manuals readily available through every library.

The Wyoming State Library developed a campaign to introduce the Chilton Auto database to Wyoming library customers throughout the state. Individual county libraries distributed promotional material for the campaign. The target audience for the campaign was men (a target audience that libraries set out to reach). This campaign is benefit focused, with the goal of raising awareness among the male population of the accessibility of auto repair information through the public library.

Real social change strategies often need to focus efforts on influencing markets upstream from the targeted market—men. Wyoming libraries also needed to focus on politicians, media figures, donors, community activists, corporations, schools, and foundations. Wyoming State Library is keenly aware of the need to develop a strong focus on those upstream segments of the state legislators who are influential in funding libraries. The legislators and county officials live in those Wyoming communities. These legislators also drive long distances and are positively aware of the branding and positioning efforts of the libraries. Wyoming has historically been a boom-and-bust state, and the legislature works hand in glove with the state library to provide a stable funding environment.

figure 6.2
Mudflap Girl

Columbus Metropolitan Library

ACCORDING TO ALISON CIRCLE, director of marketing and strategic planning at Columbus Metropolitan Library, "Libraries need to get real about what's out there in the form of competition. Think of Netflix: 'What You Want before You Know You Want It.' Competition keeps libraries innovative, aware of opportunities, and constantly moving forward."

Determining How to Position Your Brand

Branding is the process of first developing a brand identity as discussed in Section I of this book—one that enables you to speak as narrowly or as broadly as possible to all that you do. Next is the development of a personality to go with the identity, one that converges the human, emotional dimensions to which your audiences can relate. Finally, you want to establish a brand image that captures both identity and personality in a way that sets a new standard and establishes market-relevant expectations amid competing choices—all of which translate to how your audiences come to think, feel, and act in relation to and in the presence of your brand. Determining how to position your brand with your target audiences is directly related to all three steps in the branding process—and especially this last step. Your brand image is determined by how your target audience actually ends up thinking, feeling, and acting relative to your brand and the competitive landscape. The positioning statement provides an operational means of clarifying your *what* and *for whom* in the context of your competition. The positioning statement provides guidance for your decision making regarding your products and services, buildings and facilities, websites, and access points, as well as your promotion and communication.

The Positioning Statement

The positioning statement operates like a miniature business plan. It forces the organization to consider what it must do to be successful. The positioning statement reflects whom you serve, what services you provide, and how you provide those services. It also reflects the competitive advantage that you deliver. It is developed from the mission, vision, and core values of the organization. The positioning statement is an internal document and not necessarily a public one.

POSITIONING DRIVES THE CREATIVE PROCESS

Developing elements of the brand such as name, logo, graphics, unique value proposition, messaging, and communication is driven by the positioning statement. The positioning statement also dictates key marketing strategies of product, price, place, promotion, and people. The development of the positioning statement usually precedes the development of brand elements like logo, graphics, packaging, and communication.

CRAFTING A POSITIONING STATEMENT

Positioning statements are not easy to create. If they are done right, they require a great deal of research and thought. It is very challenging to arrive at that one paragraph, especially as it requires the consensus of so many within the library environment. The first step is to determine your current position within the community.

Ask yourself and ask your customers what value they get from your services? How are they better off after using the library? What makes library services so valuable to customers? Write, listen, and record the value customers derive and the attributes your library services offer to create a draft of your position. Notice how your target markets perceive and express the value of the library—in their own words. Philip Kotler and Nancy Lee, in their book *Social Marketing: Influencing Behaviors for Good*, say that "one way to develop a positioning statement is to fill in the blanks to this phrase, or one similar to it: 'we want (TARGET AUDIENCE) to see (DESIRED

Repositioning the Adams County Public Library

WHEN IT IS important to change the image of a library or organization, we reposition the image of the organization. For the Adams County Public Library in Colorado, it was not difficult to understand the library's position in the marketplace, having been tagged the worst system in the state by the *Denver Post*. The board and leadership of the library recognized that they had a unique opportunity to rebuild the library system from the ground up and create a new brand that was relevant, represented the future, and would help inspire innovation. In the course of creating a new brand, they were determined to do

so in a way that repositioned the library at the same time—as not only new but also very different from the previous system. The concept of repositioning was the key to the new brand. Their choice was, especially for libraries, big and bold, with an element of whimsy. The new brand moniker, Anythink, set up the complete value proposition—"A Revolution of Rangeview Libraries"—and clearly signaled the repositioning of the entire system (see figure 6.3).

figure 6.3 **Revitalize Our Offering from the Anythink Brand Book**

DON'T FIND US, WE'LL FIND YOU

You can spot Anythink guides, concierges and wranglers by their bright orange lanyard and name tag. We didn't pick orange because it's flattering, we picked it because you can see it from 30 feet. Which is exactly what we want. No matter what their job title the first priority of any Anythinker on the floor is to help you find inspiration and support it with information.

ANYTHINK IS MORE THAN BOOKS

Books are great. And we work very hard to make sure all types of them are available to you at all times. But we also put a lot of energy and funding into our new Anythink library services. Like Mac labs, Wii gaming consoles, fireplaces and more music and movies than we've ever had before.

NO FINES EITHER

Fines aren't fun. Neither is enforcing them. Besides, what's the point of being a library if you have to tell seventh graders they can't check out a book because they owe a few cents. Now that doesn't mean an Anythink library is a free-for-all. It just took some new thinking to get around an age-old library problem.

AROUND HERE, SHHH IS A FOUR-LETTER WORD

An Anythink library is designed for people of all ages and mindsets. If you want quiet space, you'll find all kinds of great hideaways. Like the company of others? Park yourself in one of the big comfy chairs around the fireplace. Want to crush someone in a game of Wii tennis, take in a puppet show, or sit in for story hour? We've got places for all that, too. The point is that an Anythink library is designed to be enjoyed. We guarantee there's a perfect space for everyone.

BEHAVIOR) as (DESCRIPTIVE PHRASES) and as more important and beneficial than (COMPETITION)'" (Kotler and Lee 2008, 187). Note, of course, that this is a very brief version, and that as you consider your positioning statement you will likely want to address multiple audiences, a range of desired behaviors and perceptions, and a variety of benefits that compete with all of the alternatives available.

Value Propositions

A *value proposition* is a short statement that tells your customers why they should use your library. Unlike the internal positioning statement, the unique value proposition is a public declaration and, as previously discussed, a key element of your brand. As you have seen, the Anythink brand is one that ties the identity element "Anythink" to an extended value proposition, "A Revolution of Rangeview Libraries," implying a sudden, radical, and complete change in what you might have expected in a library. It focuses on and implies a benefit or host of benefits the might be realized and in a manner that is memorable and evocative. When possible, the value proposition should address unmet needs as well as the aspirations of customers. Unlike positioning statements that can be developed within the organization, value propositions are carefully conceived, typically requiring the involvement of communications experts knowledgeable about branding and marketing strategy.

VALUE PROPOSITIONS AND TAGLINES

The value proposition, as reflected in the examples from Anythink libraries and Queens Library, grows out of your brand and expresses your true uniqueness in a sentence or two. The tagline is a word or short phrase, based on your value propo-

Developing Strategic Positioning at Queens Library

THE MARKETING TEAM at Queens Library developed a strategic positioning statement describing exactly what the library is and should be in the eyes of its constituents—the public and its supporters. It is a statement in keeping with its identity as a library while being communicative of a personality and an assertive image. It differs from the library's mission statement and embraces elements of vision and values. It is designed for all audiences, internal and external, as it accommodates the four strategic directions of the library. The branding and strategic positioning effort also differentiates Queens Library from the other New York City libraries—key to addressing the diverse needs of Queens and to generating public support through advocacy.

Beginning with early site visits, observations, and conversation, marketing staff formulated the positioning statement by using the Socratic method of guided questioning. In the process, they unearthed the essence of the library—its past, present, and future and living legacy. Feedback came in many forms, but soon the content began to converge into common themes and insights. People tended not to talk about the library and libraries as just repositories of books, but rather as communities, as gathering places where people, information, and ideas come together. Libraries are places where people come for help, to solve problems, and to improve their lives. Libraries are not so much physical spaces or "branches" but rather a resource (of people) dedicated to helping others make their lives better. The idea of "Enrich your life" as a theme or tagline emerged naturally and organically from these conversations.

sition, that prompts your customers to consider why they should use your library. Like value propositions, taglines are more artfully crafted, typically requiring the involvement of communications experts. In Chapter 7 you will learn more about value propositions and taglines and how to develop them.

WHERE TO BEGIN

Begin with the development of your brand. This process will identify your mission, vision, and core values and determine your unique brand essence—your value proposition. Branding defines the enterprise; it defines the organization and identifies for whom it matters and what the organization values. Positioning defines how you want the library to be perceived and by whom. Therefore, you need to know the brand before you can begin to develop a positioning statement. If you have the brand correctly defined and position the organization correctly, you will be able to successfully develop your promotional strategies in a manner that accurately expresses the value you offer to the markets you seek to serve, via value propositions, taglines, and key messages.

There are many examples of taglines or slogans and the value propositions behind them, many of which are known to you. As you review each tagline try to interpret the value proposition behind the tagline that provides the rationale for the tagline and is prompted by the tagline. Keep in mind that value propositions tend to emphasize one of three brand advantages: uniqueness, price, or service. While every good brand, or every good library for that matter, seeks to address all of these advantages, effective positioning and efficient promotion require that you give primary emphasis to one advantage to effectively differentiate your brand. Achieving relative market advantage in one area allows you to compete more effectively in

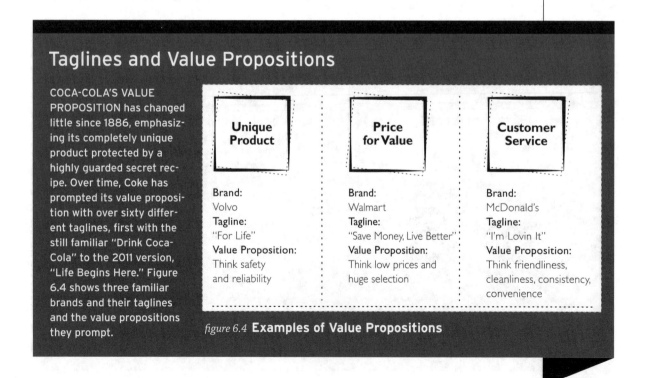

Taglines and Value Propositions

COCA-COLA'S VALUE PROPOSITION has changed little since 1886, emphasizing its completely unique product protected by a highly guarded secret recipe. Over time, Coke has prompted its value proposition with over sixty different taglines, first with the still familiar "Drink Coca-Cola" to the 2011 version, "Life Begins Here." Figure 6.4 shows three familiar brands and their taglines and the value propositions they prompt.

Unique Product	Price for Value	Customer Service
Brand: Volvo	**Brand:** Walmart	**Brand:** McDonald's
Tagline: "For Life"	**Tagline:** "Save Money, Live Better"	**Tagline:** "I'm Lovin It"
Value Proposition: Think safety and reliability	**Value Proposition:** Think low prices and huge selection	**Value Proposition:** Think friendliness, cleanliness, consistency, convenience

figure 6.4 **Examples of Value Propositions**

others without having to invest so heavily in those areas. For example, Volvo positions itself primarily on the basis of uniqueness—a market leader in delivering an exceptionally safe vehicle, as captured in the tagline "For Life." Thus, Volvo does not have to compete as aggressively on price, or perhaps even on service beyond the aspect of safety, as other car companies might.

RELATIONSHIP OF THE POSITIONING STATEMENT AND THE UNIQUE VALUE PROPOSITION

Both are components of the branding process, one to guide internal strategy and the other to enhance the communications power and reach of the brand externally. A tagline is an artfully crafted word or phrase that derives from the value proposition and serves to prompt—by evocation or provocation—the value the market can expect to realize. To review, the platform for developing the positioning statement is the branding process and the brand itself. The positioning statement derives from the mission, vision, and core values of the organization and a clear understanding of the market or markets to be served. It becomes an internal statement to guide the brand strategy and promotional messages, and not necessarily a statement the public will ever see or have reason to see except for purposes of public transparency. The

The Apple iPhone

AS APPLE WAS considering launching the iPhone, it developed the following positioning strategy objectives ("iPhone Marketing Plan" 2007):

> Objective 1—To capture 10 percent market share in the U.S. smartphone market over a course of two years.
> Objective 2—To extend Apple's brand name and build an image of innovations, quality and value.
> Objective 3—To satisfy the needs and wants of smartphone customers and guarantee satisfaction through value delivery.
> Objective 4—To manage a successful, focused launch without budgetary wastages.

Apple developed a complete marketing plan for the iPhone, identifying the target audiences, completing a SWOT analysis, and conducting necessary research that included a competitive analysis. It established goals and objectives, developed marketing mix strategies including product price, and created distribution plans as well as a communication and implementation plan.

The positioning segmentation strategy was to target professionals and corporate users who needed to record information on the go and who needed to receive input and access critical data on the go. The corporate and professional target markets also included entrepreneurs (who needed to organize contracts and schedule details) and medical users (who needed to exchange medical records). Apple also targeted students who needed to perform many functions and didn't want to carry multiple gadgets.

In reviewing the SWOT analysis, Apple listed innovation, compatibility, ease of use, and brand awareness among its strengths. Opportunities included increasing demand and expansion to new target audiences and partnerships, among others.

The primary business target audience included large cell phone service providers AT&T, Verizon, Sprint, and Cellular One. Apple also targeted large software firms where information was critical to the end user. A secondary business target was small to midsize corporations that wanted to help managers and employees stay in communication. To experience the complete marketing plans for the iPhone, visit www.iphoners.com and search "iPhone marketing plan."

positioning statement and value proposition are integral to the brand platform and drive the creative process when developing all forms of brand expression from logos to key messages, from advertising to web design to direct marketing—essentially all considerations related to product, price, place, people, and promotional strategies.

The positioning statement is generally a sentence or two, or perhaps a series of bullet points at most. You use the positioning statement to develop your unique

Anythink Strategic Goals

RANGEVIEW LIBRARY DISTRICT (RLD) began with the establishment of communications goals before they began their branding process. Those goals were as follows:

- Rebrand the library system.
- Increase the number of library cardholders by 30 percent.
- Increase circulation by 100 percent.
- Enhance the district's online presence and increase web usage by 50 percent.
- Turn the negative library image into a positive.
- Receive national press coverage. Receiving national press coverage was a bold, dramatic initiative, demonstrating the belief that the team would accomplish and exceed their expectations.

RLD measured Anythink's success by monitoring general awareness, library card registrations, online and in-person visits, positive reception of the new brand, and awards recognition. To achieve these goals, the district needed a new logo, brand guidelines, and website that reflected the transforming library and projected this new library concept. The brand guidelines would help the district create cohesive branding at all touch points, from library cards and signage to the design of the libraries' interiors. With these tools in hand, RLD could move forward with an internal as well as external rollout of the new brand, complemented by an aggressive advertising campaign orchestrated by the creative consultants at Ricochet Ideas. The initial budget for the project was $135,000.

What does Anythink mean? *Anythink is a new style of library—a place of unlimited imagination, where play inspires creativity and lifelong learning. It is a place where anything and everything is possible. Anythink is anything you can invent or imagine.* "We think it is a perfect name for a library, because no matter what you might want or need to know, you can find it at Anythink. Anything you can think of, the library can connect you with that idea or information," says Director Pam Sandlian-Smith.

Anythink is a *stretch brand.* It is committed to something big and different. There is a feeling of innovation, of becoming a resource for library innovation as well as a local resource for business innovation. Anythink broadcasts an optimistic attitude that anything is possible.

STRATEGIC INITIATIVES

RLD has identified six strategic initiatives with related goals that will enable it to achieve its strategic outcome for improving the quality of life in Adams County.

Initiative I: Deliver Superb Customer Service, Products and Programs

Our libraries are recreation centers for the mind and spirit, and our high level of customer service together with a top-of-the-line array of library products will become our hallmark.

> *Goal 1:* Design libraries that are user-friendly and easy to navigate. Build in convenience services to expedite efficiencies.
> *Goal 2:* Deliver programs and products that anticipate customer needs.
> *Goal 3:* Create innovative ways for customers to "open doors" to intellectual adventures (listen to music, video, create media, learn life skills, read for skills as well as pleasure, connect with other people).
> *Goal 4:* Create a new paradigm for library fines.

Initiative II: Build Beautiful and Inspiring Environments

> *Goal 1:* All of our new planned facilities are inspiring, Colorado-influenced environments and are completed and open to the public.
> *Goal 2:* Our legacy facility renovations are accomplished.
> *Goal 3:* All of our environments are unique "experience" places that celebrate the positive power of words, images, sounds and emotions and become popular cultural destinations.
> *Goal 4:* All of our environments and operations utilize responsible and sustainable environmental practices.
> *Goal 5:* All facilities proudly and professionally display the RLD look and brand, are well maintained and sparkling clean.

value proposition, usually in the form of a short phrase or single sentence. Positioning statements and unique value propositions are difficult to develop. Creative expression of the value proposition, sometimes referred to as slogans, taglines, or key messages, is best accomplished by employing creative talent well-versed in the artful crafts of copywriting and graphic design—and with a solid understanding of branding and positioning.

Goal 6: Leadership evaluates impacts of new facilities in the community with regard to future growth.

Initiative III: Deliver Convenience and Innovation through Technology

Goal 1: Build a technological infrastructure that supports customer and staff needs.

Goal 2: Utilize technology to deliver innovative library services and products which assist people in creative expression and connections.

Goal 3: Integrate technologies to manage efficient use of resources and to expedite speedy delivery of services and products. Create new, easy and entertaining ways of accessing information online.

Initiative IV: Create Meaningful Communications

Goal 1: Develop and deploy consistent internal and external communication plan which conveys the RLD experience. Develop support functions to effectively implement these communications.

Goal 2: Create brand identity and implement this consistently in our environments through the RLD cohesive graphics system, including displays, signs, colors, staff mode of dress, electronic designs and furnishings.

Goal 3: The new RLD vision will be delivered holistically through brand messaging, guerrilla marketing, public relations, media relations, partnership development, staff and word-of-mouth by everyone who walks through our doors.

Initiative V: Provide Highly Effective Organizational Development

Goal 1: Work with the library Board of Trustees to create a culture of innovation, creativity and optimism.

Goal 2: Create challenging, productive work that is rewarding and inspiring.

Goal 3: Create, implement and live new service standards and job expectations.

Goal 4: Create a continuous learning environment that supports staff intellectual growth and fosters highly effective interpersonal skills.

Goal 5: Create job perks and benefits that support our values and our transformational culture.

Initiative VI: Create Financial Sustainability for the Future of RLD

Goal 1: Allocate and expend resources through the annual budget to accomplish key goals and strategies of RLD. Maintain fiscal discipline that creates a sustainable financial future.

Goal 2: Develop alternative streams of funding including grant and foundation support.

Goal 3: Complete our capital construction projects within budget.

Goal 4: Maintain the highest financial integrity of the institution by consistently providing our community with an excellent value for their financial support.

STRATEGIC OUTCOME

Enhance the quality of life in Adams County by providing opportunities for transformational experiences that spark learning, adventure and inspiration for the mind and soul.

SUCCESS INDICATORS

We intend to evaluate our successes in achieving our strategic outcome in these ways:

- Adams County ranking by citizens of their library as a key asset in the community
- Public libraries ranking in the top one-third in Colorado
- Favorable regional and national press coverage
- National library and civic awards finalists
- Foundation support
- High industry ranking as a great place to work

Developing Goals and Objectives for Target Audiences

You have determined the three primary target audiences. You have completed research to understand the needs and wants of your target audiences. You have discussed positioning strategies and developed a positioning statement. You have discussed and identified how the library can uniquely meet customers' needs and wants. You have discussed how the library has an advantage over its competition or how the library can cooperate with perceived competition to provide an advantage to the customer. Setting goals and objectives for your organization is the next challenge.

There is a strong relationship between a successful library and an effective goal-setting process. By setting goals, you will engage the staff and encourage employees across the library to focus and successfully achieve the goals together. Goals and objectives also allow for the proper allocation of resources. The staff look at the library's most important goals and objectives and make important decisions regarding priorities. Goals and objectives provide the groundwork for linking a reward system with individual and team performance.

Setting goals without objectives and an action plan is not effective. Libraries have an endless stream of challenges; goals and objectives act as a rudder to steer through the challenges. Goals and objectives are crucial, especially in times of crisis.

It's a good idea to involve staff in the goal-setting process in such a way that they are committed and can help keep the library accountable. You might brainstorm around the following:

- Your goal
- The strategy to achieve your goal
- How to measure your success by virtue of specific objectives
- Your objectives should be measurable, realistic, and achievable, as well as stamped with a date for achieving your targets. It's often necessary to revise goals and objectives as you learn more about your target audience.

Summary

Why is positioning so important to libraries? Libraries that take the time to develop their brand and their brand positioning strategy won't find that their challenges disappear. They do develop a better understanding of who they are, of their strengths and their purpose. They become stronger, more focused, and united and have a clarity of purpose to move forward to meet the challenges of the future.

According to the OCLC study *From Awareness to Funding*, "The proposed solution is to create and promote a brand—not a library product brand focused on marketing library consumption (usage) but a library support brand. The brand must do more than position the library as relevant—it must activate citizen participation and drive positive funding behavior."

Philip Kotler and Nancy Lee in their book *Social Marketing* define positioning:

> Positioning is the art of designing the organization's offering in such a way that it lands on and occupies a distinctive place in the mind of the target market—where you want it to be. . . . The research on your target audience's barriers, benefits, and competitors will provide the inspiration you need. It will also help build consensus among your colleagues . . . ensuring fewer surprises and disappointments as you move forward to developing your strategies. Take time and care to develop this positioning statement as you will refer to it frequently when developing each of the 4 Ps. (Kotler and Lee 2008, 197)

Seth Godin reminds us that there is a problem with the cow:

> If being a Purple Cow is such an easy, effective way to break through the clutter, why doesn't everyone do it? Why is it so hard to be Purple? *The Cow is so rare because people are afraid.* . . . Once you have managed to create something truly remarkable, the challenge is to do two things simultaneously:
>
> - Milk the Cow for everything its worth. Figure out how to extend it and profit from it for as long as possible.
> - Create an environment where you are likely to invent a new Purple Cow in time to replace the first one when its benefits inevitably trail off. (Godin 2003, 45)

Jim Collins in his book *Good to Great* uses a parable of hedgehogs and foxes to talk about organizations:

> Foxes pursue many ends at the same time and see the world in all its complexity. They are "scattered or diffused, moving on many levels." Hedgehogs, on the other hand, simplify a complex world into a single organizing idea, a basic principle or concept that unifies and guides everything. It doesn't matter how complex the world, a hedgehog reduces all challenges and dilemmas to simple hedgehog ideas. For a hedgehog, anything that does not somehow relate to the hedgehog idea holds no relevance. . . . What does all this talk of hedgehogs and foxes have to do with good to great? Everything. Those who built the good-to-great companies were hedgehogs. They used their hedgehog nature to drive toward what we came to call a Hedgehog Concept for their companies. (Collins 2001, 92)

Dare to become a great library by developing your brand, your positioning strategy, and your positioning statement.

REFERENCES

Collins, Jim. 2001. *Good to Great: Why Some Companies Make the Leap . . . and Others Don't.* New York: HarperBusiness.

Godin, Seth. 2003. *The Purple Cow.* New York: Penguin.

"iPhone Marketing Plan." 2007. Apple iPhone Forums, May 22. www.iphoners.com.

Kotler, Philip, and Nancy R. Lee. 2008. *Social Marketing: Influencing Behaviors for Good.* 3rd ed. Los Angeles: Sage.

Lee, Nancy R., and Philip Kotler. 2011. *Social Marketing: Influencing Behaviors for Good.* 4th ed. Los Angeles: Sage.

SECTION III

PROMOTION

Positioning and Marketing Strategies

Introduction to Positioning and the Marketing Mix

YOUR POSITIONING STRATEGY DRIVES DECISIONS regarding products and services, collection development, design of facilities, partnerships, customer service policies, distribution of materials, budget allocations and priorities, design of the website, and promotional materials, as well as the strategic plan. You have identified your target markets and have developed a rich description using demographic, geographic, psychographic, and behavioral variables. You have also developed a positioning statement that will guide decision making. Your branded identity, image, and personality are clear and understood by staff and customers alike. It is now time to express your brand most effectively with your target audiences.

The *marketing mix* can be viewed as a toolbox because it contains all of the strategies and tactics that can be developed to meet your marketing goals. The strategies are usually considered to be product, place, price, or promotion—the four Ps; however, there can be additional strategies. One additional strategy, the fifth "P," one the authors consider especially important in the library setting, is the *people* strategy. In libraries, it is people who drive and in many cases deliver customer service and perceived value. Within each strategy are a variety of marketing tactics that can be employed. Each of the strategies and related tactics must be given careful thought. The marketing strategies of product, place, price, promotion, and people are expressions of your brand and must be treated as such. The strategies are to be integrated and complementary, because together they create a successful, visible expression of your brand. This chapter will discuss product, place, price, and people strategies. Promotion strategies are addressed in Chapter 8. The sidebar example of Columbus Metropolitan Library illustrates how selecting a specific target audience influences the strategies and tactics selected.

What Is the Marketing Mix?

The marketing mix is probably the most famous of marketing terms, and the four Ps are widely recognized when discussing marketing principles. As discussed previously, the four Ps are the basic elements within a marketing plan and include product, place, price, and promotion. To this mix is added a fifth "P" to assert the impor-

Columbus Metropolitan Library and the Young Minds Target Audience

AN EXAMPLE OF target audience and positioning strategy driving the product mix is evident with Columbus Metropolitan Library (CML) and one of its target audiences, Young Minds. In 2006, Young Minds became the number one strategy to come out of the CML strategic planning and positioning process. CML developed a positioning strategy targeted to its Young Minds audience and committed resources and talent to address this target market. Using the business world framework of a product line, the library packaged Young Minds products into a cohesive whole that followed children from infancy through teen years. The simplicity of this story makes it easy to share with media, funders, legislators, and the public. The Young Minds product line includes Ready to Read, Summer Reading Club, Homework Help Centers, Storytimes, Teen Centers, Bookmobiles, and the VolunTeens program.

Columbus Metropolitan Library adapted the curriculum of the Public Library Association's Every Child Ready to Read and took it even further. The library set a goal of kindergarten readiness of 90 percent or greater. The library committed resources to the program and supplemented it with staff training in the six prereading skills that make up the Ready to Read program. The library used every opportunity to promote Ready to Read among parents and caregivers, and expanded the pro-

gram beyond the walls of the library and into daycare centers.

Columbus Metropolitan Library surveyed the Central Ohio landscape and discerned and discovered that there was a lack of programs and services designed to provide parents and caregivers with critical school readiness information. In response, the library developed its first pilot project in the Greater Parsons/Weinland Park area of Columbus and secured funding for the first Ready to Read Corps (which included two Ready to Read specialists and a van) from the United Way, Siemer Family Foundation, and Columbus Metropolitan Library Foundation. JPMorgan Chase provided funding for an additional van as well as materials for families. In 2010, the library expanded the program to six total teams, thanks to a generous gift of $500,000 from the Nationwide Insurance Foundation.

Columbus Metropolitan Library expresses its transformational capacity through programs like the Ready to Read Corps and Homework Help Centers (see figure 7.1). These centers are bright and welcoming spaces and provide students with everything they need to complete their homework, including staff and volunteers to provide help as well as essential computers, printers, on-site school supplies, and a collection of resources. In 2011, 52,000 students received help through the Homework Help Centers.

figure 7.1 **Columbus Metropolitan Library Homework Help Centers**

tance of the significant role of people. There is flexibility within this definition of the marketing mix; however, these are the basic, tactical, and integrated components of a marketing plan. It is important that every step of the development of your marketing mix reflects and reinforces your desired brand identity, personality, and image. This framework, despite its simplicity, has proven to be strong and effective.

MARKETING MIX, BRANDING, AND POSITIONING

Marketing mix decisions are heavily influenced by the library's brand and positioning. And conversely, the library brand and positioning are expressed through a balanced mix of product, place, price, promotion, and people strategies.

figure 7.2 **The Marketing Mix**

SELECTING THE RIGHT MARKETING MIX FOR YOUR LIBRARY

The five Ps are at the heart of ensuring a value exchange with the marketplace. Marketing is a complex collection of activities, and the marketing mix refers to exactly that, a mixture of strategies. Studying the five Ps allows you to develop your own mix that responds to your own situation and to needs and wants of your target market.

In the sidebar example of Columbus Metropolitan Library and its Young Minds strategy, you can see the CML product and service strategies through the Ready to Read programs and the Homework Help Centers. The *place* strategies are evident through facilities within libraries as well as bookmobiles, vans, and staff. The *pricing* strategy offered an opportunity to allow partners to join in the cobranding experience of mutual benefit and exacted an exchange for all involved. *Promotion* strategies were expanded through additional partnerships outside the typical library channels.

The marketing mix strategies are related and complementary to each other (see figure 7.2). Consideration must be given to each strategy and its effect on other strategies as well as the overall program. The creativity in which you embrace the strategies makes all of the difference. And the fifth "P," people, is the glue that ultimately holds all of your strategies together.

Product/Service—The First "P"

A product is anything that can be offered to a market to satisfy a want or need. It isn't just a tangible offering like soap, tires or hamburgers. It can be one of several types: a physical good, a service, an experience, an event, a person, a place, a property, an organization, information, or an idea. (Kotler and Lee 2008, 205)

The term *product* refers to the tangible, physical products as well as the services of the library. As you are developing products/services for the library, it's important to realize that the initial stages of product or service development require the most deliberation and effort. You must build credibility and trust. Your products and services reflect the quality and consistency of your brand. Consider ways to make your product unique, one that distinguishes your product/service from others available to the target market.

In marketing, a product or service is more than its objective or experiential and observable features. In developing the product or service, it's recommended that you consider developing the *core product, actual product, augmented product,* and *potential product* (see figure 7.3).

THE CORE PRODUCT

The *core product* comprises the benefits that your target market wants and expects from your product or service. The word *benefits* is key! It's essential to know that you are always striving to provide benefits that your target audience desires. People buy benefits! What problems will your product solve for the customer? What wants and needs will it satisfy? The great Harvard marketing professor Theodore Levitt knew that people buy products in order to solve a problem. He was known to have told his students, "People don't want to buy a quarter-inch drill. They want a quarter-inch hole!" (Levitt 1983, 76).

figure 7.3 **Core Product, Actual Product, Augmented Product, Potential Product**

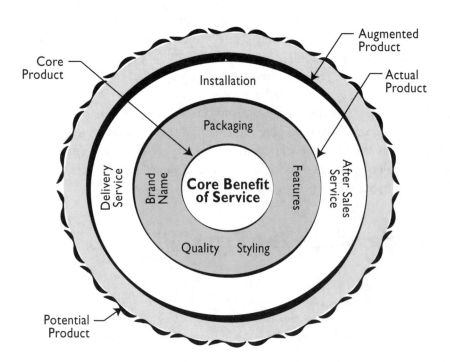

THE ACTUAL PRODUCT

The *actual product* includes the features, styling, quality, and packaging of the product or service. Customers have expectations that are set or established by the marketing of the product or service and those expectations are continually being reset, generally upward, as a result of increased competition and ongoing innovation.

THE AUGMENTED PRODUCT

The *augmented product* might include an exceptional customer experience, augmented by an unexpected level of service, delivery, check, renewal, and online access—all going beyond the basics of making information available. It's important to give customers what they expect and continually work to go beyond their expectations—always innovating, always augmenting. The process of providing augmentations educates the customer as to what can be reasonable to expect and look forward to. The augmented product surrounds the generic product with attributes that are designed to attract and hold customers. Customer expectations rise when customers know what is possible. Customer engagement is strengthened by developing augmented products, and with greater engagement come habit formation and dependence on a product.

THE POTENTIAL PRODUCT

According to Theodore Levitt, there is also the *potential product,* which is perhaps the most powerful dimension of product strategy and the most difficult to develop and deliver. This potential product consists of everything potentially feasible to attract and hold customers, including the perception of future value associated with

The Apple iPad

THE LEGACY OF Steve Jobs and Apple lies in the creation of the *potential product.* Jobs wasn't known for doing focus groups to understand what people wanted. Instead, he focused on the quality of the product to position Apple atop the competition. He did research on what was out there and sought to deliver what was not—always pushing beyond mere augmentation by creating a new vision for every product.

When developing a product, there are three areas of concern—quality, cost, and customer service. For Jobs, quality became the driver, and pricing and customer service were secondary. The quality of the product is evident in the iPad introduced by Apple in early 2011, perhaps the best commercial example of a potential product. Initially criticized by many as a device without a clear purpose,

the customers quickly defined the iPad by its value to them. "The name iPad is . . . more than a product—it's a statement, an idea, and potentially a prime mover in the world of consumer electronics . . . if Apple delivers on its promises. And those are some big promises; the company has been tossing around words like 'magical' and 'revolutionary' to describe [it] . . ." (Topolsky 2010, 1).

"The buyer of an iPad is one of two people; the first is someone who sees not just the present, but the potential of a product like the iPad. And believes in and is excited about that potential. . . . The second is an individual who simply doesn't need to get that much work done, and would prefer their computing experience to be easier, faster, and simpler . . ." (Topolsky 2010, 13).

a product. "Whereas the 'augmented product' means everything that has been or is being done, the 'potential product' refers to what may remain to be done, that is, what is possible" (Levitt 1983, 84). Homebuyers who choose a home based on how it meets the needs of their family today, but who decide to stretch their budget a bit in anticipation of future needs, are imagining the potential value of the home as a product. Likewise, parents of the young child who commit to investing time in an early reading program are doing so in part because they are imagining the future or potential value of investment today that will have payoffs for their child well into the future. It is the potential value of the product that offers the greatest opportunity to develop loyalty on the part of customers. The essence of the library brand is all about "potential" and aligns well with the notion of the transformative as discussed in the OCLC publications.

It's important to note here that the concept of positioning relies on the underlying principle of differentiation. As the product definition migrates from core product to augmented product and ultimately to potential product, greater product differentiation occurs. In other words, the product or service becomes more unique and is differentiated from others.

THE PRODUCT LIFE CYCLE

All products and services go through a four-stage *life cycle*. To the extent that organizations and institutions choose to be exclusively identified by their product strategies, they are destined to be defined by their product life cycles. Marketing-oriented businesses constantly monitor the life cycle of their products and services.

Wyoming State Library and the Chilton Auto Manual Database

THE WYOMING STATE Library conducted survey research of library cardholders who had not used their cards in the past two years. The surprising element was that women made up 81 percent of the respondents. Their conclusion was that men do not find libraries as relevant to their lives as women. Therefore, their target audience for the campaign was men.

The product selected to meet the needs of men was the Chilton Auto Repair database. In this state of long distances and few automobile repair shops, the Chilton Auto Repair database was an important asset. The core product of this database is defined by the benefits it provides—a useful, reliable reference for auto repair. The actual product was the online database that contained up-to-date information regarding the repair and maintenance of a vast variety of automobiles. The augmented product included the multimedia video presentations,

the photographs and diagrams, and the customer service that accompany the database, thus making the product readily accessible, convenient, and easy to understand and use. The potential product was enhanced through the partnerships of libraries with automobile parts stores throughout the state, providing information about the availability of this product for no charge to library patrons. Libraries also engaged with parts stores and repair shops in communities and with target audiences through an overt but more subtle word-of-mouth promotion.

The Chilton Auto Repair database service strategy was an important part of the Wyoming libraries positioning strategy to reach their targeted audience of men ages 18 and older. The branding strategy of the Wyoming libraries is to bring the world to Wyoming, and they have strengthened their brand strategy by implementing this service.

figure 7.4 **Product Life Cycle Curve**

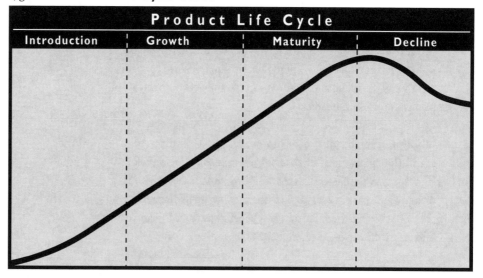

1. *Introductory stage* is when a product first appears in the marketplace. The product requires a great deal of investment in its development and loses money at this stage.

2. *Growth stage* is when the product or service begins to grow and is successful. Competitors can even make improvements.

3. *Maturity stage* is when the product or service is most highly utilized. In the profit world, it is the most profitable stage of a product.

4. *Decline stage* is indicated when the market shrinks and profitability falls.

Some products like Ivory Soap and Arm and Hammer Baking Soda have been at the mature point in their product life cycle for years. Whenever sales begin to slip, a new advertising program appears to remind the customers of the benefits of these products, often introducing something entirely new.

Libraries need a mix of new and growing products along with the old and stable ones. Yesterday it was printed books; today it may be e-books, databases, videos, and electronic services. The products continue to expand. The cyclical manner in which products and services go through is demonstrated in figure 7.4.

Libraries as a whole have enjoyed long product life cycles. However, libraries are in the mature stage of their product life cycle and are in danger of slipping into the decline stage. Thus, libraries must proactively evaluate their product strategies, while concurrently taking care to address the other Ps in a balanced manner. Imagine the product life cycle within the high technology industry in which a life cycle of eighteen months is considered long (Walters 2004, 77).

Place Strategies

According to *Library Journal:*

> Our winning libraries are regarded as community living rooms for self-learning, experiencing culture, connecting, communicating, and

tapping into information and entertainment. . . . after they are built they garner widespread community support, see rapid growth in use and often transform the neighborhood or community. Perhaps as a counterpoint to the increasingly virtual experience of life, these library centers offer what we all yearn for most—to share a common yet uplifting space in pursuit of core needs.

Libraries are the new economic engines. Community leaders understand that placement of a library spurs economic development, revitalizes decaying areas of town and stimulates neighborhood growth. Few understand that the design of the library itself has the potential to lift the spirits of the people. That is what makes the difference between good and iconic libraries. (Schaper 2011)

IKEA: Using Space as a Strategic Weapon

"PLACES AND SPATIAL issues are central to the life of every company. A relocation, the opening of a new branch office, factory or store, maybe in a foreign country, and the start of a relationship to a supplier from a certain region: all this signs often important moments in a company's life that can signify key turning points in its history. Such historical moments are however just the top of an iceberg: every company interplays *constantly* with various places, even without being fully conscious of this in every moment. Places affect companies' lives, but companies, alone or in interaction with others, also affect places. . . . IKEA is no exception to this rule. But what makes IKEA peculiar is the *many ways* in which it relates to space and places" (Baraldi 2003).

IKEA is an international furniture distributor, purchasing products from over fifty countries and selling them in over thirty countries in four continents. The company connects more than 2,000 suppliers with 180 retail stores and requires at least 20,000 transport corridors. All of the space-related aspects of the corporation matter for IKEA's costs and revenues. IKEA uses spaces as "strategic weapons" to accomplish certain goals.

IKEA purchases materials from low-wage countries. IKEA products are very transport-sensitive; its furniture products are transported in flat packs that allow easier and more economical transportation. Place is considered when obtaining suppliers worldwide, as IKEA is aware of the potential negative effect deriving from obtaining raw materials. The corporation refuses wood from rainforests and areas that are endangered or overexploited. Its products are distributed through retail facilities/warehouses in key locations throughout thirty countries. Most retail facilities are grouped within a radius of 600 kilometers from a hub to contain transport costs and ensure deliveries. These retail outlets are typically painted blue and yellow and are visible from a highway with heavy traffic. IKEA traditionally selects locations on the outskirts of major cities, and these locations quickly become filled with infrastructures and so much human activity and traffic that other retailers choose to locate there, too. The facilities can cover large surfaces; IKEA has conceived and shaped these retail outlets to have customers flow through the ideal path. This path funnels consumers through a showroomlike environment to the warehouse, a cafeteria, and the checkout lines. All IKEA retail stores reproduce the basic, tested and developed architectural, aesthetic, and functional features.

The idea of place is not limited to physical places and spaces. It can also be networks, business relationships, partnerships, and IT relationships. All of these are important and strategic for IKEA. The IT systems allow IKEA to communicate across large distances. These systems are standardized from one country to another, allowing the company to link operations easily. The company is engaged in strategically using places but also in creating and shaping them. Place strategies are the primary strategy for the organization (Baraldi 2003).

Columbus Metropolitan Library— Three External Target Audiences

IN 2011, COLUMBUS Metropolitan Library developed a new strategic plan and identified three external target audiences, including My Library, Young Minds, and Life Skills (see figure 4.7). With a combined focus on physical and virtual spaces/environments, the library is concentrating on ensuring the ultimate experience for all audiences.

Columbus Metropolitan Library is constructing a *technology branch* to focus on computers that will be 100 percent self-service, offering computer classes and technology training. The library has updated its website and developed an ongoing communication with 25,000 people via Facebook. Columbus Metropolitan Library will focus on place strategies in terms of buildings and facilities, electronic and self-service delivery systems, and state-of-the-art communication through its website and social media.

Place strategies refer, of course, to physical locations as well as online locations. Library buildings represent place strategies. New library buildings are inspiring, both as functional and inspirational centerpieces of the community. Those buildings establish themselves as the "flagship, hub, oasis, crossroads, anchor, intersection, civic presence, fabric, destination, living room and 'important campus place' to the constituents of their communities and institutions while meeting the needs and sensibilities of the 21st century library service" (Schaper 2011). Libraries as a *place* represent the centerpiece of a community, a singular and standout source for information about everything and for everyone in the community; if effect, they represent the heart and soul of the community.

DISTRIBUTION CHANNELS AS PLACE STRATEGIES

It is easy to see the impact of the physical buildings and spaces that are called libraries; however, place also refers to distribution systems. "Place is where and when the target market will perform the desired behavior, acquire any tangible objects and receive any associated services" (Kotler and Lee 2008, 247). As a distribution channel, the place strategies for a library may include:

- Physical locations including bookmobiles and kiosks
- Hours of operation
- Mail access
- Delivery systems, including interlibrary and intralibrary loans
- Distribution systems
- Online access and services, including websites, database access, and e-books
- Automated systems, including checkout services and reserve services
- Physical placement and organization of materials, departments, and furniture within the library
- Furniture, displays, meeting rooms, amenities for meeting rooms, community rooms, and bookshelves
- Telephone communication
- Circulation technology and desks
- Partnerships
- External signage and advertising
- Placement of billboards
- Library presence with facilities and websites of partners in the community, including schools, businesses, government, and nonprofits

OBJECTIVES FOR PLACE STRATEGIES

The objective with place marketing is to develop strategies that will make it as convenient, pleasant, and appealing as possible for the target market to have access to the desired product or service. As with commercial enterprises, there are certain key concepts that libraries need to keep in mind as they examine their place strategies:

- Make your location convenient and as close as possible to your target audience. Bookmobiles, Internet access, delivery systems, and partnership tactics strive to bring convenience to library use and to overcome target market barriers to access.
- The hours of operation are extremely important for customers to be able to access library services. The hours should mirror the life, work, and play cycles of the community. The library should be in tune with these cycles. Ask yourself who you are cutting out when the library closes or reduces its hours. The use of multiple place strategies can be helpful in making library services available 24/7.
- Make the location more appealing. If the library's customers are to participate in programs and services, they need to feel that the environment is inviting, supportive, convenient, and easy to understand and navigate, and intentionally designed to guide an engaging experience. IKEA is an excellent commercial example of how a very complex retail environment is designed to ease navigation and guide the experience of the customer.
- Overcome the psychological barriers associated with place. The newness of any environment poses qualities of intimidation. Often, your customers encounter substantial barriers regarding their perception of place. Certain ethnic groups are uncomfortable in facilities that resemble government buildings and that may suggest intrusiveness or risk to their safety and

Sense of Place and Development of the Brand at Queens Library

MARKETING STAFF QUICKLY realized that everything had to be changed, from the logo to the business cards, from the building signage to interior communications to the website. Every place and space of Queens Library needed to reflect the brand and to develop a similar look, while still allowing for the individuality of customers and the community. Prior to the establishment of the Queens Library brand, many of the programs and services were promoted by staff at the local community level. Flyers and posters depended heavily on the individual abilities of those who created them. Since individual employee creativity was involved, it was essential that all communications produced on behalf of the brand have a similar look and feel. Although it took some effort by the marketing department "brand police," eventually the department was able to get the vast majority of promotional and communication tactics and publications to reflect the Queens Library brand's look and feel. A major part of the solution was to create brand templates for community library staff to use. A very significant piece in building the brand was developing consistency in the sense of place as well as consistency in promotion.

security. Individuals can be uncomfortable with processes, including the process to get a library card or to reveal personal information. Recognizing these barriers as they relate to each target market is the first step to identifying ways to overcome, prepare, mediate, work around, or find alternative paths to serve your customers.

- Leverage all the dimension of place to design an experience the customer will savor. Customer experience as a holistic process depends on well-conceived place strategies. Making sure the environment is designed to produce the customer experience you seek requires that you step back and look at place from the vantage point of customers—how they experience it, in what order they experience it, and at which decision or engagement points. One effective way to assess your place strategies is to develop what is commonly referred to as a "customer experience map" that anticipates and traces each step of the customer process—each emotional or sensation touch point along the way—and that designs the total experience you intend for the customer to have, including careful integration of the other Ps.

Legend of Unbelievable Service at Nordstrom

AN EXCELLENT COMMERCIAL model for the Anythink approach to place is Nordstrom. When you enter a Nordstrom store, you experience an expansive openness that guides and encourages browsing while offering view lines for sales personnel to immediately acknowledge your presence and on a signal from you to offer their assistance.

Nordstrom is a fashion specialty store founded in 1901 as a shoe store in Seattle. Today, Nordstrom operates more than 150 stores in the United States and is committed to the principles of exceptional service, selection, quality, and value. Nordstrom service helps to differentiate Nordstrom and continually draws customers out of the regional malls. They "thrive on providing legendary experiences through unbelievable customer service, which results in customer folklore and the most powerful word-of-mouth marketing possible" (Andrlik 2007, 2).

Price Strategies

Pricing strategies are perhaps the most critical and most misunderstood and underutilized when it comes to libraries. "Everything of value comes at a price—to those who offer the value and to those who consume the value. . . . We're in the value business. . . ." says Ed Rensi, former president and CEO of McDonald's.

PRICING STRATEGIES AND VALUE

Pricing is the only strategy that primarily communicates and translates value for both the organization and the customer. Think about how pricing and value relate to libraries. In the introduction of the 2008 OCLC study *From Awareness to Funding,* the idea that "free and open access transforms communities and it transforms societies" is punctuated by the balancing reality that "free access transforms, but transformation is not free." The study goes on to say, "While the majority of residents of the United States have visited their public library and have used its services, most cannot describe how their library is funded." This survey strongly suggests that libraries are not effectively utilizing pricing strategies in their marketing mix to convey the true value of what they have to offer to the public they serve. While it is true that libraries, like many public institutions, have an elevated transparency when it comes to tracking and publicly reporting the costs for the services they provide, they tend not to communicate these considerations at the point of exchange with customers, in a manner that is measured and specific to the exchange the customer is experiencing.

HOW ORGANIZATIONS DECIDE ON PRICING STRATEGIES

How organizations decide to price a product or a service, or indeed an entire customer experience, can depend on a variety of factors. First, it is important to understand the concept of "price" in both monetary and nonmonetary terms, including the actual monetary amount to the consumer. The monetary price is the dollars and cents customers pay directly, and the nonmonetary price is what they pay indirectly in time, effort, and related psychosocial costs. Pricing strategy includes but is not limited to the actual marginal cost of the product or service, and extends to the relative or comparable price or value you seek to establish in the eyes of the consumer. The well-established exchange theory in marketing postulates that "target markets must perceive benefits equal to or greater than the perceived costs" (Kotler and Lee 2008, 161). Costs are not limited to financial exchanges but rather include all exchange elements of value, including time, effort, and an implied commitment or promise to perform or pay back. Although it would be reasonable to assume that all consumers act rationally in balancing perceived benefits with costs, research related to pricing in the context of branding, positioning, and promotion is quick to suggest otherwise. In fact, research suggests that how pricing strategies are developed and implemented has much to do with how they are perceived and acted upon by the

Anythink: Positioning through Place Strategies

THE BOARD AND staff of the Anythink libraries identified in their branding process the importance of developing place strategies. They realized that place strategies created the brand identity for the organization. The goal was as follows: "Create brand identity and implement this consistently in our environments through the RLD cohesive graphics system, including displays, signs, colors, staff mode of dress, electronic designs and furnishings."

The district has built four new library buildings and has conducted three renovations within a three-year time frame. These buildings reflect the brand identity, personality, and image of Anythink. The color palettes and construction are complementary to the selected colors of the library brand. There are no circulation or reference desks, as the library has implemented the roving model and consciously included lots of open space in its designs. Each of the libraries has zones to which staff are assigned; they rove throughout their assigned zone, staying in touch with the people and workflows of each area. There are perches throughout the library where staff can assist customers via the ILS. "Anythink-

ers" wear bright orange lanyards and name tags that are highly visible. Customers can easily identify staff members who are always looking for customers that look like they might have a question.

There is no circulation desk. Anythink believes that the interactions have become more positive since the barrier of a large reference or circulation desk is not part of the transaction. The library meets people on their own territory and on their own terms. While there is no circulation desk, there is a front perch—a small stand-up desk that accommodates up to two staff members. It is designed as a service point where staff members greet people, register customers for library cards, and orient people to the library. Its simple design allows for staff to stand and then move around the library, depending on the traffic and customer needs.

A critical element of Anythink and its Anythinkers is the attention to how the library looks, including the presentation and the hospitality of the staff. Many libraries do this as well; however, in others it is something that doesn't always receive top priority. Hospitality is how people feel when they visit your business. Anythink consuming public. Variables that directly influence perceptions of price and related value include:

- **Price/value referencing**—What the consumer deems as an appropriate price or value based on past experience, current comparables provided, manner of price presentation, and even order in which prices are presented.
- **Price/value sensitivity**—How consumers respond to changes in the price or value, what their thresholds are for accepting price/value changes, and factors that serve to increase or decrease price sensitivity.
- **Price/value segmentation**—How price and value are perceived differently by different market segments and the factors that can influence perception, including segmenting price by time, location, volume, product, or service attributes, bundling of products and services, and perhaps most important, by market segments such as demographics and psychographics.

LIBRARIES AND THE COMMON POSITIONING PREMISE—"FREE" FOR ALL

Libraries begin with the common positioning premise that most if not all of what they have to offer is "free" to all. Remember the adage that began this discussion and the disconnect identified in the 2008 OCLC study? Subsequent articles appearing in the Geek the Library campaign are addressing with a broad brush the many myths that plague the economic viability of libraries (http://geekthelibrary.org/geek-the-library/misconceptions.html). While the pricing strategy of "free" is common

wants people to feel welcomed, empowered, energized, and connected when they visit the libraries. Director Pam Sandlian-Smith says, "When I walk into our libraries, I always want to feel like I'm receiving a hug, metaphorically speaking."

Another thing that the library concentrates on is a cohesive presentation and style. The libraries are designed to be comfortable and intuitive. Everything works together—the colors, furniture, signs, graphics, library cards, and library bags. Everything reinforces the messaging, which is fun, curious, approachable, and energizing. Anythink libraries have a playful, supportive service style. There is a place for everyone at Anythink. Customers can sit quietly by the fireplace and gaze out the windows, or they can play in the "tree houses" or special entrances to the children's area. There is even a place for teens to play Wii, watch movies, or listen to music. The exteriors of the new Anythink libraries are contemporary and simple in design. They are very much in keeping with the young audiences to which Anythink is appealing, and the facilities are not what you would expect a library to look like.

However, the interiors sing the language of the library. They include wooden shelves, fireplaces, elegant lighting, and dramatic tree houses in the children's areas. They are discernible as libraries but with some major tweaks. Most important, there is no reference desk but a "front perch" and a "back perch," stand-up stations where librarians—or guides—and concierges offer quick assistance.

The GASP visioning process, first introduced by Peter Robinson for the hotel industry and used by Anythink, helped to define the characteristics of the library personality and guide decisions regarding space planning, furnishings, and services. The common vision and brand that was developed influences the library's ambience and extends to the general style. From this process, a document was created that guided the library in advising architects, designers, and artists. The initial vision helped define the essence of the brand as it was developed. From there, the brand was and continues to be consistently executed in the development of the Anythink website, publications, business cards, newsletters, and program flyers.

to libraries and increasingly common among for-profit enterprises, we must consider the complexities and challenges that go along with such a pricing strategy:

- Although the offer of free pricing tends to dramatically increase demand in number of customers for a specific product or service, it has been shown to conversely decrease the quantity of what they consume and the qualitative extent to which they consume the product or service. *Free may bring customers in the door or to the website, but it does not mean that they will leave with more than they came for, nor actually use what they take.*

- The precedent of offering something for free sets up barriers to the introduction of more strategic approaches, including opportunities to establish reasonable price/value references, address price/value sensitivities, and utilize sophisticated approaches to price/value segmentations. *Free makes it very difficult to compare the true value of what the library has to offer, inclining the market to compare the library with only the cheapest alternatives available and making it very difficult to adjust and differentiate price or value based on who is being served. If you are offering a database service free to individual patrons of the library, it may be hard to establish a pricing strategy to market the same service to for-profit enterprises at a reasonable cost.*

For more insights regarding pricing strategy and a glimpse at the research on pricing strategies and related topics, the reader is advised to review the early work of Theodore Levitt (1983) and the more recent works of Chris Anderson (2009) and Dan Ariely (2009). The research of Ariely is most interesting as he has great insight into how price influences the perception of value (see his blog at www.danariely.com).

There is tremendous opportunity to utilize creative pricing strategies in libraries and to carefully consider what it is that each customer must pay to realize the true value (actual, augmented, and potential) of a product or service—and then to determine how that price is communicated to the customer. For example, parents who give an hour a day to help their child learn to read, utilizing the resources of their library, will realize an immediate connection with their child's improved ability as well as the future potential for their child. By resisting the temptation to take the easy way out by promoting a product or service as free, pause and consider how you might address pricing in a manner that allows you to promote the *mutual value* of the exchange.

This does not require abandonment of a core strategy that focuses on free products and services. But it does require consideration and incorporation of pricing strategies that wrap "free" with a true exchange of value (monetary and/or nonmonetary) for associated products and services.

ENHANCING THE BRAND THROUGH PRICING

The pricing strategy for a library affords huge opportunity to enhance your brand, positioning, and promotional capabilities. By simply abandoning the addictive tactic of promoting the offerings of the library as "free" and committing to a disciplined way to always communicate the mutual exchange of benefits, libraries can seize the attention of existing and new markets in a manner that fully expresses the value of the exchange. Doing so, however, is not an easy task. It first requires an objective analysis of the true costs associated with the exchange on behalf of both the library and the market, including monetary and nonmonetary consideration. Then with the brand and positioning strategy in mind, select the appropriate messaging to convey the exchange value in a manner that addresses the value orientation of the market and the library. Before taking these next difficult steps, consider additional dimensions that relate price strategy to product, place, and promotion.

MONETARY AND NONMONETARY COSTS

Price is also the cost that the target market associates with using the library. "Pricing is the amount of money charged for a product or service, or the sum of the values that consumers exchange for the benefits of having or using the product or service" (Kotler and Lee 2008, 227). There are monetary and nonmonetary incentives and disincentives to using the library. Perhaps a monetary incentive would be the availability of a publication, book, and material for no actual expense to the borrower. A monetary disincentive might occur because of library fines. There are also nonmonetary costs to the customer, including the time and effort required to use the library.

COMPETITIVE BEHAVIOR AND PRICING

There are situations in which increases in pricing for competitive reasons can affect the positioning of the library, especially with price-sensitive markets. For example, the recent recession and rise in unemployment can serve on one hand to drive customers to the library for resources, assistance, and guidance, considering the informational needs they have and limitations or cost factors that make competing sources less attractive. At the same time, persons/households experiencing economic downturns will often find themselves challenged with transportation, working two and sometimes three part-time jobs, which can compromise their ability to pay the price of getting to the library or fitting their busy schedules in the limited

Starbucks Pushes Job Growth Program

STARBUCKS HAS BEGUN collecting donations of $5 or more from customers to stimulate U.S. job growth through its Jobs for USA program. The Seattle-based coffee chain is collaborating with the Opportunity Finance Network, a nonprofit that works with community development financial institutions to provide loans to small businesses and community groups. Starbucks says 100 percent of the donations will go toward loans for firms and organizations that can add jobs or stem job losses. "This is about using Starbuck's scale for good," said Howard Schultz, Starbucks CEO. The Starbucks Foundation is giving $5 million to get the program started. The Starbucks brand is positioned as a responsible community partner by seed-funding and promoting mutual participation by customers in the form of individual contributions to a community-based jobs growth initiative managed by Starbucks. The intent is to encourage regular customers to both purchase their products at regular prices and to concurrently donate as a joint venture partner to the socioeconomic cause of job creation (Skidmore 2011).

hours of the library. These are all price-competitive factors that can have an impact.

Traditionally, library services are provided without charge to the customer. Rapidly rising costs, changing political philosophy, and increasing expenses for technology are forcing administrators, funders, and policymakers to reexamine policies for library service. Users are continually questioning the quality of service. Libraries have rapidly been growing away from being from identities as pure repositories of information and into much more of a service-oriented enterprise. As they do so, market expectations rise in terms of all monetary and nonmonetary price-related considerations.

> ### Amazon Launches Kindle Owners Lending Library
>
> AN ARTICLE IN *USA Today* announced that Kindle owners can borrow books for free through a new Lending Library launched by Amazon. Thousands of books are available on the Kindle Owners Lending Library, including current and former *New York Times* best sellers— to owners who have an Amazon Prime membership (which costs $79 a year) (Molina 2011).

PRICING STRATEGIES BUILT ON THE BRAND AND POSITIONING STATEMENT

Pricing strategies in the commercial environment are built on the brand, the positioning statement, and the objectives of the organization. Is the objective survival? Is the objective cost recovery? Are there objectives for return on investment or cash flow? Some corporations build their positioning in the market based on their pricing strategies. Walmart, Costco, and Best Buy would be examples of organizations for which price is the differentiating characteristic. When low cost is the dominate pricing strategy, the enterprise will typically find itself competing with fewer entities for the same market but against competitors that are solidly positioned with a larger share of the most cost-conscience markets they are pursuing. Amazon recently entered the low-cost/no-cost arena by offering its Kindle owners/subscribers books for free through its lending library. Note that its books are not in fact free, but rather complimentary to those who own a Kindle and who also subscribe to the Amazon Prime membership program.

PRICING STRATEGY BASED ON PRODUCT OR SERVICE

The pricing strategy is also based on the product or service. What are the costs of production, advertising, promotion, and delivery of the product or service? What is the value of the product or service to the customer, and how do the nonmonetary costs factor in, including accessibility to products and services?

Cost-Plus Pricing

The most elementary pricing method and the one traditionally used in many nonprofit organizations is cost-plus pricing. Many people feel that cost-plus pricing is fair to both buyers and sellers in that the customer is paying for the true cost of the product or service plus a margin to cover service-related overhead and profit (or a margin for reinvestment and reserve for the nonprofit). It is relatively simple to design and does not fluctuate with demand.

Columbus Metropolitan Library

TARGETING A SPECIFIC market and developing programs in-depth leads to partnerships with outside funding agencies, thus increasing the power of the library to affect the outcomes. Obviously, it also leads to increased revenue for library services and programs to meet the needs of the targeted audiences. Columbus Metropolitan Library, through its Columbus Metropolitan Library Foundation, secured funding from many sources for the Young Minds programs as well as its Homework Help Centers. The library was able to secure over $2 million in private support and partnerships for these programs. The pricing strategies enabled program expansion beyond the library's individual capability.

Premium Pricing

Premium pricing is defined as asking a high price that is commensurate with the perceived value of the product and with demand for the product—as high as the market will consider. Premium pricing typically relates directly to promotable product or service qualities that far exceed competitive offerings. For example, a library that offers a unique collection applicable to the interests of a very discrete and discerning audience, perhaps researchers, historians, attorneys, or business interests, may be in a position to offer access and service support based on a premium pricing model. Premium pricing strategies are built on strong brand recognition and tend to forge enduring loyalty. Luxury items like automobiles, watches, cruises, hotels, designer clothing, and concierge services are commercial examples of premium pricing strategies for high-end products and services.

A Solid, Recognized Brand Commands a Higher Price

Generally, the extent to which the brand signifies quality, consistency, and dependability is the extent to which its products and services can command a higher price. And interestingly, there is a circular benefit to premium pricing—it elevates the perceived value of the offering and reduces the overall sensitivity to price fluctuations in the marketplace. Again, keep in mind that pricing considerations include both monetary and nonmonetary considerations—access to a primo library collection may be restricted to those who have a library card, are willing to reserve their time to access the collections and service assistance, and agree to very rigid use requirements. While there may be little or no monetary cost involved, the nonmonetary costs are substantial and speak to the elevated value of the offering.

People Strategies— The Fifth "P" for Consideration

Building relationships with customers as strategic partners with the library enables the library to realize its potential. The focus and priority should be on pleasing your current customers and building those loyal, committed customers into your most passionate advocates. Strategies to develop these relationships with customers begin with staff members who understand and have the capacity and intuitive insight to anticipate the evolving life cycle needs and aspirations of customers. An intense customer-centric life cycle focus is one that requires substantial understanding of your customers and the markets they represent. Libraries, with their data-rich resources, are in a prime position to leverage life cycle strategies and to integrate them via people-oriented strategies—utilizing incredibly well-trained, resourceful, passionate, and personable librarians who can be found among and developed within the organization.

THE CUSTOMER LIFE CYCLE

The customer life cycle has similarities to the product life cycle. The customer life cycle focuses on the creation and delivery of lifetime value to the customer, addresses needs and desires that benefit each stage of life from infancy to old age. Libraries seek to develop lifetime relationships with their customers; therefore, this concept is worth understanding. The *customer life cycle* is a term used to describe the steps a customer goes through to consider buying, using, and developing a loyalty to a product or service. In a service organization, this customer life cycle is heavily influenced by an integrated approach to product, place, pricing, and promotion strategies that fit the life cycle needs and aspirations of the customer. Life cycle relationships are also substantially reliant on the people within the organization who are responsible for the delivery of customer services (www.customerlifecycle.us).

The Anythink People Strategy

ANYTHINK STAFF WERE in survival mode prior to 2007. Working with an annual budget of less than $4 million for a population of 300,000 people meant that resources were scarce; there were limited funds for books, staff, buildings, and operating materials. That sense of frugality and scarcity shifted when the mill levy increase passed in November 2006. The future began to look promising with a sense of possibility and expansion. A new staff manifesto was created that bonded the organization.

Human Resource Director Susan Dobbs spent most of her career in pre-IPO high-tech companies and likens Anythink "very much to a start-up" with a lean staff working long hours, fueled by passion. Together with Public Services Director Ronnie Storey-Ewoldt, the staff created task forces to rethink and standardize policies in a system where branches—some quite distant—were operating as individual entities.

Job descriptions were revised. The library moved from a very traditional set of job descriptions to a competency-based job description and performance review system for the staff. All frontline staff were asked to reapply for these new positions. There were three caveats: Everyone would have a job, no one would see a decrease in salary, and everyone would have an opportunity to participate in the job decision. Some employees

> { ▲ ● ♀ }
>
> ## You are not
> just an employee,
> volunteer or board member.
> You do not merely catalog books,
> organize periodicals and manage resources.
> You are the gateway into the mind of the idea people
> who come to our facilities to find or fuel a spark.
>
> Part **WIZARD**
> Part **GENIUS**
> Part **EXPLORER**
>
> It is your calling to trespass into the unknown and
> come back with a concrete piece someone can hold
> onto, turn over, and use to fuel their mind and soul.

figure 7.5 **Staff Manifesto of Anythink**

moved down the totem pole, while others moved up. New positions were created, including the role of the *guide*, described as "part education, part reference advocate, and part event planning." Of the seventeen staffers working as guides, nine have MLS degrees and one has a master's in education. Adult, children's, teen, and tech guides design and deliver programs and experiences. The staff manifesto says (see figures 7.5 and 7.6):

You are not just an employee, volunteer or board member. You do not merely catalog books, organize periodicals and manage resources. You are the gateway into the mind of the idea people who come to our facilities to find or fuel a spark. Part WIZARD, Part GENIUS, Part EXPLORER. It is your calling to trespass into the unknown and come back with a concrete piece someone can hold onto, turn over, and use to fuel their mind and soul.

Upon examining the role of the librarian, it became apparent that librarians are really guides to information, interactions, and experiences. That is an important shift in thinking about the relationships with customers and with information.

Summary

According to Al Ries and Jack Trout (2001), "Positioning is a revolutionary idea precisely because it cuts across the other four Ps. It informs each of the Ps and adds consistency to them." Positioning affects products and can affect the price of products. Positioning can also affect the place where products and service are sold or the sale occurs. Positioning also affects the promotion of the product.

The positioning strategy determines the product and service offerings. As Columbus Metropolitan Library targeted the Young Minds segment, the majority of the resources of the library went to develop programs, products, and services to meet its positioning strategy and primary target audience.

Products and services are considered the first of the four Ps. Each product contains the core product, the actual product, the augmented product, and the potential product. The core product, the center of the product platform, is concerned with the benefits that customers will receive. The actual product or service objectively describes the offerings and the specifics of its features that extend from the product or service and its benefits to be realized by the customer or user of the product or

The busywork of checking books in and out was replaced with the role of "You're the essence of the customer's experience at the library. You greet people with a smile and welcome them into our library. You enrich people's lives through meaningful dialogue about our products and services. You earn trust by being knowledgeable about our products and making recommendations that connect with the customer. You help our library customers find the fuel and the spark to unlimited ideas and opportunities."

Achieving culture change is never simple. The original visioning of the new library personality through the GASP (Graphics, Ambience, Style, and Presentation) process jump-started a sense of optimism and set the direction for a new way of perceiving the library. A library task force charged with building a healthy, happy culture named themselves the "Yellow Geckos." The Yellow Geckos plan weekend hikes, snowshoeing, bowling, and trivia nights. By creating opportunities for staff and their families to have fun and be silly, relationships are formed that transfer to a work environment built on these positive relationships.

Anythink seeks clever ways to make the pot sweeter. Because the library pays many bills with credit cards that accrue points, it can send staffers to conferences and training events, says Finance Director Mindy Kittay, a former CFO and consultant for many small businesses who began a new library career eight years ago. Also, staffers can partake in a technology lending program—iPads, e-readers, Flip cameras, and so on—and buy technology at the library's discount, with the payment deducted from their paychecks over several

figure 7.6 **Staff Manifesto of Anythink, Part Two**

months. Being associated with Anythink has its perks.

Good ideas in the library world are often borrowed, and the decision to drop Dewey came after a staff visit to the Maricopa County Library District in Arizona, which pioneered such a plan in 2007. "We were completely bowled over at how simple it was," recalls Rachel Fewell, Anythink's former collection development manager.

Anythink expects people to be flexible problem solvers, continuous learners, innovators, and leaders. The library hires for these qualities and evaluates staff based on these qualities. Anytime someone has an innovative idea, the library tries to support it or find a way to incorporate it into the work plan. "We believe everyone can live a creative life; we just need to find ways to support and celebrate creative thinking," says Director Pam Sandlian-Smith.

service. The augmented product focuses on delivery systems, warranties, service, and other augmentations that surround the objective product or service. The potential product consists of everything that is potentially feasible and imaginable—what customers want to buy into in advance of realization. Remember, as Theodore Levitt says, people don't buy products, they buy solutions and potential solutions to their problems.

Place strategies are not just targeting the physical locations for libraries. Place strategies include distribution systems, library card systems, websites, Internet delivery systems, displays, signage, placement of billboards, checkout and renewal systems, delivery systems, hours of service, and every element of library service that can be associated with the delivery of service to customers including access to library services. Your positioning strategy affects the design, implementation, efficiency, consistency, and professionalism of all of your place strategies.

Can Mickey Mouse Teach Libraries about Customer Service?

THE SECRET TO Disney's success isn't magic dust. It is a well-trained, enthusiastic, and motivated workforce. Walt Disney himself recognized, "You can dream, create, design and build the most wonderful place in the world, but it requires people to make the dream a reality. You can build the best product. You can give people effective training to support the delivery of exceptional service" (www.JustDisney.com).

The Disney approach to people management has set the standard for industries far and wide. "We have always tried to be guided by the basic idea that, in the discovery of knowledge, there is great entertainment" (Kinni 2001, 12). "The magic of a Disney vacation is the magic of quality, the magic of innovation, the magic of beauty, the magic of families coming together, the magic of our cast members. All of these things kind of bundle together," says Michael Eisner, former chairman and CEO of Disney (Kinni 2001, 18).

All of Walt Disney World's "cast members" begin their career at the casting office. Disney takes great care with its casting department. Cast members go through a training program called Traditions, where they learn the basics of being good cast members. Walt Disney World has defined and refined its four service standards, and the Traditions program teaches cast members how to achieve them (Kinni 2001, 84).

Disney realizes that 70 percent of visitors are repeat visitors and that the quality of the service makes a difference. They try to exceed the expectations of visitors. They believe that every person within the organization is responsible for customer service. Disney has developed the Guestology Compass and taken a closer look at the elements of that guiding philosophy. They strive to understand the *needs* of guests and find the *wants* to be less obvious. "Guestology is the work of learning who your customers are and understanding what they expect when they come to you. Guestology techniques include surveys, listening posts, focus groups, utilization studies and the feedback customers give to employees" (Kinni 2001, 66). Disney uses a guest profile including demographic and psychographic information to create service quality.

Obviously, brand management is the key to Disney's success. The brand is everything and is maintained by the employee customer service training programs. Disney provides a set of quality service cues for all organizations, including:

Build a service organization greater than the sum of its parts by integrating, aligning, and distributing your service standards.

Meet guest expectations with headliners; exceed guest expectations with landmarks.

Make the integration maker a part of your organizational toolbox.

Manage every service moment.

Choose service solutions that demonstrate high touch, high show, and high tech.

Disney University is available to corporations and institutions—yes, even libraries—to learn the principles and service standards that make the Disney organization and brand so strong (Kinni 2001).

Price strategies include traditional monetary strategies as well as nonmonetary incentives and disincentives. Libraries deal with monetary pricing strategies when purchasing materials and services and with nonmonetary incentives that encourage use. Libraries must set prices for tangible objects and services while examining price incentives in all areas of service.

REFERENCES

Anderson, Chris. 2009. *Free: The Future of a Radical Price*. New York: HarperCollins.

Andrlik, Todd. 2007. "Legends of Nordstrom Service." *ToddAnd*, February 18. http://toddand.com/2007/02/18/legends-of-unbelievable-nordstrom-service.

Ariely, Dan. 2009. *Predictably Irrational, Revised and Expanded Edition: The Hidden Forces That Shape Our Lives*. New York: HarperCollins e-books.

Baraldi, Enrico. 2003. *The Places of IKEA: Using Space as a Strategic Weapon in Handling Resource Networks*. New York: Science History Publications. www.impgroup.org /uploads/papers/4289.pdf.

Kinni, Ted. 2001. *Be Our Guest: Perfecting the Art of Customer Service*. New York: Disney Editions.

Kotler, Philip, and Nancy R. Lee. 2008. *Social Marketing: Influencing Behaviors for Good*. 3rd ed. Los Angeles: Sage.

Levitt, Theodore. 1983. *The Marketing Imagination*. New York: The Free Press.

Molina, Brett. 2011. "Amazon Launches Kindle Owners Lending Library." *USA Today Technology Live,* November 3. http://content.usatoday.com/communities/technologylive /post/2011/11/amazon-launches-lending-library-for-kindle-owners/1#.UKar_IfBFWM.

Ries, Al, and Jack Trout. 2001. *Positioning: The Battle for Your Mind*. New York: McGraw-Hill.

Schaper, Louise. 2011. "LJ's New Landmark Libraries." *Library Journal*, May 15. www.libraryjournal.com/lj/ljinprintcurrentissue/890109–403/the_new_icons.html.

Skidmore, Sarah. 2011. "Starbucks Pushes Job Growth Program." *Yahoo! Finance*, October 3. http://finance.yahoo.com/news/Starbucks-pushes-job-growth-apf-1602029736. html.

Topolsky, Joshua. 2010. "Apple iPad Review." *AOL Tech Engadget*, April 3. www.engadget .com/2010/04/03/apple-ipad-review.

"Walt Disney Quotes." 2005. www.justdisney.com/walt_disney/quotes/index.html.

Walters, Suzanne. 2004. *Library Marketing That Works!* New York: Neal-Schuman.

Promoting Your Brand

THIS CHAPTER BEGINS WITH A DISCUSSION OF YOUR brand architecture, including the use of strategic touch points and tactics that apply to brochures, signage, building design, vehicles, name tags, library cards, collateral materials, advertising, social media, public relations, and website design. All of these strategies and tactics build on the foundation of your brand and your positioning strategy. The chapter then moves to a more how-to discussion of promotion, the shaping and deployment of messages consistent with your strategy, and leveraging the best tactics available. Those tactics can be clever, "whiz bang," creative, and expressive; however, they must also be rationally based and emotionally consistent with your overarching brand and positioning strategy.

Concept of Promotion

The concept of promotion begins with understanding the difference between strategy and tactic. In short, a strategy is a concept, an idea about how to accomplish a major goal or objective. A tactic, on the other hand, is a specific action or set of actions to execute a strategy. As you have now learned, your brand is about knowing who you are and what you seek to be in the minds of those you serve over the long term—your *depth, demand,* and *desire.* Your brand expresses your *premise*—largely comprised of your *depth* and reinforced or validated by the *demand* for what you do.

Your brand also expresses your *promise*—reflected in the *demand* of current markets and inspired by the *desire* to serve future markets. Effectively, within your brand reside the goals and aspirations expressed in your vision. Your positioning strategy is a conceptual approach or design to achieve your goals—moving progressively toward your vision. Your positioning will typically include these considerations:

- A complete understanding and appreciation for the brand—past, present, and future—including the articulated goals for the brand
- A clear understanding of the markets you serve and seek to serve—who they are demographically, geographically, and psychographically
- A precise knowledge of the benefits to be realized by the markets you serve and the competing choices available to them

So, your brand and your positioning are clearly conceptual and strategic in nature. Promotion as a broad concept and as the fourth P embraces your brand both as a strategy and an integration of the many tactics at your disposal. Generally speaking, having a solid brand and sound positioning strategy is more important than the tactics you choose, so getting brand and strategy right is critical. From time to time a big tactical idea may come along—the Internet for instance—that can profoundly influence strategy or may evolve into a strategy itself if critical to your positioning. But generally it's the branding and positioning strategies that come first and that matter most.

With that said, the world of promotion is fascinating and creative. It's where the paint splashes on canvas, where words and graphics find their rightful place in a well-turned and compelling message, and where the rubber meets road. In effect, your promotional efforts are your "moments of truth"—where and when all that you are and by your intentional design you seek to be. Promotion is very declarative and very public, and therefore commits your entire organization to fulfill on both the premise and promise of your message. There are specific elements of your brand that we discussed back in Chapter 1 that have substantial promotional implications—your brand name, aesthetic, and value proposition, for example. Each of these is an important tool to use when employing tactics that make the most sense.

Behind the most basic of brand expressions are the tangibles that actually make up a brand—the quality of products and services, the attitudes and personalities of people, stakeholders and customers who affectively align with the brand, and ultimately, the *experiences* they associate with the brand. The visual experience, the interactive experience, and the transactional experience need to be carefully designed, orchestrated, highly personalized, obsessively consistent, and readily adaptive to change. The design of these experiential elements, or brand touch points, is often referred to as the *brand architecture* because it provides the conceptual framework for promotional tactics.

Brand Architecture and Promotion

The Anythink library serves as an example of brand architecture. You might think that the name Anythink is clever. Anythink serves as a naming element for the

Queens Library

QUEENS LIBRARY CONDUCTED research to identify a strategy to communicate its relevance, uniqueness, and coherence in the borough of Queens. A new logo communicated a more current and relevant brand identity, personality, and image. Through research, Queens Library discovered that the primary, unifying value for customers was the difference the library made in their lives. This led to a succinct tagline to pair with the name: Queens Library, "Enrich your life." The next step was to develop an advertising campaign to introduce the new brand. Queens County in New York is the most diverse county in the United States. Residents speak more than sixty different languages. It is a major portal for immigrants from all over the world. Having pictures of Queens Library's employees represented in advertising material was a big plus for its promotional strategy. These photographs demonstrate that the staff are as diverse as the people they serve. Warm, welcoming, personal photographs encourage newcomers to come to the library, while reinforcing a highly personalized value proposition that positions the brand to serve a broad audience, including those new to the country.

Rangeview Library District and sets up a strong and declarative *value proposition*: "A Revolution of Rangeview Libraries." This "smashup" of the adjective *any* with *think* as either verb or noun combine with a very creative graphic treatment, Anythink evokes a stream of possibilities for the marketplace to ascribe to the library. Through a visioning process, Anythink was born to represent a new style of library that focuses not just on books but also on imagination, creativity, and lifelong learning. Once the identity was defined, it was translated into a cohesive concept. The concept was used to guide all decisions in creating spaces, selecting colors, lighting, materials, integrating interior furnishings, graphics, style of services, and programs. In short, by defining the desired characteristics of the library brand, decisions regarding space planning, furnishings, and services adhere to a specific integrated vision.

Consider, too, the brand and positioning strategy behind the Mudflap Girl campaign in Wyoming. Here is an eye-catching, clever, and creative graphic that cuts through the clutter and lands squarely in the psyche of the target audience, the Wyoming man. It all ties nicely with another reality of Wyoming—the preponderance of auto parts stores and the inclination of most men and many women to revere and repair their own vehicles. The campaign was an integrated promotional and database collections strategy that focused on making Chilton Auto Repair database manuals readily available to every resident. Yes, this campaign was built on the foundation of a carefully thought-out positioning strategy. The campaign has captured the attention and imagination of libraries around the world.

DEVELOPING YOUR BRAND ARCHITECTURE

The brand architecture serves to frame the big ideas and specific emotions around which you want to build your brand. "Just as a distinctive architectural style sets the tone or establishes the nature of a building, so too are brands perceived in terms of their architecture" (Knapp 2000, 95). Brand architecture is the foundation for your promotional strategy, beginning with a conceptual framework for expressing your brand identity, personality, and image by integrating your positioning strategy through your marketing mix. Brand architecture also addresses the structure and interrelationship of brands within your library, including distinctive subbrands like branches, special collections, and perhaps unique service initiatives designed to reach specific audiences. Your brand architecture also addresses strategies for cobranding with strategic partners like schools, museums, and corporate entities. The brand architecture serves to frame the big ideas and specific emotions around which you want to build your brand.

> The Brand Blueprint or architecture can be defined in this way: 1. The disciplined, detailed plan required to create, design, and communicate the intended brand perception. 2. That which determines the character or style of a brand. 3. A plan that reflects the Brand promise and outlines the underlying collective architecture for the brand name, byline, tagline, graphic representations and the brand story. (Knapp 2000, 96)

APPLICATIONS TO NEW AND EXISTING BRANDS

The idea of brand architecture applies not only to the development of new library brands, but also to updating, refining, and repositioning, and the consistent expression of a well-established brand. The purpose may be to renew or reveal the emotional verve and connection of the brand to reflect the evolving reality of what the brand represents and whom it serves. Revisiting the existing brand architecture,

Brand Architecture and the Rangeview Library District

THE RANGEVIEW LIBRARY District (RLD), rebranded as Anythink, took up the challenge to become a transforming power within the community, within libraries, and among the educational, social, and cultural organizations with which it partners and interacts. RLD selected the creative team that eventually became Ricochet Ideas to lead the rebranding efforts. John Bellina, founder of Ricochet Ideas, said to the staff and board of Anythink, "We need to first understand your DNA, your essence—and then we can translate it into a brand."

Anythink was designed to be a "challenger brand" strong enough to compete or perhaps partner with the likes of Starbucks, Google, and Barnes & Noble. These brands are seen to be direct competitors of libraries, so Anythink must be instilled with a sense of ingenuity. It was also designed to be a "declarative brand," identifying the library as essential and vital to life of the community. The new brand embodies creativity, ideas, and discovery—all things the RLD wanted the community to associate with Anythink as a place, a resource, and an experience. It established Anythink as a relevant and highly expressive brand that increases awareness with a shift in perception— to increase usage and build engagement and loyalty

that leads to an informed community and a higher quality of life.

Anythink is a new style of library—a place of unlimited imagination where play inspires creativity and lifelong learning. It is a place where anything and everything is possible. Anythink is anything you can invent or imagine. Anythink is a stretch brand. It is committed to something big and different. There is a feeling of innovation, of becoming a resource for library innovation as well as a local resource for business innovation. This is the brand strategy—the conceptual architecture for Anythink libraries is summarized beautifully in the "Anythink Staff Manifesto" (see figures 7.5 and 7.6) and "Brand Guidelines."

The brand architecture or blueprint for Anythink represented a total way to set the foundation for the other components of the brand. The brand architecture aligned the brand's identity, personality, and image. The brand architecture combined the premise and promise, the story, and the visual and operational requirements into a single structure that is expressed through customer service, community partnerships, and effective use of technology, facilities, signage, programs, and collections—mindful of every touch point.

Developing the Queens Library Brand

A NEW LOGO was needed to communicate the brand's evolving identify, personality, and image. Everyone had to be "singing from the same hymnal" to ensure that Queens Library was understood by all of the stakeholders served by all of its branches. Time and time again, employees of the library provided anecdotes of how the library and staff supported the new Americans arriving daily in Queens in a variety of ways to enable them to adapt to their new country. Staff worked with the unemployed to craft a résumé or properly answer a want ad. Staff taught individuals to speak English and helped the illiterate learn to read. Staff supported children with after-school homework help and provided guidance and resources to parents and educators—as partners in learning. Queens Library made an important difference in people's lives. This was the value trigger that led to a succinct and meaningful value proposition, where none existed before, that could be linked naturally with the name, Queens Library, and the tagline "Enrich your life."

The old logo was a blue, corporate-looking seal. The new logo needed to reflect the welcoming nature of Queens Library and its warm, caring, and engaging staff. The warm colors of yellow, orange, and red were chosen to express this warmth and convey the personal/emotional touch of the library. Queens Library also wanted to reflect the changing nature of the public library, especially from a technology and nonprint collection standpoint. It was then that one of the staff members said, "One hundred years from now, public libraries will still be about books." She was right. Though the form and mode of delivery might change, Queens Library would continue to be "about books." So the marketing department worked to develop a more contemporary "book look" for the logo. The new logo, combined with a personalized and embracing value proposition, served to renew the brand and provided helpful architectural elements for repositioning the library through the good works of its people.

identifying areas of strength and weakness, and making the necessary adaptations can be the key to success. Consider the Queens Library brand—in need of renewal with a focus on communicating value to a widening audience.

REVISITING BRAND ARCHITECTURE TO BRING CLARITY AND FOCUS TO THE BRAND

Brands are like people. Left to the pressures of the moment and the constancy of change swirling about us, we can easily get disconnected—running here and there, putting out fires, responding to never-ending demands and an ever-widening group of people, and losing our sense of purpose and focus. And we can get sloppy in the process—not always thinking about who we are, what we are doing, and how we are coming across to others. That's why for some libraries, as with people, the biggest challenge is to pause and revisit the brand and the infrastructures used to express the brand. Columbus Metropolitan Library had cause to do just that.

INVESTING IN BRAND IDENTITY

As seen with Queens Library and Columbus Metropolitan Library, the brand is a powerful communications tool to the extent that it conveys authenticity, personality, commitment, and value. Visual expressions of the brand typically begin with the name itself and extend to aesthetic treatments, including the use of what Alina Wheeler refers to as "brandmarks" in her discussion of brand elements. "Designed with an almost infinite variety of shapes and personalities, brandmarks can be assigned to a number of general categories. From literal through symbolic, from word-driven to image-driven, the world of brandmarks expands each day" (Wheeler 2009, 50).

To the extent possible, brand elements should also be protected by trademark or service mark. Often, there is no need to protect a highly descriptive and established name like Columbus Metropolitan Library, but any symbol and/or value proposition or tagline that is uniquely tied to that brand is a good candidate for legal protection. Remember, awareness of your brand will grow and become more valuable as the association with value is strengthened. It thus becomes a communications asset to the library and to the community it serves. To the extent that the brand is compromised or confused by what other competing institutions or enterprises are doing with similar images or taglines, both the library and the public suffer the erosion in value.

As the brand takes on a certain value, it serves as a virtual and conceptual starting point to guide all expressions, including a host of decisions that extend well beyond

Clarifying the Columbus Metropolitan Library Brand Identity

COLUMBUS METROPOLITAN LIBRARY (CML) distilled the brand down to its essential elements—what the library is about, its identity. They formulated this simple statement that expressed the essence of the CML brand—its heart and soul: "You can create opportunity + we are stewards of knowledge = Opportunity through knowledge."

A brand review of Columbus Metropolitan Library showed that the library had diluted the power of its brand identity through an unwieldy "house of brands" approach. Every program or service had its own look and feel, sometimes its own brand, disconnected from the library's overarching brand. It was time to return to a singular brand—one that embraced all program and service dimensions and the customers they served.

Next, Columbus Metropolitan Library built a messaging map. Through an animated session with the team, and using customer research as a foundation, the library created a map to build a hierarchy of core messages in terms of attributes, what they offered, their values, and the benefits they delivered to customers. This map led the library back to its brand's identity, what they promised to deliver to the customers—*opportunity through knowledge.*

Next, Columbus Metropolitan Library explored all the dimensions of its brand's personality to better define and ultimately express who it is—to find a voice, a look, and a consistent feel. The team identified traits that distilled the brand personality. Keywords floated to the top—*smart, accessible, trusted, alive, approachable,* and

But what does it mean?

One way to talk about our brand personality is by comparing our brand to other brands. This exercise helps to inspire us visually and verbally because each of these brands has strong associations that are "more like" or "less like" where our brand should go.

	MORE LIKE	LESS LIKE
SIMPLICITY	APPLE	IBM
RESPECTED	DISCOVERY CHANNEL	E!
FUN	TARGET	WALMART
INSPIRATIONAL	WHOLE FOODS	IGA
INVITING	PANERA	BURGER KING
AUTHENTIC	DISNEY WORLD	UNIVERSAL
ORGANIZED	CRATE & BARREL	BED, BATH & BEYOND
APPROACHABLE	HONDA	MERCEDES
ACCESSIBLE	USA TODAY	WALL STREET JOURNAL
SOPHISTICATED	HBO	FOX

figure 8.1 **Columbus Metropolitan Library Brand Personality**

what is commonly viewed as marketing communications. Consider how broadly the Anythink brand is applied.

Using Graphics and Color

Graphics as a communication tool are essential to brand architecture and come in many forms, serving the purposes of branding, informing, illustrating, or entertaining. They can be effectively utilized for purposes of objectively communicating a brand identity, or more subjectively to express the brand's personality and image. However deployed, it is important that graphics align with the brand and the audiences to be served by the brand. Where possible and when used primarily to promote the brand, graphics should be unique to the brand and therefore not commonly found in other commercial uses that may confuse or confound the brand message you are trying to convey. The inclination to use free downloadable graphics, videos, and clip art, for example, can serve to cheapen the brand image by the lack

human. The team returned to one word over and over—*alive.* CML is vital, noisy, ever-changing, and full of activity. The team identified six traits that express the brand personality, including how one thinks about the library and what one feels toward the library. Brand personality was described in human terms, much as you might describe a person. The personality needs to resonate in a meaningful way with the staff delivering the brand and the customer experiencing the brand.

One path Columbus Metropolitan Library chose to consider when examining brand image was to compare the library brand to other brands (see figure 8.1). This exercise inspired the team visually and verbally because each of the brands had strong associations that were either "more like" or "less like" where they wanted to go.

What does Columbus Metropolitan Library look like? In the process, they declared, "This is not your grandfather's library! Once upon a time, the library was a place to visit occasionally and perhaps borrow a book or two. Today, it's a destination. The place to be. An experience. And CML sought to declare it loudly and proudly!"

REVISITING THE LOGO

The current library logo is considered by Columbus Metropolitan Library to be the most recognizable symbol of the brand, and when combined with the name, the most important element in unifying the brand. "It should be considered a sacred mark and treated with respect," according to Alison Circle, director of marketing and strategic planning (see figure 8.2). The original logo was designed in the 1970s and was conservative, education-centric, and difficult to work with.

At first, the library sought a graphic solution, something abstract and eye-catching. But what the team came up with seemed too confusing and not helpful to

figure 8.2 **Columbus Metropolitan Library Logo**

the task of elevating the communicative power of the brand. Then they worked on designs that expressed specific ideas like a "third place" to be. But the images that emerged just did not seem to resonate and were difficult to explain to customers. Reflecting on the OCLC perceptions study that indicated library users overwhelmingly associate the library with books, Columbus Metropolitan Library wondered why it was running away from such a strong core identity. The team agreed unanimously.

The ultimate logo design suggests the essence of a book, the pages within, and a feel that is contemporary, light and airy, and visually complementary to the name. The new logo works well with a variety of applications, including those in "lockup" with the name (i.e., when the logo and name are part of the same graphic element).

When the team unveiled the new logo to staff two things happened. The staff heaved a huge sigh of relief that the team hadn't done something totally wacky, and then they discovered on their own a range of relevant meanings associated with the graphic, including ideas like movement, sails and sailing away, energy, and inspiration or a rising up. They had discovered a newfound symbolism in the logo with ample room for meaningful interpretation. They considered their new brand complete.

of relevance to specific audiences, overuse in the marketplace, and disconnect with the brand and its related aesthetics.

Color is an important tool in addressing the visual qualities of the brand. At Columbus Metropolitan Library, the primary palette is bright and vibrant. It represents the warm, friendly, exciting, and approachable nature of the library. The palette selected by the library signals vitality as well as a crisp, modern approach.

At Queens Library, the old logo was a blue, official seal. The new logo needed to reflect the welcoming nature of Queens Library and its caring staff. The warm colors of yellow, orange, and red were chosen to reflect the exciting and changing nature of the public library, especially from a technology and nonprint collection standpoint.

At Anythink, the primary branding color palette was selected to express high energy and intensity, yet in a manner that also conveyed a sense of calm. Anythink libraries are a wonderful gathering place, full of energy, community interaction, and constant movement and activity. It is also a quiet, private place of retreat. The palette recognizes both: a vibrant orange, crimson red, and warm gray. The branding guide gives specific criteria for matching colors across a variety of color/reproduction processes. Anythink employs a secondary palette that extends creative opportunity without sacrificing brand consistency. The secondary colors are complementary to the primary colors and provide a spectrum of warm and cool options that align with influences of nature and particularly the front range landscape of the Colorado Rockies.

Anythink Libraries, Brand Strategy and Brand Identity

AS PAM SANDLIAN-SMITH of Anythink libraries says, "Once the identity is defined, this identity or definition is translated into a cohesive concept. This concept is unique to a particular library, product, or company. The concept is then used to guide all decision making in creating spaces, selecting colors, lighting, materials, integrating interior furnishings, graphics, style of services and programs, use of technology and web presence, engaging and cobranding with community partners, and extending to advertising and public relations" (see figure 8.3).

figure 8.3 **Anythink Banners**

Using Typography

Each of the case libraries was careful in choosing type fonts/styles that would serve the purposes of their new or enhanced brands. At Columbus Metropolitan Library, the house font Gotham was selected because it shifts away from the classic textbook or newspaper look. This font keeps the library looking fresh and in line with current marketing trends. It was chosen because of its contemporary style, multiple weights, and adaptability.

At Anythink, the brand guidelines call for the use of the Vertag font in headlines and subheads and Archer for body copy. This combination offers a variety of weights and styles, allowing for great flexibility in type layout that can be used to aid readability. Recognizing that electronic communications can alter fonts across different platforms, Trebuchet is used for headlines and subheads, and Georgia is used for body copy. The use of fonts and the very specific guidelines that apply are an example of the importance of maintaining consistency across all aspects of your communications.

Unique Value or Selling Propositions and Taglines

Value propositions, as introduced in Chapter 1 and discussed in Chapter 6, are designed to provide a powerful means of conveying the unique value your brand affords—capturing the essence of your brand identity, personality, and image in a single phrase or sentence. It is the perfect backdrop to your brand and should provide an embracing rationale for the expressive elements of your brand—name, aesthetic, and tagline. Your value proposition should, in effect, serve as your elevator speech or your thesis sentence, with versatile application for messaging internally with leadership, staff, and volunteers and externally with cardholders, donors, and partners. Value propositions should be used carefully and sparingly in marketing communications, not because they lack power and punch but rather because they do. Overuse can serve to trivialize the value proposition, fatigue the audience, and engender skepticism. This is where good and creative taglines come in.

Taglines are creatively expressive words or short phrases that serve to prompt your value proposition with and among your primary audiences. Apple's "Think Different" is a very good example of a tagline used to facilitate the repositioning of Apple in the marketplace. Not all brands require the use of taglines. The value proposition itself may be succinct and versatile by itself, or it may include the essentials for the tagline to express it, either in a pairing with the brand directly or in association with its offerings, its services and benefits. State Farm's "Like a Good Neighbor . . ." is a tagline that pulls from a more complete value proposition, "Like a Good Neighbor, State Farm Is There," and is a good example of how the two work together.

Crafting creative taglines is not easy and should generally evolve from a carefully conceived process and involve creative talent accustomed to highly market-sensitive word crafting. Generally, taglines will follow one of several paths—serving as either simple descriptors of value (the benefit you realize), differentiators of value (how your benefits are different or are set apart), or the future anticipation of value (the benefit you can expect to realize in the future or aspire to realize). It is important to keep in mind that good taglines should not seek to say too much or overpitch the brand. The best taglines and even slogans are those that evoke (as opposed to explain or provoke) the engagement of the customer, allowing the customer to apply his or her own judgments about levels of quality, service, or performance of the brand. Furthermore, taglines that are overly pitchy tend to put customers off and elevate skepticism (Laran, Dalton, and Andrade 2011, 34). David Heitman provides a good tip when he says, "Let nouns and verbs do the heavy lifting in your new tagline, and avoid too many adjectives" (Heitman 2010).

Aligning Promotion with Your Target Audience

Your promotional strategies and communication tactics draw directly from your brand and your positioning strategy and must resonate with your target markets. Every word, graphic, photo, video, audio, and environmental tactic you employ as an honest expression of your brand must also, and in equally honest fashion, address the uniqueness of your target audience. Positioning strategies support brand strategies. You have already identified your target markets in the process of developing your positioning strategy. That strategy in turn guides development of product, place, price, promotion, and people strategies to guide communications tactics. At each step, you must revisit the target market and keep these customers in the forefront of your thinking. This is where the use of a creative brief comes in (discussed in "Developing a Creative Brief" later in this chapter).

Staying on Message

'Stay on message' is the brand mantra. The best brands speak with one distinctive voice. On the Web, in an advertisement, and in conversations, the company needs to project the same unified message. It must be memorable, identifiable, and centered on the customer" (Wheeler 2006, 48). Staying on message requires a high level of discipline premised on buy-in within the entire library organization. It is helped by

Consistency at Anythink

CONSISTENCY IS VERY important at Anythink. With a minimal budget and facing spending levels among competitors like Starbucks, Barnes & Noble, and larger libraries and museums, Anythink needs a consistent communications expression if it hopes to stand out and "box above our weight" as Ricochet's Bellina puts it. He goes on to emphasize that "Consistent communications make it easier for our target to recognize our messages. We want to train their eyes and earn their attention. Keep in mind an old advertising adage: 'You will get bored with your campaign communications before your customer ever sees them.'" Touch points for Anythink that reinforce brand consistency include customer greetings, library signage, staff and community newsletter, e-mail signatures, press releases, and PR interviews, to name a few.

Communication strategies at Anythink are driven by branding and positioning strategies. The communications department reaches deep into the library's activities. It creates newsletters, press releases, and advertising. The department also writes speeches for staff and board members and coordinates special events, signage, and the public art program. Integrated communication strategies are developed through brand and positioning.

The creative team at Ricochet Ideas devised stealth ways to get the word out without a big budget. Staff members' name tags ask, "What do you think?" hung from easy-to-spot orange lanyards, and T-shirts include slogans like 'Shhh is a four-letter word.' Then there are the banners in the parking lots. To rethink summer reading, Bellina helped the staff put on their "Anythink goggles," as one Anythinker termed it.

Anythink is continually working on the emotional connection between the library and the brand. The library seeks a sense of engagement, feeling and connection, ownership and contribution, present value or takeaway, and future potential (see figure 8.4).

figure 8.4 **Brand Touch Points**

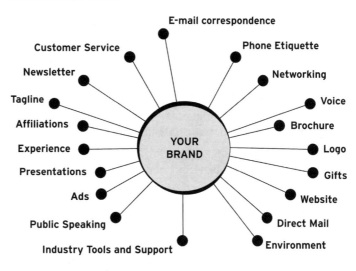

use of clear and easy-to-use communications policies and guidelines, as well as the centralization of brand communications management. Most important, however, is having a process that internalizes the brand and engages the entire library culture.

Creating Brand Touch Points

Touch points represent everything "touched" by the brand and consumers of the brand and may include letterhead, business cards, brochures, library cards, and collateral material such as hats, banners, and tote or book bags. Touch points also include the website, signage, vehicles like bookmobiles and automobiles, staff dress or uniforms, name tags, and facilities. At Anythink, when the new brand was introduced to staff, each staff member was given a specially designed T-shirt and a fleece vest to celebrate the new image. However, the only required uniform is the branded name tag. Anythink T-shirts continue to be incentives for the staff, as are baseball hats, mugs, and blankets. In fact, the demand for these items by the public has the library exploring opportunities to sell them to the community. The library provides messenger bags with the logo at cost to members of the public and sells coffee mugs and travel mugs in the Anythink Café at the Wright Farms location.

At Queens Library, the brand was personally introduced to each staff member through the gift of a high-quality branded T-shirt. A committee of staff members joined together to pick the T-shirt color. It was an immediate hit, and something personal for each employee that reflected the new brand. In subsequent years, staff received a branded baseball cap, folding umbrella, and zippered canvas book bag. Each of these brand items became so popular that the library established an online store to sell the merchandise, not only to employees but also to library patrons who kept asking for them. The Queens Library has sold thousands to date and has extended the line of branded merchandise.

Both of these examples demonstrate the importance of touch points and brand identity. It is imperative to express your brand identity at every opportunity, and with consistency.

Your Website as a Strategic Touch Point

In this Internet-driven world, the websites for most institutions and enterprises have become more than a communications tactic, rising to the level of a "place" strategy as important as, if not more so than, physical buildings and locations. The website serves as a portal of entry for new and returning customers, a platform for virtually all "calls to action" and a place where your target markets can feel at home as they search catalogues and databases, explore new offerings and services, make transactions, arrange for delivery of materials and inter- and intralibrary loans, download materials, and discover new ways to engage with the library. As a strategic touch point for the brand, the website is a platform for marketing communication and must be aligned and carefully integrated into the organization's marketing efforts. That significance may suggest a different organizational structure for the leadership and management of your website. As a "place" strategy, your website also provides a powerful venue to introduce customers to messages they might not have been looking for or expecting, to address their tangential needs or appeal to latent needs or wants, and to introduce and precondition them to offerings, services, promises, and partnerships now and in the future. Leveraging this power begins with having a profound understanding of your customers and appreciating how they utilize the Internet in their daily lives.

"The best websites understand their customers and respect their needs and preferences. A company's website should quickly answer these questions: Who is this company? What's in it for me?" (Wheeler 2006, 138). At the same time, the best websites reflect the brand in all of its dimensions and fully express the value proposition throughout.

When designing your website, keep in mind your goals, audience needs, key messages, and brand personality as you make every decision regarding the site (Wheeler 2006, 139). You should anticipate future growth, measure usage (web hits), and change, update, and evaluate your website. Conduct tests to understand your customers' ability to navigate the site and retrieve information needed. Keep in mind that the marketplace of popular websites from Amazon to Apple to Disney establishes customers' expectations for what a good website experience can and should be.

Develop a plan and position resources, either in-house or outsourced, to monitor, maintain, refresh, and continually update your site. In the process, make sure you are continually optimizing your site to concurrently attract and hold the attention of your target markets based on the information they are seeking and utilizing. Use analytic tools available, including those available for free (www.google.com /analytics), that can help you track site usage and patterns. Websites, like all other place environments, require management that includes the analysis of traffic in, around, and out of the site to measure traffic trends and control traffic so you are certain you are attracting and serving the markets you seek and avoiding or minimizing unwanted traffic or traffic overload.

Anythink continues to develop its website. Future development is focused on seamless integration between the website and the catalogue to allow for an easy, functional, and fun user experience. The library is regularly conducting usability testing and discussing with customers their online needs. Two-way interaction continues to build as plans are in the works for staff blogs, community discussion boards, and customer comments and ratings.

Facilities as Strategic Touch Points

Library facilities, including main or central libraries, branches, storefront or satellite settings, kiosks, vehicles, and even booths at special events, are by definition strategic brand touch points. Exterior design, landscaping, signage, and external and internal displays all contribute to the brand experience of customers and provide a means for the library to promote the brand. Perhaps most important, facilities are designed not only to serve the external customer but also to provide a venue to effectively deploy "people" strategies—leveraging the immense resource, talent, energy, and personality represented by the library staff and volunteers. So in a very real way, library facilities provide the environment for the most critical brand touch points of all—those that are human. Arguably, of all the touch points a customer will experience along the path of interaction with the library brand, it will be the human touch points that make the most difference, and of those it will be the face-to-face touch points that are the most impactful and enduring. And those touch points will generally occur in context to a place in the form of a physical facility.

Vehicles Reflect Your Branded Image

Automobiles, bookmobiles, vans, and service mobiles reflect your branded image and can be traveling billboards for your service while also performing important place functions (see figure 8.5). Vehicles offer a unique, effective, and exciting way to advertise to and engage customers. Vehicles should have a consistent brand image and identity. Those who operate them, whether driving safely down the road, delivering products or services to customers, or formally representing the library in off-site locations, should be brand aware and properly prepared to represent the brand accordingly.

figure 8.5 **Anythink Bookmobile**

BRAND ARCHITECTURE IN SUMMARY

Brand architecture is the conceptual framework for expressing your brand. It integrates your positioning strategy and deploys your marketing mix. The process of developing or refining the brand architecture applies equally well to new brands or to the refurbishment or repositioning of existing brands, and extends beyond the utility of improving communications to include the building of a valuable and enduring organizational asset. In this section we have reviewed key elements of brand architecture, including the use of graphic visual elements, typography, value propositions and taglines, and the critical importance of aligning and staying on message and creating powerful brand touch points, with particular emphasis on websites, facilities, and vehicles. People are also part of your brand architecture. Just as an architectural rendering of a building will typically include people to express the human dimension, so must your brand architecture factor in the people—customers, librarians, volunteers, and partners.

Developing Your Promotional Plan

Development of your promotional plan is the final step prior to implementation and begins with getting your messaging strategies clear, selecting the best tactical approaches available to you, and evaluating the effectiveness of both. Your promotional plan will involve making decisions in four key areas, plus the establishment of benchmarks or measures for evaluating each (Lee and Kotler 2011, 320):

1. **Message**—What do you want to communicate?

2. **Messengers**—Who will deliver your messages?

3. **Creative strategy**—What will you convey in your messages and how do you want to say it?

4. **Communication channels**—Where and when will your messages appear?

Anythink Positions through Incredible Spaces

THERE IS A place for everyone at Anythink. The libraries are designed to meet multiple needs and activities, quiet or active, solo or communal. Customers can sit quietly by the fireplace and gaze out the windows, or they can play in the tree houses or special entrances to the children's area. There is even a place for teens to play Wii, watch movies, or listen to music.

The exteriors of the new Anythink libraries are contemporary and simple in design. They are very much in keeping with the young audiences to which they are appealing and not what you would expect a library to look like. However, the interiors sing the language of the library. They include wood shelv-ing, fireplaces, elegant lighting, and a dramatic tree house in the children's room. They are discernible as libraries but with some major tweaks. Most important, instead of a reference desk there are "service perches"—stand-up stations where guides and concierges offer quick assistance. In planning these spaces, the key decision-making criteria were anchored to a keen sense of hospitality, intuitive wayfinding, and the creation of spaces for people to interact with information and collaborate with their community. This is a distinctly different direction from regular space planning, which centers on space requirements for shelving, tables, and chairs.

DEVELOPING A CREATIVE BRIEF

The most effective way to establish your message, identify clear messengers, inspire dynamite creative strategies, and select the right communication channels is to develop a *creative brief*. A creative brief is, as the name implies, a distillation of your branding and positioning strategies, including a clear description of your target audience, to guide creative talent in the development of specific communications campaigns and related tactics. The creative brief helps to make sure your communications will be meaningful, believable, and distinctive (Lee and Kotler 2011, 320).

Elements of the Creative Brief

Begin your creative brief by identifying the purpose of your communication. Identify the target audience as well as your communication objectives. Your positioning statement is an essential part of the brief, as are clear statements regarding your brand premise (why the brand is the best choice based on objective or comparative measures) and the brand promise (why the brand is the best choice based on emotional assurances and future/potential value). Finally, your creative brief should identify openings or opportunities suggested by your branding and positioning strategies and the target market research that supports those strategies.

Format and Presentation of the Creative Brief

A creative brief should be developed for each major promotional tactic or combination of tactics, sometimes referred to as a marketing campaign, to which you are committing your organization. The process of developing a creative brief imposes the duty to carefully plan and research the effort before committing resources to the creative process, especially to costly implementation. A good creative brief should be just that, brief. A page or two at most, the creative brief should clearly and quickly summarize all of the essentials to frame and stimulate the creative process.

MESSAGES AND MESSENGERS

Identify what you want your target audiences to do, what you want them to know, and what you want them to believe (Lee and Kotler 2011, 328). An effective message should lead to one or more calls to action. As for messengers, consider people or organizations that align with your brand and the audience you are seeking to reach. Due diligence is critical, ensuring that your messenger is capable of communicating with your audience in a manner that resonates with them while conveying the message easily and naturally and in a manner that reinforces your brand—identity, personality, and image. One way to assess the qualifications of messengers is to compare their expressed values with that of your organization and to critically evaluate how effective they will be in conveying your message. If you seem to have insufficient information about either, no matter the popularity of the messenger, you are not ready to engage this messenger in the important task of carrying your message.

CREATIVE STRATEGY

Your creative strategy includes the content of your message and the careful word crafting of the message, including graphic elements to complement the written or spoken word. It also includes everything from logos, typeface, taglines, headlines, copy, visuals and colors, and sounds (in broadcast media). It also can include social and new media. Above all, strive for elegant simplicity, clarity, and a careful balancing of emotional and functional appeal. Have fun and keep strategy always in mind. Engage the most creative individuals on your team and seek outside resources to complement your internal talents. Finally, manage the creative process in a manner that encourages creative thinking and imaginative leadership within the team by establishing trust, fostering collaborative analysis and synthesis, and employing techniques that encourage a "yes, and . . ." approach to idea generation and development. See "A Final Word about Leadership" at the end of Chapter 9 for more on this subject.

Selecting Communication Channels

Professionals within the marketing/advertising world have migrated beyond traditional channels, such as television, radio, outdoor, and print advertising, to a more integrated mix that now includes social media on mobile phones, interactive websites, Facebook pages, YouTube, blogs, Twitter, podcasts and webcasts, online forums, wikis, and others. Libraries too have evolved in their use of communications channels, favoring those most directly aligned with the markets they serve, the partnerships they develop, and the limited resources they have available. Luckily, the evolution of communication channels, including social media and new media, presents options that are not necessarily cost intensive. However, effective use of such channels requires careful considering of strategy and the commitment of supportive resources to ensure success. This section guides you through the final step in developing your promotional plan—deciding on the most efficient and effective mix of media channels to reach and inspire your audiences.

VARIETIES OF COMMUNICATION CHANNELS AND MEDIA VEHICLES

As you are selecting the communication channels you will use, you will be faced with decisions regarding (1) types of communication channels, (2) specific media vehicles within those types, (3) the timing for your communications, and (4) budget considerations for both dollar and people resource requirements. Let's begin with the types and implications for each.

Types of Media

In the broadest sense, there are basically four types of media as defined by the medium employed, including print, electronic, web, and personal. Print media addresses a huge range of traditional approaches to marketing, and while print still has its place, it is increasingly combined with more personalized and direct approaches enabled by the Web. Print media include ads, posters, banners, postcards, direct mail, brochures, flyers, news releases, business cards, classifieds, billboards, catalogues, and so on.

Electronic media is often associated with mass media—designed to reach large groups of people primarily via television and radio. Although there is a mass quality to television and radio, they increasingly focus on niche audiences with their combination of programming content and advertising. Television affords visual impact, while radio offers advantages in cost and the ability to target niche audiences and align with localized events.

The Web is now among the most ubiquitous and personalized of media, with reach potential into nearly every household in every market. Once considered a limited media with a highly defined niche audience, the Web is now accessible from home, work, school, community centers, libraries, and coffee shops and via computer, phone, or other smart devices hitting the market daily. A web presence, optional just a decade or so ago, is now essential for every organization, particularly those in the information and education sectors. The Web serves as a powerful integrator of marketing messages and mix. Social media is an outgrowth of the Web, affording highly personalized access to markets and the ability to engage with the brand in a highly personalized manner.

Despite the rise in electronic media, however, personal face-to-face connection has never been more important, especially for libraries. The fifth "P," people, captures the importance of human contact in cultivating and establishing relationships with customers and with target markets of present and future customers. Libraries are particularly well positioned to leverage their people resources as a primary marketing media.

Electronic Media and Mass Media Channels

Mass media channels are used when you want to reach large groups of people quickly. These media types typically include newspapers, television, and radio. If you are more selective in your target audience, you can use direct mail, flyers, brochures, posters, and the Internet. The more personalized media channels include social network sites like Facebook, blogs and microblogs like Twitter, podcasts and webcasts, life workshops, seminars, and training sessions. The infomercial is another form of mass media that offers a personalized experience for both participants and viewers.

Television and Radio Stations

If you are selecting television as your medium, which stations will you select and for what reasons? If radio stations were the chosen marketing channel, again you would have to choose specific stations as well as consider specific geographic, demographic, and psychographic market segments. Such choices are made by careful analysis of your viewer or listener audience and the penetration or listenership among a target audience, as well as significant cost/budget considerations. Other communication channel types of particular relevance to libraries might (continued on page 150)

Advertising at Queens Library

AN ADVERTISING CAMPAIGN was developed to introduce the new Queens Library brand. Many new Americans so prevalent in the Queens Borough do not have a cultural heritage of public libraries in their home countries and are reluctant to enter an official-looking building flying the U.S. or New York State flag. Enticing these individuals and their families into the library with its many benefits is a big challenge. Again, the pictures reflecting the diversity of Queens Library employees in advertising material were a plus. The marketing staff used bus posters and community newspapers that featured photos of actual employees. Those employees had come from Puerto Rico, Trinidad, India, and China, as well as the United States. The headline for these ads was, "I Am Your Queens Library." Residents saw familiar-looking faces in their new environment with the names, titles, and library locations listed. The initial campaign created confidence for customers to come into the library and get a library card.

There was also a surprise benefit. Staff members responded enthusiastically to the new Queens Library brand campaign that featured them. They applauded the fact that senior management recognized the essential role all employees play in the library's success by featuring them in the ads. Shortly after the campaign launched, more staff members appeared at the marketing department offering photos of themselves for the campaign. Internal research showed that employee morale had substantially increased as a result of the ads.

Many of the staff not only work in Queens but live there as well. A funny thing began to happen. Employees featured in the ad campaign began being stopped on the street or in supermarkets. "You're the library lady on the side of the buses," people would say. One staffer started to get ardent fan e-mail. Many customers were proud that "their" librarian was in the campaign. A key part of the brand strategic positioning statement—"Queens Library has a friendly, supportive, and professional staff"—was successfully communicated by highlighting and including the employees. There also was a circular benefit here: by staff publicly declaring their commitment to service, they were raising the bar for their own performance and that of their colleagues.

Queens Library had not had either an advertising budget in the past or a significant advertising program, even when advertising space was donated. In fact, the entire operating budget of the library was only slightly more than the advertising budget for corporate giant General Electric. There are many communities within the Queens Library system, and each community has local weekly newspapers, both free and subscription based. Marketing staff called on the publishers of these neighborhood publications and explained that the library was developing its brand and needed a means of communication that would be of benefit to both newspaper and the library. Marketing staff were able to negotiate rates with the local publications, sometimes up to 50 percent off, to get the ball rolling. Developing highly targeted and creatively visual ads, marketing staff satisfied local newspapers that the library was indeed localizing its focus and at the same time enhancing the look and feel of their publications.

The library could not afford TV or radio advertising, so the staff focused on outdoor and transportation advertising—a good fit for the markets it served and much more approachable for pricing advantages. The transportation district was asked to provide the library with free ad space, knowing that it was January and advertising revenues were predictably down for buses and subway. It addition to prevailing on them as good corporate citizens, the Queens Library marketing staff promised good visual ads that they could use to fill the voids of vacant ad space. The placement was successful, and six months later the library ads could still be seen in prominent spaces that had not otherwise sold (see figure 8.6).

BAITING THE HOOK: GRABBING THE ELUSIVE NONUSER WITH ARRESTING ADS

The Queens Library focused on reaching as many people as possible, particularly elusive nonusers. Although people between the ages of eighteen and thirty-four are notoriously difficult to reach, there is an entire group of people both younger and older who simply have no idea what a public library has to offer. Research reveals that nonusers tend to have a very dated or incomplete view

figure 8.6 **Transit Ad for Queens Library**

figures 8.7, 8.8, 8.9 **Love, Eat, and Surf** @ **Queens Library**

of public libraries, typically reaching back to their childhood. Some of these nonusers imagine elderly librarians in glasses with hair tied back in severe buns. They remember being shushed or told to leave the library because of boisterous conversations with friends. They envision catalogues with yellowing, typewritten cards. Younger nonusers may have little if any connection with libraries and simply assume that their portable devices with access to search engines and social media give them all the access to information they need. Still other nonusers may be from countries where public libraries do not exist, are few and distant, or have very limited collections or services.

The marketing and communications department saw these misperceptions as a challenge worth taking on and asked, "How do we change the perceptions of nonusers? How do we give them a more contemporary and relevant sense for what the library offers them?" Pursuing those local, neighborhood newspapers was a first step. They developed crisp, communicative, and highly targeted ads that by visual design and unexpected headlines disrupted the traditional view of libraries and spoke directly to the interests of nonusers. Here are some examples.

FIND LOVE @ QUEENS LIBRARY

The Love @ Queens Library ad campaign was an attention grabber, with a visually arresting image of a female vampire taking a bloody bite out of the shoulder of her half-clothed male companion. The copy, "Love might bite, but not at Queens Library," drew nonusers in, making them rethink their traditional view of libraries.

A rollout of accompanying collateral materials was coordinated to coincide with the print ads. When customers came through the doors of the sixty-three neighborhood libraries, they saw full-color, oversized posters and stand-up tent cards featuring the ad. In this way, the ad reinforced the themes and messages and made an immediate connection between external advertising and the user experience. The campaign was timed to coincide with the major theatrical release of the film *Twilight* (see figure 8.7).

WHET YOUR TASTE BUDS

The next ad addressed something else that Americans love to do—eat! With the success of TV shows like *Top Chef* and magazines like *Every Day with Rachael Ray*, it is clear how many people prioritize buying, preparing, and eating food. Immediately after the Love campaign, Queens ran its Eat @ Queens Library campaign during the holiday season, promoting the vast collection —46,000 cookbooks available—a literal feast to be had by just asking (see figure 8.8).

HANG TEN

Some nonusers are well versed in technology, particularly blogging, tweeting, and other forms of social networking. A third ad, titled Surf @ Queens Library, was introduced in January 2010, featuring surfboards in warm and inviting rainbow colors on a beautiful ocean background. The copy lets viewers know that they can "ride the technology wave" with more than 1,500 computer workstations and fast Internet access (see figure 8.9).

(continued from page 147) include transportation channels like buses and light rail, transportation hubs, or congregate areas like bus stops, shopping malls, schools, senior centers, health care settings, and corporate environments.

Timing of Your Promotional Strategies

The timing of your communication is another consideration. You will need to make decisions regarding the months, weeks, days, and hours when campaign elements will be implemented or aired. Your decisions are guided by when your target audience can most likely be reached and in context to the milestones and events that relate to your brand and your offerings, including new program announcements, new releases and introductions of materials and services, and important events in the life of the library and the community (Lee and Kotler 2011, 159).

Advertising and Your Promotional Strategies

Advertising is traditionally any form of paid presentation of ideas. The most common channels for advertising include television, radio, newspapers, magazines, direct mail, and a variety of outdoor opportunities such as transit signage, kiosks, and billboards. Organizations that regularly buy advertising usually employ an advertising agency to design and negotiate placement of the advertisements. Public radio sponsorships offer libraries an opportunity to reach influential and loyal customers through cobranding opportunities. Although considered advertising, public radio sponsorships provide for mutual promotion of services and causes important to the community.

THE WEBSITE

The website has become more than a communications tactic; in fact, in many libraries it is considered the "online branch." The website serves as a portal for new and returning customers, as well as a platform for virtually all calls to action. It also serves as a place where customers can feel at home while searching catalogues and databases, exploring new offerings and services, making transactions, arranging for delivery of materials and inter- and intralibrary loans, downloading materials, and discovering new ways to engage with the library. The website is an essential touch point for the brand.

FACILITIES AND PHYSICAL ENVIRONMENTS AS COMMUNICATION TOOLS

Library facilities, including branches, kiosks, booths, and other permanent or temporary physical environments, are strategic brand touch points. Exterior design, landscaping, signage, and displays also serve external customers by drawing them in. They provide a venue to effectively deploy people strategies by leveraging the immense resources, talent, energy, and personality of the library staff and volunteers. Library facilities and the people who staff and utilize them provide the environments and social contexts for the most critical brand touch points of all.

Public Relations

Public relations as a communications tactic is distinguishable because the mention and coverage of your library brand can be "earned" but not necessarily at a direct cost or expense. While you may pay for public relations advice or even representation, much of what falls under the broad heading of public relations is a shared responsibility of the organization's leadership team, management team, marketing team, frontline staff, volunteers, and community partners. Libraries should do planning for *crisis communication,* as indeed it is better to be trained, prepared, and informed. Libraries are involved in lobbying and media advocacy and need to develop strategies in line with their brand. Many libraries and other organizations employ public relations specialists who are highly skilled and can develop specific public relations programs complete with goals, objectives, strategies, target audiences, and tactics. Here are some tips to guide your public relations initiatives.

PUBLIC RELATIONS TOOLS

Tools for public relations include press releases, press kits, news conferences, editorial boards, letters to the editor, and strong personal relations with key reporters and media representatives, as well as key influencers in the community and the organizations they represent.

Build Relationships

Build relationships with the media, know who covers which areas, and position the library as the reliable source of information to enable the media to do its job. Consider writing regular columns for local newspapers to provide continued recognition of the library and partner with educational and corporate entities in the community to be a source to assist them in their public relations efforts. Libraries are in a particularly good position to align with other organizations as an information source without having to align with those same organizations in other partnership endeavors that may not be compatible with the library brand.

Build Partnerships

Build partnerships (cobranding opportunities) with organizations, including your local chamber of commerce, the League of Women Voters, Rotarians, Lions, and other service clubs, as well as other public and private institutions that will find significant cobrand advantage in the affiliation. As noted previously, carefully assess and select your cobrand partners to ensure that you are value aligned internally and with your target markets. Remember that a strong library brand is your best means to acquiring strong and aligned cobrand partners.

Create News

Create news through special events, receptions, and demonstrations. Participate in community events, fairs, parades, and festivals. Convene a press conference on the library's successes. Create "good news" that enhances the brand and brand strategy of the library and share the good news with your cobrand partners. Be mindful that "bad news" can be powerful as well when considered in the proper light as an opportunity. Recall how Anythink was able to spring-board from the negative news story of a failed library system.

Coordinate Your Public Relations Campaigns

Coordinate public relations campaigns with paid advertising campaigns. Newspapers, for example, are more inclined to print a positive story on an event or program at the library when that story or event accompanies paid advertising.

Advertising and Public Relations in the Wyoming Libraries Campaigns

THE ADVERTISING AGENCY for Wyoming State Library was Barnhart Communications, the same agency that designed and implemented the very successful Wyoming Tourism campaign. The first advertising campaign developed was an awareness campaign to remind Wyoming residents that libraries are an important part of their communities and their lives.

Barnhart did an excellent job in creating a new logo and slogan for all Wyoming libraries, as well as designs, strategies, and campaign tactics for implementing the message. The logo for Wyoming libraries is a cowboy on a bucking book, reminiscent of the bucking horse and rider that is the official trademark of the State of Wyoming. Because the logo is similar to the unique Wyoming logo, it creates a link between libraries and the dispersed residents of Wyoming communities.

Barnhart also created a campaign around the slogan "Bringing the World to Wyoming." In their designs, artists showed elements of something from another part of the world that you would learn about at the library and put it in a Wyoming setting. For example, in one design an image of the Eiffel Tower as a windmill is shown in a field of sheep with the tagline "Bringing the World to Wyoming." In the corner of this image is a stack of books with one titled *Paris* on top.

The other image is of a Trojan horse being pulled by an old pickup truck through a wheat field. This image has a pile of books with the DVD of the film *Troy* on top. Both of these images have been used for numerous marketing materials, including posters, bookmarks, and mouse pads. These images were also designed as billboards and newspaper advertisements, both black-and-white and color. Customers can also order items at the Café Press website with one of these images on them (see figures 8.10 and 8.11).

To supplement these materials, Barnhart also wrote two radio ads with the same message as the print ads. These radio advertisements also described elements of something from another part of the world that you would learn about at the library and put it in a Wyoming setting. The first radio ad has two men hunting for elk, and one hunter begins speaking with a New England accent and talks

figures 8.10, 8.11 **Wyoming Trojan Horse and Wyoming Windmill Eiffel Tower**

Develop Printed Material

Develop necessary printed materials such as newsletters, brochures, bookmarks, catalogues, and other appropriate materials. These materials serve as reminders of library services and programs, but remember that they must be designed to meet the brand guidelines and communication strategies of the library.

PUBLIC RELATIONS AND LIBRARIES

Public relations (PR) programs are designed to further the image and the brand of the library. PR programs are an art used to maintain goodwill for the library. A PR program is essential for your library to stay connected to its various publics, to

about things he has learned at the library. The other ad is about two men fishing on the Snake River, with one man speaking in an English accent about things he has learned at the library. Both of these ads appeal to Wyomingites, especially to men because they are about hunting and fishing. The professional quality of these ads makes them very engaging and humorous.

The launch of the campaign was in February 2006. The Wyoming Library Association hosts a legislative reception every year and invites legislators and the five state elected officials. It is a very popular event hosted by librarians from across the state, and most legislators and elected officials attend each year. As an invitation to the event in 2006, each legislator received a small box with his or her name on the front and a piece of chocolate shaped like a cowboy boot inside, along with a special library card with the legislator's photograph, name, and address on the front. On the back of the card, it said, "Do you have your library card?" The cards were a hit, and more legislators attended than ever before, many of them with their cards in hand to show one another.

During the months of March, April, and June, placement for the marketing campaign involved three areas of the state—Laramie, Fremont, and Sheridan Counties. There were radio ads, billboards and quarter-page ads in the Sunday papers in each of those counties. In September, a statewide launch of the campaign was implemented, with radio ads on at least one radio station in each county, several billboards strategically placed across the state, and a newspaper advertisement placed in every newspaper in the state. September was chosen for the statewide launch because it is library card sign-up month. A guest editorial written by State Librarian Lesley Boughton was also sent to every newspaper in the state to emphasize the importance of "what your library card can do for you." This letter was included in the newspapers at the same time as the rest of the campaign.

The unique element of this campaign involved send-

ing each library in the state a marketing kit, including the twenty-three county libraries, the community college libraries, the University of Wyoming libraries, and all high school libraries in the state. Each marketing kit included fifty posters, one of each design (Eiffel Tower windmill and Trojan horse); twenty mouse pads; fifty plastic bags; twenty-five canvas bags; one hundred bookmarks; and one CD with the logos, radio ads, and newspaper ads for libraries to customize and use themselves. These kits are invaluable to the smaller, rural libraries in the state, where some counties have only three staff members, two of whom are part-time. These libraries do not have the resources to create materials for their own promotional purposes, so these items can be used as part of their local marketing. The libraries also have the option of ordering more materials through the state library.

MUDFLAP GIRL CAMPAIGN

Barnhart Communications, the advertising agency that designed the statewide marketing campaign, also designed the Mudflap Girl campaign. Although a bit controversial, the state library decided on the mudflap girl reading a book. The ad agency designed posters and shiny silver mudflap girl stickers that were mailed along with a letter about the online product to auto parts stores throughout the state. The posters were 12 inches by 18 inches, a size that works well for business doors. The library had a great response statewide, and the mudflap girl stickers can now be found on pickup trucks across Wyoming.

The state library realized that this campaign could cause some controversy; therefore, it allowed the individual counties to opt in or out. Twenty-one of the twenty-three counties decided to participate in the campaign. The University of Wyoming Libraries also participated in the campaign, going so far as to adopt the theme for its homecoming parade float.

listen to the pulse of the community it serves, and to develop positive programs to communicate the brand.

Nontraditional and New Media Channels

Within the context of the Web, social and new media are an evolving and higher personalized media channel. This section expands on the specific application to the library environment.

SOCIAL MEDIA

"To use social media successfully, we must become collaborators, conveners, facilitators, brokers and weavers" (Lee and Kotler 2011, 369). By collaborators, Lee and Kotler suggest that it's important to work *inside* what others have created, including existing blogs and social network sites, and create platforms for group participa-

Columbus Metropolitan Library Levy Campaign and Social Media

IN THE FALL of 2010, Columbus Metropolitan Library (CML) faced a significant levy in an unfortunate economic climate. Its current ten-year levy was expiring and for the first time in twenty-four years an increase was requested of voters. The levy increase would add 0.6 mills, or an average of $5.24 per month on a $100,000 home.

Like many libraries throughout the state, Columbus Metropolitan Library was impacted significantly by state budget cuts. After making $11 million in cuts to deal with the state's funding decrease since 2008, the library knew that this levy was imperative to maintaining customers' demands. The election also marked a governor's race, and CML staff knew the campaign needed to be grassroots in order to share its message in a saturated market. Chief Executive Officer Patrick Losinski said, "I don't want any of us to wake up on November 3 and wonder what we could have done differently."

So the marketing and communications campaign committee got to work developing a social media plan. Social media was only one component of what made the levy a success, but it allowed Columbus Metropolitan Library to directly answer questions on Facebook and Twitter. Although social media offers amazing tools, it can fuel negativity—the last thing a campaign needs. Thus careful management was critical. Social media does offer the perfect forum to rally support and awareness, and that's exactly how it was

utilized for Issue 4, the levy campaign for Columbus Metropolitan Library (see figure 8.12). In the end, Issue 4 was on the ballot in 619 precincts throughout Franklin County and passed in 591 of them.

Here is a snapshot illustrating how the campaign used Facebook leading up to election day:

- The campaign developed a Facebook page to share information with staff, volunteers, and supporters.
- The campaign encouraged people to write on the "Keep Columbus Metropolitan Library Strong" Facebook page wall to keep momentum going.
- By the end of the campaign, almost 3,000 people had "liked" Keep Columbus Metropolitan Library Strong.

figure 8.12 **Issue 4, Levy Campaign**

tion from the beginning. "We must think about using social media in new ways to bring people of common purpose together to get things done" (Lee and Kotler 2011, 369). The library must become a broker, a dynamic resource center where people can exchange advice and information. Libraries need to think of themselves as network weavers, pulling together a number of diverse groups. The creative use of social media and mobile technologies moves past the actual technologies and focuses on how they fit into the lives of people you serve.

Social Media Marketing Is Not Selling

Social media marketing is not about selling. It is about creating relationships and making people feel as if they are a part of your community and your brand. While it is tempting to pitch and promote in the context of social media, nothing will quiet the conversation faster than unwanted solicitation. Social media requires strategies and consistent management to build success. Your brand and your reputation depend on your consistency and management of the social media networks you decide to employ.

Social Media Sites

There are many social media sites; however, the most commonly used sites include Facebook, Twitter, LinkedIn, and YouTube. Beyond these external branded sites, there is the opportunity to develop your own social media venues, including blogs, forums, listservs, and so on. It is good to develop a target market profile for each venue you choose and to design a social media program that fits your objectives, expresses your brand, and addresses the target market. Social media sites offer the opportunity to know the library and to trust the library.

Management of Social Media Sites

Conduct day-to-day management of social media sites and assign responsibility for the management of these sites. It is critical that your brand be personally represented in the sites, stimulating and managing the flow of discussion in some cases, dropping in and offering resources and support in other cases, but always present and always monitoring and assessing the activity. Treat social media as a place strategy, no different from promoting, accommodating, and supporting meetings in your library. And be timely and current, updating postings daily.

Social Media and Your Brand

Social media allows you to opportunity to connect, listen, engage, and build relationships with your customer. This media creates a dialogue between your brand and your customers. The proliferation of social media sites will continue, so make sure that your social media goals track with your brand. Provide value, relevance, and content on your sites while monitoring participation to maximize your brand value.

Evaluation—You Get What You Measure

There is an old adage that reads, "The counter gets what the counter counts." In the world of branding, positioning, and marketing, if you can't measure it, you have not achieved it. The success of your promotional strategies and tactics, if properly planned, designed, and executed, are measurable in terms of actionable success or failure and gradients in between. They are also dynamic in their delivery and interaction and thus by virtue of careful monitoring and evaluation can be refined and modified in process. It is important to address evaluation at the outset based on your consideration of what success will look like and how it will be measured and tracked. The goals you establish early on should be tied to the organization's vision—a key element of brand strategy—and to criteria related to your cost-to-benefit ratio. It is important that the methods and criteria for measurement, tracking, and evaluation be established at the outset.

In general, monitoring refers to measurements conducted sometime after the launch of the effort, during, and before completion. The purpose is to assist you in making midcourse corrections. Evaluating takes place after the campaign is completed and should be used as a base for assessing cost/benefits of the effort and setting the stage for subsequent initiatives.

Measurements for monitoring and evaluation include the reach and frequency of market exposure to each of your campaign tactics. You can measure media coverage as well as the numbers of materials that have been distributed. You can measure the

SocialThink: The Anythink Approach to Social Media

ANYTHINK'S VENTURE INTO social networking in 2009 included a four-pronged objective:

1. Inform the public about Anythink by sharing news, events, and innovations.

2. Interact and engage existing and potential customers.

3. Make friends, followers, and fans feel like Anythinkers.

4. Make connections by connecting people with new ideas, music, movies, books. and articles.

ANYTHINK WEBSITE

As Anythink continues to develop its website, Anythink libraries.org, there are many features to be incorporated that allow two-way interaction between the library staff and users. These include blogs, which will be included on age-specific pages and maintained by staff members; comments and ratings, which can be included on news and events pages; share options on news events pages; and RSS links anywhere that the library has regularly updated content. A SocialThink page will be added to the site as well so that visitors can see all the other places Anythink exists on the Web.

TWITTER

Weekly "tweets" will occur, and then more frequently as news happens and as time allows. Twitter is not only a way to share information with the masses, but it is a great tool for strengthening the voice of Anythink. It's amazing what one can do with only 140 characters; some examples of how we will use Twitter are sharing news stories, events, and videos and highlighting Anythink heroes and Anythink in action throughout our communities and the world. Two-way interaction with followers is also possible through Twitter.

FACEBOOK

Facebook is now the fourth largest site in the world, only behind Google (1), Microsoft sites like MSN (2), and Yahoo! (3). It makes sense for Anythink to be part of Facebook because it's another venue to share Anythink happenings and also continue to strengthen and support our voice. The ways Facebook is used include sharing articles, videos, and events; highlighting Anythink heroes and Anythink in action; sharing new books and movies from our collection; and providing yet another venue for two-way communication with the public that isn't currently available on the website. This is the best example of Anythink being where the customers are, not to mention a great way to build buzz and loyalty to be where the customer will be in the future.

amount of money spent and results obtained. You can conduct surveys and focus groups to measure results in quantitative and qualitative terms. You can compare your results with those of other libraries and development benchmarks, internally and externally, to track comparable performance and trends over time.

Building Brand Champions

It is crucial to engage employees in the meaning of the brand and the thinking behind it. It will be one of the best investments that the library can make. The long-term success of the library and its brand is influenced by the way employees share in the library's culture—its values, mission, vision, stories, and symbols. Enlisting the employees as brand champions builds the success. After all, it is not just the values of the library, it is the sharing of those values that makes the difference.

Companies all around the world are beginning to develop compelling ways of sharing the brand essence with their employees. Corporations are realizing how important it is to build brand involvement among their employees and are committing significant funds to building their brands through their employees.

"This may be the place where strategy is the most important. We want to share information with our 'friends' without spamming them. It's very easy for them to 'hide' updates; we don't want that. A balance of frequency and content type is necessary for people to anticipate our updates rather than become annoyed by them," says Stacie Ledden, communications manager.

FLICKR
The value of Flickr is that the public can not only get a visual sense of what Anythink is doing, but they can also link to these photos in their blogs and social media sites. Media can also access these photos to supplement articles, forging a lasting and mutually beneficial bond between the library and local media.

GOODREADS
As ideas become the focus at Anythink instead of books, Goodreads is a great place to remember what has brought most of the staff together—a passion for reading. Not only is it a great tool for staff to keep track of what they're reading and want to read, the "I Love My Anythink" group also allows staff to bond with each other and the public through this shared passion. Bookshelves allow the public to see what Anythinkers are reading; reviews allow our staff to show off their personalities; discussions encourage interaction; polls let us tap into the public's interests; and event postings help us spread the work about great things happening at Anythink. Individual branches can use the site to show what their

book clubs are reading and spark discussion on the site with book club members outside of their meeting times. Another aspect of Goodreads that is often overlooked is the accessibility of authors. Many authors these days are responsible for promoting themselves and many do this through Goodreads.

YOUTUBE
YouTube was founded in 2005 and has since become a site ingrained in our culture. As a free, easy way to share videos, it also infers a certain status to videos, depending on how many views a video gets and its star ratings. It also makes it easy to share videos with large amounts of people through site search and linking to blogs and social networking sites. As Anythink continues to explore video as a means of sharing the story, it can continue to post classes, events, and stories to share with the world. Viewers can then provide a star rating to the videos posted.

CONCLUSION
Anythink's venture into social networking isn't a matter of *will we*—it's a matter of *when*. Anythink seeks to be where its customers are to be competitive with the many distractions in today's world and to continue to establish the relevance of the library. Beyond that, social networking is enjoyable and engaging, and so is Anythink. The strategy needs to be sustainable. The library wants to ensure that whatever it commits to, it will be able to manage with success.

USING INTERNAL AND EXTERNAL DESIGN TEAMS

Brand programs are often developed by outside firms that have the experience and qualifications to develop new branding strategies. In-house designers often implement the bulk of the brand programs once launched and brand standards have been developed. It is critical to understand the role that the internal design department will play in implementing and managing your brand. The new brand is an asset that needs to be managed and nurtured.

You must also coordinate the brand program standards between the external branding firm and the internal staff. The new program and its rationale must be introduced to the internal team. The key to success is to appoint a project manager, a person who coordinates the identity program between the external design firm and your internal design resources.

DEVELOPING BRAND STANDARDS AND GUIDEBOOKS

Brand guidebooks, often referred to as standards or guides, are created to inspire, educate, and apply brand awareness internally. A brand book will get your brand strategy out of the conference room and into the hands of staff who will communicate the brand strategy and guide implementation. The vision for your library and the meaning of a brand require that a communications vehicle be available, accessible, and personal to all employees and volunteers. The brand guide should outline who you are and what your brand stands for, as well as provide standards, templates, and guidelines.

MANAGING CONSISTENCY AND INTEGRITY OF THE BRAND

Managing consistency and integrity of a brand requires a set of standards and guidelines that are easily accessible to all staff, volunteer organizations, foundation office, and all other internal and external audiences associated with the library. Building a brand is viewed as the shared responsibility of each and every employee. Adhering to the guidelines requires discipline and vigilance. This adherence will save money and time and will help build the brand.

Libraries are in the midst of change and need to convey direction to their staff and to their stakeholders. The brand identity process sparks a new clarity about the brand and the brand essence, and the process can serve to emotionally and intellectually engage staff in ways to enable the culture to address change and new opportunities. Communicating to each employee can help build the brand and involve each employee in delivering the brand promise.

Evaluation at Anythink

OVER THE PAST two years, the community has come to view the library as an asset and essential service. Attendance at programs has grown from 4,063 in 2007 to 40,550 in 2010. Circulation of materials has increased by 300 percent since 2007, and public computing has increased by 400 percent. Awards include the 2010 IMLS National Medal for Library Service, the 2011 John Cotton Dana Public Relations Award, and the naming of the Anythink Wright Farms location the 2010 *Library Journal* Landmark Library. Anythink has been featured in articles in the *Los Angeles Times, Library Journal,* and the *Denver Post.* Local business leaders noted Anythink as one of the outstanding success stories in Adams County.

Success at Columbus Metropolitan Library

HOW DOES COLUMBUS Metropolitan Library know that its efforts have worked?

- Received the Association of Marketing and Communication Professional Gold Hermes International Creative Award for outstanding design
- Selected as the Library of the Year for 2010 by *Library Journal*
- Increased private funds from less than $500,000 to over $6 million
- Raised $4 million toward our endowment
- Won the 2011 Medal for Community Service from the IMLS
- Reached 25,000 Facebook fans

Summary

This chapter began with a discussion of the brand architecture as a foundation for your promotional strategy. The brand architecture begins with a conceptual framework for expressing your brand identity, personality, and image by integrating your positioning strategy through the product mix. The discussion included the use of strategic touch points and tactics that apply to brochures, signage, building design, vehicles, name tags, library cards, collateral materials, advertising, social media, public relations, and website design. All of these strategies and tactics build on the foundation of your brand and your positioning strategy.

The brand architecture is the foundation for your promotional strategy. It also addresses the structure and interrelationship of brands within your library, including branches, collections, programs, and services. The brand architecture serves to frame the big ideas and specific emotions around which you want to build your brand.

Discussion extends to elements of the brand, including the logo, value propositions, and taglines. Your value proposition is often known as your elevator speech, while taglines are creative, expressive words or phrases that serve to prompt your value proposition with and among your primary audiences.

Your promotional strategies and communications tactics draw directly from your brand and your positioning strategy and must resonate with your target markets. Every word, graphic, photo, video, audio, and environmental tactic you employ needs to address and resonate with your target market. Touch points represent everything "touched" by the brand and by consumers of the brand, including your letterhead, business cards, brochures, library cards, collateral material including hats, banners, and tote or book bags. Touch points also include the website, signage, vehicles like bookmobiles and automobiles, staff dress or uniforms, name tags, and facilities.

We reviewed key elements of brand architecture, including the use of graphic visual elements, typography, value propositions and taglines, and the critical importance of aligning and staying on message, and creating powerful brand touch points, with particular emphasis on websites, facilities, and vehicles.

Developing your promotional plan begins with getting your messaging strategies clear, selecting the best tactical approaches available to you and evaluating the effectiveness of both. Your promotional plan will involve making decisions in four key areas, plus establishing benchmarks or measures for evaluating each. It is important to identify the *message,* the *messengers,* and the *creative strategy.* The most effective way to establish your messages, identify clear messengers, and inspire dynamic creative strategies is to develop a *creative brief.* A creative brief is a distillation of your branding and positioning strategies, including a clear description of your target audiences, that is used to guide creative talent in the development of specific communications campaigns.

Professionals within the marketing/advertising world have migrated beyond traditional channels, including television, radio, outdoor, and print advertising, to a more integrated mix that now includes social media, mobile phones, interactive websites, Facebook pages, YouTube, blogs, Twitter, podcasts and webcasts, and online forums. Basically, there are four types of media—electronic (TV and radio), print, web, and personal. Public relations as a communications tactic is a shared responsibility of the library's leadership team, management team, marketing team, frontline staff, volunteers, and community partners. Social media marketing is more about creating relationships and making people feel as if they are a part of your community and your brand.

It is crucial to engage employees in the meaning of the brand and the thinking behind it. It will be one of the best investments the library can make. The long-term success of the library and its brand is influenced by the way the employees share in the library's culture—its values, mission, vision, stories, and symbols. Enlisting the employees as brand champions builds the success. After all, it is not just the values of the library, it is the sharing of those values that makes the difference.

Brand guidebooks are created to inspire, educate, and create brand awareness internally and externally. The brand strategy does no good sitting in the conference room or isolated in the marketing department. Managing consistency and the integrity of a brand identity requires a set of standards and guidelines that are easily accessible to all staff, volunteer organizations, foundation office, and all other inter-

Mudflap Girl Campaign in Wyoming

THERE WAS AN unexpected and overwhelming response to this campaign. The library accomplished its goals and expectations for Wyoming and did indeed reach its target audience with humor and effective communication tactics. The campaign brought humor and lighthearted response to libraries. Even the governor's staff had copies in their offices.

The surprise was the response of the library community across the nation and the world. Wyoming libraries caused quite a stir, both positive and negative. Mudflap Girl caused stronger reactions than had been anticipated. At the state library, over 200 e-mails were received within the first weeks after the image was revealed on the library listservs—about 75 percent positive and wanting to know where to get stickers for themselves.

The Mudflap Girl reading has been featured in *Library Hotline, Library Journal, American Libraries,* and the *Wall Street Journal.* Hundreds of blogs have discussed the branding image, including library blogs and marketing and business blogs. Marketing presentations for libraries use her as an example. Library marketing classes at universities include her in the curriculum. Members of the state library staff have been asked to speak at several conferences across the country about their marketing campaign and Mudflap Girl.

EVALUATION OF CAMPAIGN TO BRING THE WORLD TO WYOMING

Response to the campaign has been overwhelming. Every library in the state was included and bought into the campaign—*it was their campaign.* Wyoming libraries have seen a 21 percent increase in library cardholders. In 2005, there were 306,550; by 2007, there were 389,050 cardholders. This means that 78 percent of Wyoming residents have their own Wyoming library card in a state where the population is just over 500,000.

A surprising result of the campaign has been the response from other libraries across the country. The state library has received inquiries from all over the United States and been asked to present the campaign to other state library associations. The campaign has won the John Cotton Dana Award. Wyoming libraries really have been "Bringing the World to Wyoming."

nal and external audiences associated with the library. Building a brand is viewed as the shared responsibility of each and every employee.

REFERENCES

Heitman, David. 2010. "Here's How to Write a Great Tagline." *Coloradobix,* March 23. www.Cobizmag.com/articles/heres-how-to-write-a-great-tagline.

Knapp, Duane E. 2000. *The Brand Mindset.* New York: McGraw-Hill.

Laran, Juliano, Amy N. Dalton, and Eduardo B. Andrade. 2011. "Why Consumers Rebel Against Slogans." *Harvard Business Review,* November. www.hbr.org/2011/11/why-consumers-rebel-against-slogans/ar/1.

Lee, Nancy R., and Philip Kotler. 2011. *Social Marketing: Influencing Behaviors for Good.* 4th ed. Los Angeles: Sage.

Wheeler, Alina. 2006. *Designing Brand Identity: A Complete Guide to Creating, Building and Maintaining Strong Brands.* Hoboken, NJ: Wiley.

———. 2009. *Designing Brand Identity: An Essential Guide for the Whole Branding Team.* Hoboken, NJ: Wiley.

CHAPTER 9

Advocating
for Libraries

[Librarians] are subversive. You think they're just sitting there at the desk, all quiet and everything. They're like plotting the revolution, man. I wouldn't mess with them.
—Michael Moore (www.goodreads.com/quotes)

HY DO SOME COMPANIES THRIVE IN uncertainty, even chaos, and others do not? When buffeted by tumultuous events, when hit by big, fast-moving forces that we can neither predict nor control, what distinguishes those who perform exceptionally well from those who underperform or worse?" (Collins and Hansen 2011, 2). Brands that break through the challenges of today's environment are those able to forge strong, enduring, and resilient relationships with their marketplace—organizations and enterprises for which brand loyalty is a differentiating asset. As an institutional category, libraries have distinct advantages when it comes to the business of establishing brand loyalty on behalf of the markets they serve. At the same time, libraries that have been less than aggressive about branding, positioning, and promotion are finding themselves vulnerable to the changes in today's marketplace—vulnerable to the challenge of relevancy. This big idea of relevancy transcends increasing market share and mind share among specifically targeted audiences, extending to the even bigger idea of advocacy—supporting the transformative role of libraries in our society. Libraries are well positioned to leverage strong emotional attachments with their customers

and their communities, to advocate on behalf of their own localized transformative value, and to extend the glow of that transformative value to other organizations and institutions with which they partner.

Loyalty is defined by the *Merriam-Webster Dictionary* as being loyal, or "unswerving in allegiance," which implies that good brands create loyal followings among their customers, and in turn customers develop strong emotional attachments to the brand. When the going gets tough, it's the brand that provides the basis for a loyal relationship, the motive force that drives overt expressions of loyalty, and the organizational resilience from within and outside to expedite recovery, renewal, and redirection to capture and sustain that loyalty.

As discussed in earlier chapters, a brand is so much more than a new name or a new look or a tagline. The brand is everything and everything is the brand. The brand is your strategy, your aspiration and inspiration, and the progress you make and milestones that mark your fulfillment of shared goals. Your brand is a call to action, is reflected in your customer service, and is expressed in your website and related communication tools. Your brand is your people, your facilities, and of course, your name, aesthetic, and value proposition. "The brand is about caring about your business at every level and in every detail, from the big things like mission and vision, to your people, your customers and to every interaction anyone is ever going to have with you, no matter how small" (Pallotta 2011).

Good brands and the branding process enable the development of enduring relationships with and among people—relationships to weather seismic and threatening vectors of change, chaos, politics, economics, technology, markets, and choices available to markets (see figure 9.1). Those characteristics that we seek in trusted relationships with people we also seek in brands. Attributes of authenticity, clarity, honesty, integrity, charisma, warmth, assertiveness, approachability, passion, quality, innovation, reliability, and originality represent a few of the most salient characteristics to which people are attracted. This is true because these characteristics translate to the perceived benefits of any relationship—benefits that enable people

figure 9.1 **Brand and Chaos**

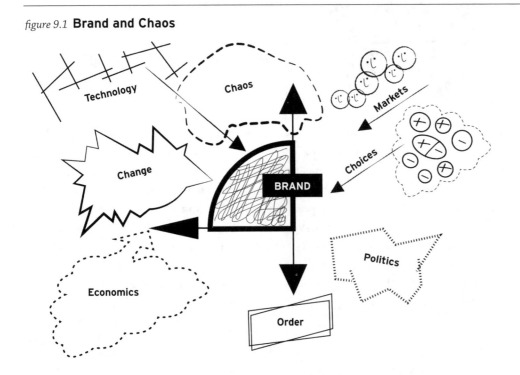

Steve Jobs and the Apple Brand

STEVE JOBS WAS largely responsible for creating, recovering, and renewing the Apple brand amid the perils of difficult economic times, the challenges of stiff competition, and problems within the Apple culture of investors and employees. He was able to leverage, perpetuate, and expand the base of customer loyalty to first survive and then invent new paths to thrive and redefine an entire industry. Launching a new ad campaign under the tagline "Think Different" in 2002, Jobs translated a simple two-word slogan to an embracing value proposition that endures to this day in the minds of loyal customers, employees, investors, and strategic partners.

to cope, solve problems, and find meaning. After all, people don't buy products or even services. According to Theodore Levitt, "They buy solutions to problems" (Levitt 1983, 76). "People also buy personalities and meanings associated with the story of those products. People will only find meanings in brands with personality" (Dawson 2011). The library brand can deliver on all of these attributes and more. Libraries enable the capacity to cope amidst difficulty, to solve the most challenging of problems, and to find meaning in all the dimensions of life and living. Leaders of libraries are in a powerful position to express these very attributes as they leverage and develop their library's brand, positioning, and promotional strategies.

This chapter will discuss the advantages of formulating a solid and enduring brand platform, a carefully honed positioning strategy, and creatively inspired promotional strategies and tactics to address the challenges of today and seize the opportunities of tomorrow.

OCLC Study *From Awareness to Funding*

According to the OCLC study *From Awareness to Funding*, "U.S. public libraries are facing marketing and advocacy challenges that have been faced by other 'super brands.' Lessons learned and successes achieved can be applied to increase library funding. Utilizing marketing and advocacy techniques targeted to the right community segments with the right messages and community programs, we can improve the state of public library funding" (DeRosa and Johnson 2008, viii). The quantitative research identified that a sizable segment of library funding supporters exists—the library's Super Supporters and Probable Supporters. They can be identified and differentiated from U.S. residents less likely to support library funding. Their perceptions, attitudes, and beliefs about the library can be documented and profiled. But can these two groups be moved to action? (DeRosa and Johnson 2008, 6-1).

The belief that the library is a transformational force in people's lives is directly related to their potential for active political and funding support:

> The most likely library funding supporters do not view the library as a source of information, but rather as a source for transformation. The rewards identified by library supporters that are more associated with information, such as "allows you to immerse yourself in another culture" and "doesn't just present facts, but rather helps them come alive," provide useful insights into the mindset held by this group. (DeRosa and Johnson 2008, 4-12)

Attributes associated with this "purposeful transformation" quadrant of the Emotional and Intellectual Rewards Framework include the following:

- Helps create who you are
- Makes you feel good about yourself
- Allows you to appreciate the beauty in life
- Lets you come away feeling like you really learned something
- Fills you with hope and optimism
- Empowers you
- Helps you seek truth
- Serves a serious purpose

The OCLC report goes on to describe how perceptions of the library as a transformative brand translate directly to funding support. "Belief that the library is a self-actualization tool is directly related to level of funding support." Library funding support is an attitude, not a demographic. According to the OCLC report, library support is only marginally related to visitation. "Advocating for library support to library users focuses effort and energy on the wrong target group. While frequency of library visitation and awareness of the full range of library services are not key determinants of library funding support, respondents' perceptions of the public librarian have a strong influence on funding support. Analysis of the responses shows that a strong positive rating for the librarian across five of these attributes has a strong influence on library funding support." The five important attributes of the "passionate" librarian—by extension the "personality" of the library's brand—identified in the OCLC report include the following:

- True advocate for lifelong learning
- Passionate about making the library relevant again
- Knowledgeable about every aspect of the library
- Well-educated
- Knowledgeable about the community

"The library occupies a very clear position in people's minds as a provider of practical answers and information. This is a very crowded space, and to remain relevant in today's information landscape, repositioning will be required . . . Elected officials are supportive of the library—but not fully committed to increasing funding. Engaging Super Supporters and Probable Supporters to help elevate library funding needs is required" (DeRosa and Johnson 2008, 4-16). The library brand, properly positioned and promoted, becomes a catalytic resource for engaging supporters in advocacy and influencing the behaviors of elected officials.

COLUMBUS METROPOLITAN LIBRARY

In June 2009, Ohio Governor Strickland addressed the $3.2 billion shortfall in the state budget. He proposed that half of libraries' state funding be eliminated. The library mobilized. Led by the Ohio Library Council and its Governmental Relations Council, of which the president was Columbus Metropolitan Library's own Chief Executive Officer Patrick Losinski, Columbus Metropolitan Library (CML) and all 251 Ohio libraries organized their customers and the media to reverse this dreadful course of events.

In forty-eight hours, Columbus Metropolitan Library had acted:

- Placing of signs in all branches announcing that the branch could close if the governor's proposal were accepted
- Handouts for customers to tell them how to contact their legislators
- E-mails to all CML adult customers telling them how to take action (32,000 responded)

Geek the Library Campaign

BORN OF THE work of the OCLC and made possible by the Bill and Melinda Gates Foundation, the Geek the Library Campaign, piloted in 2009 and 2010 and launched nationwide in 2011, highlights the importance of the following:

- Awakening potential supporters to the relevance of libraries in the 21st century
- Putting libraries squarely in the mix of critical community infrastructure
- Activating conversations about the transformative role of libraries and their value to the community's future and well-being

Geek the Library (www.geekthe library.org) is a community awareness campaign designed to assist libraries throughout the United States by highlighting the vital role of public libraries (see figure 9.2). There are materials, resources, and support available. "Libraries and library systems that decide to implement the program will receive initial training and full access to all campaign material," according to the website.

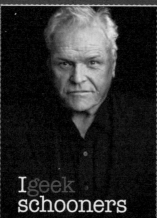

figure 9.2 **Geek the Library Campaign**

- Follow-up e-mail to this group of 32,000 because these customers are self-declared advocates. The library created a unique communication plan for this group.
- Messages on all public PCs with links to legislators' e-mails
- Messages on all self-check stations
- Messages on wireless sign-in page
- Messages on websites urging action from CML customers, Friends of the Library, and Columbus Metropolitan Library Foundation
- Daily/hourly messages on Facebook and Twitter
- Daily internal updates posted for staff on Columbus Metropolitan Library SI, the staff intranet
- Letters to all legislative conference committee members
- Extensive media coverage

Within those 48 hours, so many e-mails (30,000) were sent to legislators by the public that the State House servers crashed! As the weeks passed, 19 percent of the funding was restored, leaving the library with a 31 percent budget cut.

Remember that strategic plan and the positioning strategies? More than ever it has become the defining road map of where and what the library wants to be. Columbus Metropolitan Library has sharpened its focus in a way never done before, delivering every day on its intended promise of being a transformational agency that changes lives in the community. The brand loyalty and the emotional commitment earned through positioning its services earned positive support in the election process.

QUEENS LIBRARY: POSITIONING THROUGH ADVOCACY

In New York City, the various city services for all of the five boroughs, including health and hospitals, New York police department, fire department, and libraries, are all funded through the budgetary process for the city. Queens Library budget, the Brooklyn Public Library's budget, and the New York Public Library budget are determined by the city budgeting process. Each of these library systems is so huge that they have not been combined, although they share information and best practices. The branding process of Queens Library helps elected officials understand the unique qualities of Queens Library and differentiates the library from others, which is very important in the budgeting process. The Borough (county) of Queens is not a taxing entity and cannot issue municipal bonds; therefore, all funding is through the New York City mandate.

Queens Library organizes public events and rallies in support of public library funding. In addition, the government and community affairs department works within communities to create neighborhood ownership of their libraries. The various chapters of the Friends of the Library are very involved in advocacy efforts and are very supportive. A new website now under construction will also enhance the library's ability to communicate and build support. The library not only has to focus on the coming budget cycle, it must also keep an eye on the long term, realizing that it is not alone. In New York City, other city agencies such as police, fire, education, and schools are all experiencing budget woes. Joanne King, spokesperson, indicates that "we will rebuild and will be stronger." She comments that librarians have a quiet resiliency, that "they don't see a stop sign. They do see a detour sign." They are moving forward in service to the customer, in areas of technology, buildings, and collections. Queens Library has received $245 million in capital money from the State, with some from the city, that will be used to deploy new technology as well as build and repair/renovate branches. The library is pushing toward teen spaces and has opened a new Children's Library Discovery Center. They are initiating 24/7 exterior book drops that provide receipts for customers.

Queens Library is performing a balancing act. On one hand, if it is too forgiving of elected officials it loses face with staff and the public. On the other hand, it cannot afford to burn bridges with elected officials, realizing that the library is not the only one facing changing economic times. It is a difficult situation and one that is going to last longer than one budget season or one economic cycle .

ANYTHINK LIBRARIES AND ADVOCACY

In July 2003, the *Denver Post* published an article with a brutally blunt headline: "Adams library system worst in state." The Adams County Library System, with a collection geared more to reference than popular materials and small, musty branches, had been mired in a vicious cycle. In 2006, with articulate and visionary leadership, a new levy was passed. The board and leadership recognized that they had a unique opportunity to rebuild the library system from the ground up and create a new brand that was relevant, represented the future, and would help inspire innovation.

Anythink libraries serve as a model as they have increased awareness, revitalized their brand, and increased revenues, both from public sources and private sources.

WYOMING STATE LIBRARY: FORGING STRONG COMMUNITY GRASSROOTS ADVOCACY PROGRAMS

Wyoming is a land of beauty, of long distances and broad horizons, of wild spaces and independent people. The scenery is spectacular and the wildlife abundant. This state is home to Yellowstone and the Grand Teton national parks. Wyoming's libraries are as expansive as the state, and yet just down the street in every community.

Wyoming is one of the least-populated states in the United States, with a 2009 population of 544,270 people. The Wyoming State Library was founded in 1871, and even though Wyoming was still a territory at the time, it was one of the first of states to have a county public library system. The legislature has played a major role in managing the library system throughout its history and is therefore a key target audience to this day.

All LSTA funding that provides federal funds to Wyoming is administered through the state library. Those funds have supported OCLC products and services, interlibrary transactions and management, and databases, as well as training and travel funds for librarians. The state library plays a pivotal role in the individual county, school, and community college libraries throughout the state. Wyoming libraries work together using an integrated library system that connects the resources of all one hundred public libraries and libraries in most schools and community colleges. Wyoming libraries forge strong grassroots communities throughout the state, a quality especially important to legislators and other public officials who represent those communities.

The Wyoming State Library serves as the hub of the twenty-three county library systems. It is through the state library that one looks for government documents, patents, and trademarks, as well as the Center for the Book, an affiliate of the Center for the Book at the Library of Congress. The state library is the source for customers when they want to download e-books and for the WYLDCAT bibliographic database system. The state library produces and distributes the *Outrider* publication to stakeholders, legislators, and donors to highlight and promote the good works of authors, libraries, and the uniqueness of Wyoming. It is a voice for the entire library system.

State Librarian Leslie Boughton and her staff recognize that state legislators, as well as city and county officials, are a primary target audience for the library. Branding campaigns that create an awareness of "Bringing the World to Wyoming" catch the attention of every legislator. Those legislators live in the remote locations across the state, and the Mudflap Girl campaign reaches them in their neighborhoods. Those legislators personally experience the value of the libraries.

The state library coordinates an annual reception for legislators, provides all legislators with personalized library cards, offers personalized research service for legislators, and works closely with individual legislators to provide excellent customer service.

Turning Adversity into Advantage

Toyota, a revered automobile manufacturer with a strong brand image built on reliability was forced to suspend sales of eight models because of sticking gas pedals on its cars. More than eight million vehicles were recalled for sticky accelerator pedals. Of course, this erodes consumer confidence in the brand (Chandran 2010, 1). "Reputation is the heart of any brand. Toyota has been renowned for its high quality and vehicle reliability. . . . it became one of the top 10 world's leading brands in 2008 based on its reputation for 'reliability,' according to the Global 500 report" (Singh 2010). Toyota engaged in fixing the automobiles as well as "operating television campaigns that reiterate the strong quality record of the company and an outright apology" (Chandran 2010, 1). Can Toyota recover from this adversity and is the Toyota brand strong enough to endure?

Early signals based on industry measures revealed that a counterintuitive uptick occurred because of increased awareness of the brand resulting from recall announcements and more conversations among Toyota customers and potential customers about the Toyota brand and issues of quality. Just by focusing attention on the brand, even with the mixed messages about quality, Toyota demonstrated that a brand with an established, strong loyalty base can recover and even thrive amid adversity (Singh 2010).

USING ADVERSITY TO REPOSITION YOUR LIBRARY

Rahm Emanuel says, "You never want a serious crisis to go to waste. And what I mean by that it's an opportunity to do things you think you could not do before" (www.brainquote.com). Adversity shakes things up, it rewards strengths and creates opportunities and new ideas. You can use adversity as an opportunity to reposition your library. In fact, half of the Fortune 500 companies, including FedEx, CNN, and Microsoft, were founded in recessions.

The Greek philosopher Herodotus said, "Adversity has the effect of drawing out strength and qualities of a man that would have lain dormant in its absence" (www.brainquote.com). The very best qualities of strength, courage, character, and persistence are brought out when you face your greatest challenges and when you respond to them positively and constructively. Remember that tough times present valuable opportunities.

Adversity offers the opportunity to reposition the library for future growth. Adversity calls for innovation as well as collaboration. It provides libraries with the opportunity to review operations and facilities, to reposition themselves strategically, to explore new directions, and to establish new relationships. Adversity requires new ways of thinking and action. It demands vision and offers an opportunity to inspire and empower your team.

The pioneering spirit comes alive in adversity. Bouncing back from adversity is the key. If you can harness adversity you will achieve gains you could never have enjoyed without it. Adversity builds stronger leadership skills. Handling adversity well strengthens the role within the community. The leadership, the vision, and the galvanizing of the team working together through adversity can be truly inspirational. Understanding your brand, its origins, its core competencies and capacities, and its inherent brand loyalty can serve to frame and guide the path through times of diversity. It can also provide a "future frame" for repositioning the asset value of the brand to better align with a changing market, market conditions, and emerging market opportunities.

Adversity is the true test of leadership. Do you remember Chesley B. Sullenberger, the U.S. Airways pilot who flew into a flock of geese and lost both engines? Can you still see the news photos of the 155 passengers landing safely on the Hudson River? By staying poised and keeping a positive attitude under pressure, leaders can pass through adversity having grown in stature more than they ever could have in more comfortable times. Sullenberger said, "One way of looking at this might be that, for 42 years, I've been making small, regular deposits in this bank of experience: education and training. And on January 15, the balance was sufficient so that I could make a very large withdrawal" (CBS News 2009).

Libraries certainly experience frequent bumps in the road. Budget cuts, layoffs, and emergencies are all too common for libraries; yet, the resiliency and tenacity of libraries and librarians is to be applauded. Leaders of libraries facing adversity have a true test. They feel the pain and pressure acutely. In the middle of adversity, it can be difficult to develop a feeling of optimism. However, rising above the adversity to see the opportunity and the vision for the future is the true test of leadership. Focusing on your brand and engaging in the process of branding, as addressed in

Chapters 1–3, can be a powerful way to shake off the sense of hopelessness and establish a new footing based on the assets you have and how you see your future.

THE REBIRTH OF THE GRAND COUNTY LIBRARY DISTRICT

Grand County, Colorado, is an expansive and beautiful area in the state. It is bordered by snowcapped mountains and nestled in a valley known for its vistas and stunning sunsets. The communities within Grand County include Granby, Grand Lake (a lovely community that sits on the western edge of Rocky Mountain National Park), Hot Sulphur Springs, Winter Park/Fraser, and Kremmling.

The population in this extensive county is relatively small, numbering approximately 14,500. There is one movie theater within the county, one recreation center, no bookstore, and limited commercial development. The Grand County Library District serves as the hub of community activities, cultural events, and a children's door to learning, as well as the intellectual center for the county.

June 8, 2004, was marked by tragedy in the Grand County mountain community of Granby. The former owner of a muffler shop on the west side of Granby, Marvin Heemeyer, became enraged over the construction of a concrete plant that had been approved by the city. In a ninety-minute rampage, Heemeyer left a path of destruction through the town with a homemade "tank" that he had constructed from a D9 bulldozer. He armed the bulldozer with a 50-caliber semiautomatic rifle and two semiautomatic assault rifles, and also had a couple of handguns with him.

The first target was the concrete plant and several nearby offices and buildings. The next target was the Granby Town Hall, where the public library resided on the lower level. He mangled town vehicles, drove through children's playgrounds, tore up trees, and headed for the local newspaper, the *Sky Hi News*. After demolishing the home of the former Granby mayor, he drove to the Independent Gas Company facility, where he began firing at propane tanks.

The rampage ended as the engine of the bulldozer finally seized up and quit. Grand County SWAT team members swarmed over the vehicle as the sound of a shot from the interior of the bulldozer rang out. Heemeyer had committed suicide with one of his handguns. In all, thirteen buildings were damaged or destroyed.

In the Granby library, books and materials as well as computers were all lost. However, library shelving held up the second floor of the building, thereby saving some materials.

How does one have the courage, determination, knowledge, and understanding to stand up in the face of deep adversity? How does one confront the brutal facts, yet never lose faith? The courage comes out of a culture of discipline, of knowledge that adversity brings opportunity, that good will prevail, and that leadership must lead the way. Mary Anne Hanson-Wilcox, executive director of the Grand County Library District, realized that once presented with the destruction, she must act. She knew that the library must remain vital to the community, and that the library had a commitment to the community. As a part of that commitment, the library opened in temporary quarters within three days and began to develop plans to rebuild. Hanson-Wilcox said, "We were running out of space and really needed a larger library, but didn't plan to start work on a new library at this time." The vision was not simply to rebuild. The vision was to take this opportunity to reposition the library within the community and to build the library that would signify the rebirth for the whole community. The board and staff cemented the vision for the new library. This glass-and-steel structure would feature a community room, a fireplace, and a drive-up window that would be very popular in this community that experiences long winters. "These are things this community has never had," Hanson-Wilcox said. "In a way, [Heemeyer] did us a favor." The new library was born out of the rubble of destruction.

Money, money, money—how did they afford to build a new library? There was no time for a bond election or to accumulate gifts and grants. "We will do it by hook or by crook," said Hanson-Wilcox, her blue eyes sparkling and her visible, determined Norwegian/Irish roots shining through. Collaboration followed with the board commitment and the commitment by the community. Hanson-Wilcox found herself becoming a development director, orchestrating a major capital campaign. Various foundations assumed leadership positions, and challenge grants motivated others. There were pledges by communities, companies, organizations, and individuals who were excited and animated by the vision of a new, even grander library that would enhance the rebuilding of a community. Yes, there were crazy fund-raising events, including progressive dinners, book sales, and private parties. Even the State of Colorado offices offered assistance through the Department of Local Affairs. The library district was able to get a thirty-year lease/purchase agreement on the physical building and raise the capital necessary to complete the project. The staff joined together and said, "We can do this!" The employees began to see a vision wider than they were as individuals. Those who picked up the mantle and carried the flag went beyond and continue to go beyond today. Hanson-Wilcox finds that Jim Collins in his book *Good to Great* provides a road map to excellence, and she has adopted his philosophy. Collins remarks that great organizations have a culture of discipline. They have disciplined people, disciplined thought, and disciplined action. "The executives who ignited the transformations from good to great did not first figure out where to drive the bus and then get people to take it there. *No,* they *first* got the right people on the bus (and the wrong people off the bus) and *then* figured out where to drive it" (Collins 2001).

Together with the library board, the staff and director developed an RFP to identify the architectural firm to build the library that Granby deserved. The firm of Humphries/Poli Architects won the bid and designed a building that was so much more than the community had ever seen (see figure 9.3). It is a building of distinction and has since won the *Library Journal*

figure 9.3 **New Granby Public Library**

award for library architecture of the year in December 2006. As one library customer said, "Libraries are a haven for the residents of this small community. It is our Taj Mahal." The library is the intellectual haven as well as the cultural haven. The library also won the Colorado Library of the Year for 2005 as well as the architecture award for 2006.

The Grand County Library District and Director Hanson-Wilcox have capitalized on adversity. They had the vision and trusted that their vision would lead them forward. They have been technologically savvy, and have connected community, staff, board, volunteers, stakeholders, and donors to build collaboration with the county. The library has been repositioned through adversity.

In 2010, the Colorado Library Career Achievement Award went to Mary Anne Hanson-Wilcox, who said, "Who can plan a bulldozer event? My advice is to act with integrity, and do what you need to do. The road has a way of smoothing out and you can make it. Never play the 'cheap' card. Treat people with respect and give them an opportunity!"

Positioning the Library within the Brand of a University

Universities, motivated by a new strategic reality, are being transformed throughout the country. There is greater competition for financial and human resources, and increased student mobility demands that those providing the resources position themselves to compete. Universities are also being transformed to accommodate a more student-centered, collaborative problem-solving environment. University administrators are recognizing that they must develop their brand culture, a brand that differentiates their institution from others and promotes the unique interests of prospective students, faculty, staff, donors and volunteer supporters, strategically aligned partners from business and other institutions, and the communities they serve. Universities today are branding and positioning themselves within the marketplace.

> What about that mission issue? Done right, "institutional branding is meant to help propel an institution from its mission to its vision by creatively conveying the powerful strategy that will take it from where it is to where it wants to go," argues Barbara O'Malley, chief communications officer at the University of Akron (Ohio). "When strategy is clear and the creative and communication consistent and supportive of the strategy, branding is powerful and can benefit a university greatly." Research has tied good branding to attracting students, faculty, and staff as well as to achieving success in fundraising and in getting media coverage. (Kennedy 2008)

Within this environment, there is an opportunity to reinvigorate the library and promote the library as a source for the development of learning communities.

Libraries are shifting from the traditional role as repositories of information to places where learners meet, collaborate, and interact in the learning process.

Students respond to the environment created by the library; they react to the level of comfort and to an environment that invites and sustains a diverse range of study approaches. The library facilities, collections, database access, programs, and environment all require a new vision to match the branding and positioning strategies of the university. According to Dr. Robert Schwarzwalder of Stanford University, "The library can be, and should be, the intellectual commons of the university. To achieve that end, we need to foster and support the sort of collaboration, team-building, and inspired play in library spaces that continues our role in education. Rethinking our services and spaces is far more complex than adopting a new technology or two; it involves engaging with our community in a manner that meets real patron needs."

Of the many exciting choices that illustrate branding and positioning strategies of the library within the university, the University of Denver was selected because of accessibility to internal decision makers. Some of our contacts included members of the Advisory Planning Council; the dean emeritus of the Daniels College of Business and director of the Ethics Integration program, R. Bruce Hutton, PhD; Interim Vice Chancellor of University Communication, Jim Berscheidt; and Nancy Allen, dean of the Penrose Library.

A Final Word about Leadership

"The success of even the best of marketing plans depends entirely on the vision of the leadership of an organization and the understanding and buy-in of the staff. It takes time and organizational will to live up to this vision, but it is possible. It can result in a stronger community that understands the value of a great library," says Alison Circle of Columbus Metropolitan Library.

Investigation of the key libraries highlighted in this book found that leadership played a pivotal role for each institution. In fact, none of the libraries would have succeeded without the support of strong, capable leadership. What is the role of leadership in branding and positioning? Strong leaders within an organization recognize the power of vision, mission, and values. As Margaret Wheatley says, "The impact of vision, values, and culture occupies a great deal of organizational attention. We see their effects on organizational vitality . . ." (Wheatley 2006, 14). Wheatley goes on to assert the power of a clear vision and how it translates to the entire culture. "Vision statements move off the walls and into the corridors, seeking out every employee, every recess in the organization. . . . We need all of us out there, stating, clarifying, reflecting, modeling, filling all of space with the messages we care about. If we do that, a powerful field develops—and with it, the wondrous capacity to organize into a coherent capable form" (Wheatley 2006, 57). It is that coherent capable form that Wheatley refers to that is embodied in the organization's brand.

As you review the work of libraries featured throughout this book, consider the instances, examples, and models for leadership they provide. Consider the extent to which it took leadership to first grasp the need to pay (continued on page 178)

A Case Study: University of Denver

THE OLDEST AND largest private university in the Rocky Mountain region, the University of Denver (DU) attracts thoughtful leaders who are committed to academic rigor, community engagement, and global responsibility. The value pillars of *integrity, inclusiveness,* and *ideas* that push the limits are principles and practices for the purpose of improving the human condition at the university. Whether through art, science, or gestures of understanding, the University of Denver uses its skills, applies the knowledge, and pours the passions into tackling society's most urgent concerns.

The university enrolls approximately 11,600 students in its undergraduate and graduate programs. The Carnegie Foundation classifies DU as a Doctoral/Research University with high research activity. Committed to internationalizing its campus and curriculum, DU draws students and faculty from more than eighty countries around the world.

DU faces challenges of branding while riding the waves of change sweeping across higher education today. A branding initiative was begun in 2005 within the university. To make its brand authentic, DU invested in a communal process to define what makes the university special. The university has a wonderful story to tell, and building the brand ensured that the story would be heard. The brand would capture DU's distinctive approach to education as well as the university's role in the broader community. The brand differentiates DU from current and future competitors. The university felt that the branding process was of utmost importance and would be responsible for aligning the culture of the school or department with the identity DU deserves, both nationally and internationally.

Vision: The University of Denver will be a great private university dedicated to the public good.

Values: In all that we do, we strive for excellence, innovation, engagement, integrity and inclusiveness.

Mission: The mission of the University of Denver is to promote learning by engaging with students in advancing scholarly inquiry, cultivating critical and creative thought and generating knowledge. Our active partnerships with local and global communities contribute to a sustainable common good.

Goals:

Community: We will create a diverse, ethical and intellectually vibrant campus community to provide a challenging and liberating learning environment.

Learning: We will provide an outstanding educational experience that empowers students to integrate and apply knowledge from across the disciplines and imagine new possibilities for themselves, their communities and the world.

Scholarship: We will invigorate research and scholarship across the university to address the important scientific, sociopolitical and cultural questions of the new century.

"We will become a catalyst of positive change, fueled by hope, percolating with ideas, pulsing with the vitality of many cultures. We will be tough and determined, open-minded and optimistic, committed to students and community, to excellence and innovation, and to integrity and engagement," says Chancellor Robert Coombe ("Message from the Chancellor" 2011).

POSITIONING STRATEGY

Focus on educating the whole student.

Build educational and research opportunities with special attention to our location in Denver and the Rocky Mountain West.

Foster innovative integration of liberal and professional education and research.

Embrace innovative and more effective approaches to teaching and learning.

Educate a more diverse domestic and international student body to meet challenges of a global society.

Reinforce and strengthen a culture of civic engagement within our community and build upon that to further engage a wide range of external communities.

STRATEGIC PLANNING

Guided by the *brand* and the *positioning strategy* to be a great university dedicated to the public good, each school and area within the university were charged with strategic planning. As they began discussing the future of the university and a strategic plan, there were four important questions that helped them focus on the efforts:

• Who are we and how do we differ from others?
• In what context do we operate?
• What should we look like in five to ten years?
• How should we achieve our goals?

The changing environment of the university breathed new life for the university library—symbolically, geographically, and functionally. The library "plays an important part in the world today because of the dependency of

Design is a collaboration of H + L Architecture and the Office of the University Architect with rendering by Carl Dalio.

students, professionals and researchers of information. Lifelong learning must be supported because of the rapid technological change that is affecting more and more industries requiring more support for professional study," says Dr. R. Bruce Hutton, dean emeritus of the Daniels College of Business.

Penrose Library is embarking on a remarkable transformation to support the university and its goals. The library has completed its own strategic plan to support the branding initiative and the positioning strategy of the institution. As the university seeks to support collaborative environments, the library has recognized how students respond to the environment. Penrose Library is undergoing a complete restoration and rebuilding process. The library understands the value of providing an environment of technological support. This strategic transformation represents the goals and objectives and the positioning strategy of the university.

The Academic Commons at Penrose Library will be a dynamic center that will support social learning, interactive technologies, student-centered programs, and individual study and reflection. A digital revolution is under way at the Penrose Library, where a $30 million renovation will cut the number of bound books and journals.

"The renovation will change the building's functionality from book storage space to technology-rich people space," says Robert Coombe. "We will not only create appropriate spaces for student study and practice groups, for faculty research, but will support social learning, interactive technologies, student-centered programs, and, of course, individual quiet study. The library is a place students and faculty go for academic support; in one convenient location, they find the Writing Center, the Research Center, the Math Center, and the technology help desk, which faculty, similarly, go to the library for collaboration with the Center for Teaching and Learning. These academic support services combined with digital and tangible library collections make the Penrose Library the University of Denver's Academic Commons," according to Dean and Director Nancy Allen.

This dynamic center of the Academic Commons at Penrose Library, with the tagline "Connecting people to ideas," will be housed in a reconstructed, state-of-the-art LEED-certified building. It will be a light-filled space designed according to a new learning model, one where students can work in groups, develop team projects, use the latest technology in innovative ways, and collaborate with professors and each other. The Academic Commons at Penrose Library will be open twenty-four hours a day, five days a week, and will provide cell phone access as well as electronic books that can be checked out to computers or e-readers such as the iPad, Kindle, or Nook. The library's customers will have access to 1.7 million digital links (see figure 9.4).

(continued from page 175) attention to the library's brand. Consider the strength of conviction coupled with openness to new information required to address the positioning of the library's brand. And appreciate the leadership required to engage and manage involvement throughout the organization and to collaboratively implement a consistent and comprehensive approach to promotion.

Finally, recognize that leadership in today's environment is more than a personality style, more than a charismatic quality, and even more than a comprehensive set of competencies. Leaders today must themselves be creative thinkers and doers, skillful in managing creative processes in which they engage and develop imaginative leadership in others. In the afterword to his book *A Whole New Mind: Why Right-Brainers Will Rule the Future,* Daniel Pink (2006, 247) describes competencies necessary to perform in the new "Conceptual Age" in which we find ourselves and our organizations:

> The promise is that Conceptual Age jobs are exceedingly democratic. You don't need to design the next cell phone or discover a new source of renewable energy. There will be plenty of work not just for inventors, artists, and entrepreneurs but also for an array of imaginative, emotionally intelligent, right-brain professionals, from counselors to massage therapists to school teachers to stylists to talented salespeople. What's more, as I've tried to make clear, the abilities you'll need—Design, Story, Symphony, Empathy, Play, and Meaning—are fundamentally human attributes. They are things we do out of a sense of intrinsic motivation. They reside in all of us, and need only be nurtured into being.

What Daniel Pink describes is a new way of looking at and approaching our work. This book is about branding, positioning, and promotion of libraries—a complex process that requires engagement at all levels of the organization. It is a process that requires keen analytical thinking—the stuff that left-brain thinkers and librarians are especially good at. And it is a process that requires open, risk-taking, creative right-brain thinking—the stuff right-brain thinkers and artists, performers, and entrepreneurs are especially good at. Most important, it requires leaders who are skillful at employing both modes of thinking and uniquely capable of enabling and orchestrating the same from others in the organization. From the library boardroom to the executive office to department heads to branch managers to individual librarians and volunteers, the big idea of imaginative leadership and breakthrough branding are the keys to success.

The authors of this book are experienced in facilitating and training staff, managers, and graduate-level students in addressing organizational branding, positioning, and promotion. As proposed by Daniel Pink, these are skills requiring a merger of right-brain and left-brain thinking and the ability to empathize with and engage others in the process. The approaches the authors have developed blend sound psychology, productive group process, and methods commonly associated with the creative and performing arts, including improvisational theater. In collaboration with DiscoveryOnstage, a Los Angeles–based company, a pilot workshop was developed for insurance professionals and introduced at a national leadership conference of the Certified Property and Casualty Underwriters (CPCU) Society in 2010. The workshop served as an intensive full-day laboratory to refine a three-act process to develop and apply imaginative leadership skills to real industry challenges. Details of the process and results from this pilot workshop are presented in three articles appearing in CPCU Society Leadership & Managerial Excellence Interest Group newsletters (Jackson 2010, 7–8; Catrambone and Jackson 2010, 8–10; Grecsek 2011, 12–13).

Others like MIT's Sloan School of Management recently introduced improv training as part of their MBA programs (Flucht 2012), and well-known acting companies like Second City in Chicago and The Groundlings in Los Angeles offer corporate training programs using similar methods. What they all have in common is the unique integration of sound theory with practical exercise and application to give rise to a new form of leadership and to empower today's leaders with new skills that leverage existing competencies.

In order for our libraries to survive and thrive in today's world, it will take imaginative leaders at all levels of the organization to cut through the clutter, to clarify the value, and to deliver the benefits of breakthrough branding, positioning, and promotion. In this new age of change and opportunity, libraries that embrace the ideas presented in this book will survive as valued institutions and thrive as pivotal forces for positive and transformational change. In cooperation with the American Library Association, the authors are developing and conducting courses and related educational offerings for librarians and library organizations to implement the principles of breakthrough branding utilizing the methods of imaginative leadership.

Summary

Applying sound principles of branding and strategic positioning to advocate on behalf of libraries and the communities and institutions to which they are inextricably linked can produce powerful results. Beginning with the brand loyalty the public attaches to libraries and by promoting the big idea that libraries are transformational agents for change and self-actualization, libraries are finding paths to turn the tide of public opinion and support. This chapter, and the book as a whole, has included examples of how libraries are able to address nagging funding issues and budget cuts, frontal political assaults, the demands of diversity, opportunities for makeover and revitalization, and the ability to tell their story to those who hold the purse strings. The role of branding and positioning amid circumstances of adversity was explored as well as the role of library branding and positioning amid a larger institutional brand, the university. And the role of imaginative leadership in guiding this transforming was illuminated, calling particular attention to extraordinary examples of leadership exhibited by the libraries highlighted throughout this book and introducing improvisational methods for developing imaginative leaders and organizations.

REFERENCES

CBS News. 2009. "Flight 1549: Saving 155 Souls in Minutes." 60 Minutes, July 6. www.cbsnews.com/8301-18560_162-4783586.html.

Catrambone, Dominic, and Jeremy Jackson. 2010. "Imaginative Leadership—Developing Leadership Skills to Inspire Creativity and Spawn Innovation." *Leadership & Managerial Excellence Interest Group,* October. http://discoveryonstagecorporate .com/2010/09/leadership-institute-hosts-pre-session-imaginative-leadership-course.

Chandran, Vigneshwaran. 2010. "Total Recall: Impact Assessment of Toyota's Quality Issues on Its North American Business." *Frost and Sullivan,* February 17. www.frost.com/sublib/display-market-insight-top.do?id=192823606.

Collins, Jim. 2001. *Good to Great: Why Some Companies Make the Leap . . . and Others Don't.* New York: HarperBusiness.

Collins, Jim, and Morten T. Hansen. 2011. *Great by Choice: Uncertainty, Chaos, and Luck—Why Some Thrive Despite Them All.* New York: HarperBusiness.

Coombe, Robert. 2011. "Message from the Chancellor." *Ascend: Campaign for the University of Denver.*

Dawson, Thomson. 2011. "Four Methods of Strategic Brand Building." *Branding Strategy,* November 1. www.brandingstrategyinsider.com/2011/11/four-methods-of-strategic -brand-building.html.

DeRosa, Cathy, and Jenny Johnson. 2008. *From Awareness to Funding: A Study of Library Support in America.* Dublin, OH: Online Computer Library Center.

Flucht, Julie. 2012. "When the Art of the Deal Includes Improv Training." December 5. www.npr.org/2012/12/5/166484466/it-s-improv-night-at-business-school.

Grecsek, Ernie. 2011. "Imaginative Leadership—Developing Leadership Skills to Inspire Creativity and Spawn Innovation." *Leadership & Managerial Excellence Interest Group,* January. http://discoveryonstagecorporate.com/2010/09/leadership-institute -hosts-pre-session-imaginative-leadership-course.

Jackson, Kent. 2010. "Imaginative Leadership—To Inspire Creativity and Spawn Innovation." *Leadership & Managerial Excellence Interest Group,* July. http://discoveryonstage corporate.com/2010/09/leadership-institute-hosts-pre-session-imaginative -leadership-course.

Kennedy, Randell. 2008. "50 Best Branding Ideas: How Colleges and Universities are Successfully Creating and Communicating Their Brands." *University Business,* December 1. www.universitybusiness.com/article/50-best-branding-ideas.

Levitt, Theodore. 1983. *The Marketing Imagination.* New York: The Free Press.

"Loyalty." 2012. *Merriam-Webster's Collegiate Dictionary.* Springfield, MA: Merriam-Webster, Inc.

McGirt, Ellen. 2008. "The Brand Called Obama." *Fast Company,* 124 (April). www.fastcompany.com/magazine/124/april-2008.

Munoz, Genevieve Ann. 2009. *Emotional Branding: Obama's Bottom-Up Campaign.* California Polytechnic State University, San Luis Obispo, CA.

Pallotta, Dan. 2011. "A Logo Is Not a Brand." *Harvard Business Review,* June 15. http://blogs.hbr.org/pallotta/2011/06/a-logo-is-not-a-brand.

Pink, Daniel H. 2006. *A Whole New Mind: Why Right-Brainers Will Rule the Future.* New York: Berkley Publishing Group.

Schwarzwalder, Robert. 2011. "The Changing Face of Academic Libraries: Why Less Space Does Not Have to Mean Less Impact." *Elsevier Library Connect Newsletter,* 9, no. 1 (March).

Singh, Shiv. 2010. "Could the Toyota Recall Crisis be Helping the Brand?" *Mashable Social Media,* February 22. http://mashable.com/2010/02/22/toyota-brand.

Wheatley, Margaret J. 2006. *Leadership and the New Science: Discovering Order in a Chaotic World.* San Francisco: Berrett-Koehler.

about the authors

Suzanne Walters was the director of marketing and development for the Denver Public Library during the successful bond election and capital campaign to build the new central library building as well as to remodel and build branches throughout the city of Denver. She previously served as the director of marketing for the Regional Transportation District of Denver, responsible for the implementation of the 16th Street Mall. Suzanne also developed nationwide programs of aluminum recycling for Adolph Coors Golden Recycling Corporation and was a statewide coordinator of volunteers and events for the PBS station KRMA. Currently, she is the president of Walters & Associates Consultants and conducts marketing workshops and seminars for libraries both nationally and internationally. She also serves on the graduate faculty of Regis University, facilitating courses in social marketing. Her BA in biology comes from Wichita State University, while her MBA comes from the Daniels College of Business at the University of Denver.

Kent Jackson, PhD, CPCU, owner of Jackson Research, Strategy, Solution, LLC, provides consulting services for a variety of for-profit and nonprofit enterprises, including education, professional associations, medical and human service providers, homebuilders and developers, insurers, and professional service firms. In association with other qualified firms and individuals specializing in graphic and web design, copywriting, advertising, public relations, and market research, Jackson has developed refined methodologies and services that enable clients to better research, strategically position, and sell through their distinctive value advantage. Jackson's more than forty-year career uniquely qualifies him to address custom market research, branding strategy, and solution challenges for business-to-business and business-to-consumer enterprises and initiatives. For nearly a decade, he was a principal and director of research for a graphic design and branding company. He currently serves on Regis University's graduate faculty, teaching social marketing and organizational leadership, and as a resource consultant to DiscoveryOnstage, a Los Angeles–based theatrical education and performance company. Jackson earned bachelor's and master's degrees from the University of Northern Colorado and a PhD from Oregon State University. He is recognized for his work on behalf of business and community organizations and is a frequent speaker and author/coauthor of articles in his areas of expertise.

index

A

actual product, 112–113
Adams County Library System, 20, 98
advanced branding, 9–10
adversity, using, 170–171
advertising promotion strategies, 150
advocacy
    Anythink and, 169
    employee brand advocacy stage, 51
aesthetics, brand elements and, 7
aging process, segmentation and, 80
alignment, building, 52
Allen, Nancy, 175, 177
Amazon Lending Library program, 124
amenities as a strategy, 117
Anderson, Chris, 122
Anythink
    advocacy and, 169
    brand strategy and identity, 138
    communication consistency, 140
    development process, 42
    goals, 102–103
    logo, 63
    marketing research at, 94
    people strategy, 126–127
    place strategies and, 120–121
    policies at, 50
    positioning and, 59, 62
    Staff Manifesto, 134
    strategic planning and positioning at, 68
Apple brand, 49, 101, 113, 165
application
    and brands, 10–11
    sequence and, 28–30
    surveys and, 11–14
Arapahoe Library District, 67

architecture of brand, 132–134
Ariely, Dan, 122
Art + Business One, 24
Asacker, Tom, 6
assessments
    about, 17–18
    brand story and, 18–19
    development and, 45
    equity and, 34
    household engagement, 33–34
    mission and values, 22
    purpose and, 20–21
    SWOT and, 23–26
    teams and, 26–27
    of vision, 22–23
assistance in research, 73–74
augmented product, 112–113
automated systems as a strategy, 117
awareness stage of planning, 47–48

B

barrier-focused positioning, 95
basics
    advanced branding, 9–10
    application to libraries, 10–11
    experiential elements, 8–9
    image of library, 13–14
    library identity, 11–12
    observable elements, 7–8
    personality of library, 12–13
    three dimensions of branding, 10
behavior
    competitive types, 123–124
    segmentation of, 80–81
behavior-focused positioning, 95

believers, employee brand advocacy stage, 51
Bellina, John, 42, 63
benefit-focused positioning, 95–96
benefits, core products and, 112
Berscheidt, Jim, 175
Bill and Melinda Gates Foundation, xv
billboards
    as a strategy, 117
    as touch points, 143
Blink (Malcolm), 19
blogs as communication, 154
bookmobiles
    as a strategy, 117
    as touch points, 143
BrainReserve, xvii
brand guides, 48
brand image, 82
Brand Manners (Pringle and Gordon), 43
branding
    about, 3–4
    action and, 6–7
    advanced elements, 9–10
    basics of, 7–8
    concept evolution, 5–6
    experiencing, 4–5
    experiential elements of, 8–9
    libraries and, 10–14
    positioning integration and, 64–67
brandmarks, 135–136
brands
    advocating and, 163–180
    assessing, 17–36
    concept of, 3–15
    crafting strategies, 93–105
    developing, 39–53
    marketing mix, 109–129
    positioning and strategies, 57–69
    promoting, 131–161
    segmentation and, 71–91
Bubble Room (blog), 11, 19–20, 84–85
business plans, 21

C

campaigns
    Geek the Library, 121–122, 167
    Mudflap Girl, 96, 160
    as PR tool, 152
causal research, 29
change
    design and, 9
    nexus for, 20–21
choice, branding and, 9–10
Circle, Alison, 11, 58, 97
Claritas, 81, 88
classification systems, 81–82
A Clear Eye for Branding (Asacker), 6
cluster systems, 81–82

cobranding
    architecture and, 134
    strategies for, 80
Collins, Jim, xviii, 45, 105, 173
color, using, 137–138
Columbus Metropolitan Library
    brand identity, 136–137
    logo, 66, 137
    market segmentation research, 86–90
    OCLC study, 166–168
    planning process, 46
    social media and, 154–155
    transformational agency, 35
commercial marketplace, positioning and,
    61–62
commonalities, brands and, 5
communication
    Anythink and, 140
    plan for, 50
    promotional plan and, 144
    protocols for, 44
    selecting channels, 146–150
    strategic focus and, 26
    as a strategy, 117
community, positioning and sense of, 64
competition
    evaluation criteria, 82
    identifying, 58
    positioning and, 59, 96
competitive markets, 32–33
concentrated marketing, 86
concepts
    brands specific, 3–15
    creative types, 46–47
    promotion of, 131–132
conclusive research, 29
consultants, using, 17
context, honoring, 9
convenience, strategic focus and, 26
Coombe, Robert, 176
copywriters, discovery process and, 45–46
core products, benefits and, 112
cost-plus pricing, 124
costs, monetary and nonmonetary, 123
Cowley, Don, 6
creative concepts
    creating briefs, 145
    developing, 46–47
    discovery process and, 45–46
    promotional plan and strategy, 144–146
crisis communication, 151
cultural considerations
    change, 21
    library mission and, 22
    plan for, 50
    relevancy of, xvii–xviii
    segmentation and, 80
Curtin, Mike, 66

customers
  challenges facing, 11–12
  choice and branding, 9–10
  life cycle of, 126

D

Dalio, Carl, 177
declarative outcomes, 36
decline stage, product life cycle and, 115
delivery systems as a strategy, 117
demand
  internal strengths, 24–25
  promotion and, 131
demographic segmentation, 78–79
depth
  internal strengths, 24–25
  promotion and, 131
descriptive research, 29
design
  change and, 9
  charrettes of, 46
  as a strength, 25
  teams for, 158
Designing Brand Identity (Wheeler), 36
desires
  internal strengths, 24–25
  promotion and, 131
development, Anythink and, 42
differentiated *vs.* undifferentiated marketing,
    60–61, 85–86
dimensions of branding, 10
disciplined approach to development, 45–49
discovery, brands and, 45–46
DiscoveryOnstage, 178
disincentives, 123
Disney, customer service and, 128
distribution channels, 117
Dobbs, Susan, 50, 126

E

e-books as a strategy, 117
Earls, Mark, 6
economic considerations
  changes in, 21
  segmentation of, 80
effort as a cost, 120
electronic media, 146
elements of brands, 7–14
Elements of User Experience (Grant), 8
Emanuel, Rahm, 171
Emotional and Intellectual Rewards
    Framework, 165–166
emotional attachment, positioning and,
    64–65
emotions
  assessments and, 18

emotions *(cont'd)*
  brand architecture and, 134
  brands evoking, 5, 64–65
employee brand advocacy, 51
engagement stage of planning, 48
environment
  personality and, 12–13
  strategic focus and, 26
equity
  assessing, 34
  building, 52
Esri/Tapestry (information resource), 82
ethical concerns in research, 30
evaluations
  components and development, 49
  measurable results, 155–157
  segments of, 84
experience model, 23
experiences, creating, 8
experiential elements, 8–9
exploratory research, 28
external opportunities/threats, 26, 40

F

Facebook, social media, 155–156
facilities
  as communication tool, 150
  personality and, 12–13
  as touch points, 143
feelings
  assessments and, 18
  brand architecture and, 134
  brands evoking, 5, 64–65
Flickr, social media, 157
focusing brand, 20–21, 135
format of creative brief, 145
four Ps, marketing mix and, 109–110
free for all positioning, 121–122
From Awareness to Funding (findings study)
  about, xv
  advocacy challenges, 165–166
  brand perceptions, 10
  perceptions of libraries, 32
  pricing strategies, 119
  Rangeview Library District, 23
furniture as a strategy, 117

G

Garden Party survey, 11–12, 19–20, 84–85
GASP process, 23, 121–122, 127
Geek the Library campaign, 121–122, 167
geographic segmentation, 80
Gladwell, Malcolm, 19
goals
  developing, 104
  establishing, 50

Godin, Seth, 93–94
Good to Great (Collins), xviii, 45, 174–175
Gordon, William, 43
Grand County Library System, 45, 172–174
Grant, Jesse James, 8
graphic designers, discovery process and,
    45–46
graphics, using, 137–138
The Groundlings, 179
growth
    assessment of, 18
    evaluation criteria for potential, 82
    product life cycle stage, 115
guidebooks, development and, 48, 158
guiding principles, 50

H

Hanson-Wilcox, Mary Anne, 45, 173–174
Harvard Business Review (journal), 21
Hastings, Reed, 59
Heemeyer, Marvin, 172–173
Heitman, David, 140
hours as a strategy, 117–118
household engagement, assessing, 33–34
Humphrey, Albert, 24
Hutton, R. Bruce, 175

I

identity
    Anythink and, 138
    Columbus Metropolitan Library, 136–
        137
    of library, 11–12
IKEA, space as a strategy, 116
image
    dimensions and, 10, 13–14
    evaluation criteria, 82
impact, building, 52
incentives, 123
information
    resources and personality, 12–13
    source and type, 30–31
initiatives, 36
intellectual relationships with brands, 5
intentional elements, 9
internal perspectives, 40
internalizing brand, 49–51
introductory stage, product life cycle, 115
involvement, protocol of, 44
iPad, potential products and, 113
iPhone
    brand loyalty and, 64
    positioning strategy and, 101

J

Jackson, Kent, xvi
Jobs, Steve, 19, 113, 165

K

Keller, James, 58, 65, 72
King, Joanne, 169
Kotler, Philip, 51, 95–96, 98, 154

L

Lance Jackson and Associates, Inc., 24
leadership, 175, 178–179
learners, employee brand advocacy stage, 51
Lee, Nancy, 51, 98
Leo Burnett USA, xv
Levitt, Theodore, 112–113, 122, 165
libraries
    brand dimensions and identity, 11–12
    card database, 73–74
    image of, 13–14
    personality of, 12–13
    using public relation programs, 153–154
Library Branding (Jackson), 11
Library Journal, 115–117
life cycle of products, 114–115
life stages, segmentation and, 80
LinkedIn, social media, 155
location
    as a strategy, 117–118
    as a strength, 25
logos
    Anythink, 63
    Arapahoe Library District, 67
    Columbus Metropolitan Library, 66, 137
    OCLC, 61
    Seth Godin's Purple Cow, 94
Long Overdue (report), xv
longevity of brands, 5
Losinski, Patrick, 35, 154, 166
loyalty
    defined, 164
    evaluation criteria, 82
    positioning and, 64
    stage of planning, 48

M

mail as a strategy, 117
mall intercept interviews, 87
management
    of brand, 51–52, 158
    of social media, 155
market research
    about, 27–32
    Anythink and, 94
    Columbus Metropolitan Library, 86–90
    external and internal markets, 32
    positioning and, 63
    sequence and application, 28–30
    sources of information, 30
    target markets and, 72–73
    types of information, 30–31
    using professionals, 74

market share
    assessing, 33–34
    brand value and, 4–5
marketing
    concentrated, 86
    identity and, 11–12
    understanding, 32–34
    undifferentiated *vs.* differentiated,
        85–86
marketing mix, 58, 109–129
marketplace
    library position in, 62–63
    positioning and, 59–60
mass media channels, 146
maturity stage, product life cycle, 115
May, Eloise, 67
media types, 146–150
messages
    prioritizing, 9
    promotion plan and, 144
    promotional considerations and, 140–
        141
    target audience and, 145
Mestis, Joyce, 59
methodology, market research positioning,
        63
Mildly Delirious Design, 23
mind share
    assessing, 33–34
    brands and, 4–5
    defined, 33
mission and values
    assessments and, 22
    positioning strategy and, 100–101
monetary costs, 123
morals, segmentation and, 80
Mudflap Girl campaign, 96, 160
mutual value, 122
My Library, target audience, 90

N
names, brand elements and, 7
Netflix, 59
*New International Dictionary of the English
        Language* (Funk and Wagnalls), 5
news, creating as PR tool, 151–152
nexus for change, 20–21
Nielsen Company, 81
nonmonetary costs, 123
nontraditional media, 154–155

O
objectives, developing, 104
observable elements, 7–8
O'Malley, Barbara, 174
Online Computer Library Center, Inc. (OCLC)
    about, xv
    advocacy challenges, 165–166

Online Computer Library Center, Inc. (OCLC)
        (cont'd)
    logo, 61
    perceptions of libraries, 32
    Rangeview Library District, 23
opportunities
    assessments of, 18
    defined, 24
organizational development
    brands and, 6
    strategic focus and, 26
origins of intent, 9
outside experts, development and, 41

P
partnerships as PR tool, 151
patron needs, personality and, 12–13
people strategy, 109, 125–127
personality of library, 10, 12–13
perspectives, external and internal, 40
Pink, Daniel, 178–179
place strategies, 115–121
planning
    implications of, 35
    relating to branding, 42–43
political change, 21
Popcorn, Faith, xvii
positioning
    focused types, 95–96
    iPhones and, 101
    market strategies and, 57–69
    marketing mix and, 109–129
    statement crafting, 97–99
    taglines and, 138–140
    target audiences and, 97
    university libraries and, 174–175
    value proposition and, 99–101
potential products, 112–113
power users, 89–90, 95
premise *vs.* promise, 17–18
premium pricing, 125
presentation of creative brief, 145
pricing
    brand enhancement and, 122–123
    competitive behavior and, 123–124
    product and strategies, 124–125
    referencing and sensitivity, 121
    strategies for, 119–121
primary and secondary resources, 74–75
primary market research, 30–31
Pringle, Hamish, 43
printed materials as PR tool, 153
PRIZM cluster system, 81–82, 88
processes
    of branding, 41
    development types, 43–44
    protocol of, 44
products
    life cycle of, 114–115

products (cont'd)
    positioning and, 60–61
    pricing strategies and, 124–125
    service promotion and, 111–112
programs
    assessment of, 18
    personality and, 12–13
promotion
    brand architecture and, 132–134
    concept of, 131–132
    identity and, 11–12
    plan development and, 144
protocol of development, 43–44
psychographic segmentation, 80
psychological barriers, place strategies and,
    118
Public Agenda, xv
public perception, brands and, 10–11
public relations, 151
The Purple Cow (Godin), 93–94
purpose
    brand and, 20–21
    example of, 66

Q

qualitative/quantitative research, 31, 75–78
Queens Library
    advertising, 148–149
    advocacy and, 168–169
    barriers at, 95
    developing brand, 135
    developing strategic positioning, 99
    positioning and branding, 65
    sense of place at, 118

R

radio, as communication type, 146, 150
Raimondo, Gina, 18–19
Rangeview Library District
    brand architecture and, 134
    changes to, 33
    creating a new library brand, 23
    strategic initiatives, 36
    value proposition and, 133
referencing, price and value, 121
registers, employee brand advocacy stage, 51
relationships
    brands and, 5
    build as a PR tool, 151
    strategies for, 125–126
Rensi, Ed, 119
research
    Columbus Metropolitan Library, 86–90
    ethical concerns, 30
    methodology of, 63
    professional teams for, 74
    secondary market, 30–31
    target markets, 72–73

research (cont'd)
    types of, 28–29
    . *see also* market research
research assistance, 73–74
resources
    evaluation criteria, 82
    strategic focus and, 26
resources, relevance, 82
Ricochet Ideas, 42
Ries, Al, 60–61
Robinson, Peter, 23

S

Sandlian-Smith, Pam
    Anythink libraries, 42, 63
    creating new brands, 23
    place strategies, 121
    policies, 50
    staff manifesto, 127, 138
    strategic goals, 102
Scan/US (information resource), 82
Schultz, Howard, 123
Seattle Public Library, 76–77
Second City, 179
secondary and primary resources, 74–75
secondary market research, 30–31
segments
    analysis, 78–81
    appeal of, 85
    evaluation criteria, 82
    market and, 84
    price and value, 121
    targeting, 84
selling
    brand element propositions, 7
    social media and, 155
sensitivity, price and value, 121
sequence and application, market research,
    28–30
services
    positioning and, 60–61
    pricing strategies and, 124–125
    strategic focus and, 26
"Six Design Lessons from the Apple Store"
    (article), 8–9
social beliefs, segmentation and, 80
social currency, brands and, 65
Social Marketing (Lee and Kotler), 51, 98
social media
    development process and, 45–46
    sites for, 155
SocialThink, 156
space, as a strategy, 116–117
Staff Manifesto, Anythink and, 134
stages of brand planning, 47–48
standards as guidance, 48–49
Starbucks job growth program, 123
statement crafting, 97–99
Stathopoulos, Tasso, 42

Storey-Ewoldt, Ronnie, 50, 126
strategic goals, Anythink and, 102–103, 138
strategic initiatives, 36
strategic planning, 21, 67–69
strategy
    example of, 66
    forming, 35
    purpose and focus, 26
strengths
    assessing, 18
    defined, 24
    focus of, 24–25
Sullenberger, Chesley B., 171
surveys, application and, 11–14
SWOT analysis, 17–18, 23–26

T

taglines, value propositions and, 99–100, 139–140
tangibles, 8
target markets
    aligning promotion with, 140–143
    evaluation criteria, 82
    market research and, 72–73
    marketing mix and, 111
    positioning and, 58–59
    steps in selecting, 84–85
team involvement, 26–27, 41
technology
    personality and, 12–13
    as a strategy, 117
television, communication type, 146, 150
threats
    assessing, 18
    defined, 24
3D model, 24
time as a cost, 120
timing
    promotional strategies and, 150
    protocol of, 44
touch points
    brand personality, 12
    creating, 141
trademark defined, 6
transaction stage of planning, 48
transformation, purposeful, 165–166
transit ad, 148
Trout, Jack, 60–61
Twitter, social media, 155–156
typography, using, 139

U

Understanding Brands (Cowley), 6
undifferentiated *vs.* differentiated marketing, 85–86

unique value, 139–140
unique value proposition, 101–103
universities, positioning libraries in, 174–175
usage, as a strength, 25
use, stage of planning, 48

V

VALS cluster system, 81–82
value proposition
    brand element and, 7, 133
    strategies and, 99
value referencing, 121
value statement, 22
values
    brand equity and, 34
    as a cost, 120
    evaluation criteria and, 82
    example of, 66
    positioning strategy and, 100–101
vehicles as touch points, 143
vision
    assessing, 22–23
    building, 52
    example of, 66

W

Walters, Suzanne, xvi
weaknesses
    assessing, 18
    defined, 24
    putting in perspective, 25–26
web designers, development process and, 45–46
websites
    promotion of, 150
    strategies for, 117
    as a touch point, 142
Wheatley, Margaret J., xvii, 175
Wheeler, Alina, 36, 135
A Whole New Mind (Pink), 178
Wittenstein, Mike, 49
WYLDCAT bibliographic database system, 170
Wyoming State Library
    advertising and PR at, 152–153
    advocacy programs, 169–170
    Mudflap Girl campaign, 96
    product and, 114
    segmentation at, 83

Y

You Had Me At Hello (Wittenstein), 49
Young Minds, target audience, 90, 110–111
YouTube, social media, 155, 157